PRAISE FOR

BOTTOM OF THE 33rd

"Dan's Barry's meticulous reporting and literary talent are both evident in *Bottom of the 33rd*, a pitch-perfect and seamless meditation on baseball and the human condition."

—Gay Talese, author of *The Silent Season of a Hero*

"What a book—an exquisite exercise in storytelling, democracy, and mythmaking that has, at its center, a great respect for the symphony of voices that make up America."

—Colum McCann, author of the National Book Award–winning *Let the Great World Spin*

"Dan Barry has crafted a loving and lyrical tribute to a time and a place when you stayed until the final out . . . because that's what we did in America. *Bottom of the 33rd* is chaw-chewing, sunflower-spitting, pine tar proof that too much baseball is never enough."

—Jane Leavy, bestselling author of *The Last Boy* and *Sandy Koufax*

"A masterpiece. . . . Destined for the Hall of Fame of baseball books."

—*Publishers Weekly*

"A fascinating, beautifully told story. . . . In the hands of Barry, a national correspondent for the *New York Times*, this marathon of duty, loyalty, misery, and folly becomes a riveting narrative. . . . The book feels like *Our Town* on the diamond."   —*Los Angeles Times*

"An astonishing tale that lyrically articulates baseball's inexorable grip on its players and fans, *Bottom of the 33rd* belongs among the best baseball books ever written."   —*Cleveland Plain Dealer*

"Meticulously researched and tremendously entertaining!"
—*Columbus Dispatch*

"A heroic conjuring of the past."   —*New York Times Book Review*

"[Dan] Barry does more than simply recount the inning-by-inning-by-inning box score. He delves beneath the surface, like an archaeologist piecing together the shards and fragments of a forgotten society, to reconstruct a time and a night that have become part of baseball lore."
—Associated Press

"Whether you're a baseball aficionado or a reader who just enjoys a good yarn, you'll love this book."   —*Minneapolis Star Tribune*

"A worthy companion to Roger Kahn's classic *Boys of Summer*. . . . [Dan] Barry exploits the power of memory and nostalgia with literary grace and journalistic exactitude. He blends a vivid, moment-by-moment re-creation of the game with what happens to its participants in the next thirty years."   —Stefan Fatsis, *New York Times*

"Brilliantly rendered. . . . The book is both a fount of luxurious writing, and a tour de force of reportage."   —*Washington Post*

"Lovely. . . . Unforgettable. . . . Dan Barry portrays [the] limits and frustrations [of minor league baseball], as well as its pleasures, with more verve and vividness than a score of writers who have preceded him."   —*Bloomberg News*

BOTTOM

OF THE

33rd

BOTTOM

OF THE

33rd

Hope, Redemption, and
Baseball's Longest Game

DAN BARRY

HARPER ● PERENNIAL

NEW YORK ● LONDON ● TORONTO ● SYDNEY ● NEW DELHI ● AUCKLAND

HARPER ● PERENNIAL

A hardcover edition of this book was published in 2011 by HarperCollins Publishers.

HarperCollins books may be purchased for educational, business, or sales promotional use. For information please write: Special Markets Department, HarperCollins Publishers, 10 East 53rd Street, New York, NY 10022.

Grateful acknowledgment for permission to reproduce illustrations is made to the following: Pawtucket Red Sox, pages 19, 77, 129, 223, 224; Ernie Orlando/Rochester Red Wings, page 77; Bill George/Pawtucket Red Sox, page 195; *Providence Journal*, page 227.

FIRST HARPER PERENNIAL EDITION PUBLISHED 2012.

The Library of Congress has catalogued the hardcover edition as follows:

Barry, Dan.
Bottom of the 33rd : hope, redemption, and baseball's longest game / by Dan Barry.—1st ed.
         p.   cm.
ISBN: 978-0-06-201448-1
1. Baseball—United States—History. 2. Minor-league baseball—United States—History. 3. Baseball—Records—United States. 4. Pawtucket Red Sox (Baseball team)—History. 5. Rochester Red Wings (Baseball team)—History. I. Title. II. Title: Bottom of the thirty-third.

GV863.A1B3744 2011
796.357'630973—dc22   2010051656

ISBN 978-0-06-201449-8 (pbk.)

12   13   14   15   16   OV/RRD   10 9 8 7 6 5 4 3 2 1

To
Ben Mondor

BOTTOM
OF THE
33rd

PROLOGUE

Three thirty in the morning.

Holy Saturday, the awkward Christian pause between the Sorrow and the Joy, has surrendered to the first hushed hours of Easter. The cold and dark cling to the rooftops in a Rhode Island place called Pawtucket. Triple-decker houses, packed with three, four, six sleeping families, loom over its empty, half-lit streets, while the river that cascades through its deserted downtown releases a steady, dreamy sigh. Yet somewhere in the almost sacred stillness, a white orb disturbs the peace, skipping along the night-damp grass, flitting through the night-crisp air, causing general unrest at three thirty in the morning on Sunday, Easter Sunday.

Pawtucket, it must be said, is not given to the supernatural. This is a city grounded by harsh reality, a city of striving and struggle. After all, it was here—not in Boston to the north or Providence to the immediate south, but right here—that an Englishman with a genius for business, Samuel Slater, arrived at the end of the eighteenth century to create the water-powered textile industry. It was here, then, that the muscular Blackstone River began turning the gears of the American Industrial Revolution, shifting life from farm to factory, from country to city, changing everything. Young children followed their parents into the time-hungry mills and came out old, searching for the decades that were theirs just a moment ago. Time was everything. In 1824, for example, women weavers led a raucous strike to protest longer hours, shorter pay, and lives dictated by the insistent clangs of the factory bell. Not long after, the people of Pawtucket took up a collection to install a clock at the top of the new Congregational church. Precious time is not a mill owner's possession.

All those limbs lost to mill machinery, all those airborne fibers inhaled into the lungs, all those labor struggles and recessions and closings and reinventions over two centuries, would bequeath to Pawtucket more than just a poisoned river and a clutter of ghostly mill buildings, standing as dark brick taunts of what was. The city would also inherit a knowing hardness, an understanding to pass on to its children that life is a matter of endurance: Not everyone wins.

Tonight in Pawtucket, in some of the tidy colonial homes that border Providence, and in the cramped triple-deckers surrounding the Gothic hospital, and in the mobile homes clustered near an abandoned racetrack, baskets filled with green straw and chocolate bunnies, hollow and solid and wrapped in the thinnest foil, lie in wait. Beside them are nestled chocolate eggs filled with coconut-flavored goo, and those yellow marshmallow chicks so sweet you sense your teeth dissolving after the first decapitating bite. In a few hours these candy cornucopias will be discovered by children who are blessedly removed from millwork, too young to have the Pawtucket worldview, and too innocent to question what possible connection could exist between the elusive white-furred rabbit who brought these gifts and the white-robed man who rose from the dead.

Then again, to a ten-year-old, anything is possible. Animals are magical and death is just sleep and you can grow up to be whatever you want to be: chief of the Pawtucket Fire Department; president of the United States; even first baseman for the Boston Red Sox. All possible.

But, now, at three thirty in the morning on April 19, 1981, these children are asleep, as are their parents, as is Pawtucket—save for one radiant swath, across from the Chinese restaurant called the Mei-King and beside the bookmaker's social club called the Lily. There, in middle-aged and tired McCoy Stadium, powerful lights shine down on small clutches of people, two dozen, three dozen at most, huddled like straggling immigrants in the steerage of a ship, watching that white dot dance through the night. Some are drinking coffee and hot chocolate, even champagne and Chivas Regal, as a cold Easter wind slaps their faces for the audacity of their presence. They will not leave.

It is a baseball game; an early-season professional baseball game of no particular importance; an International League game between the Rochester Red Wings and the Pawtucket Red Sox. But why? Why are they playing now, at three thirty in the morning, on the holiest day of the Christian calendar? In frigid, unconscious Pawtucket?

To begin with, the game is tied, inextricably, maddeningly knotted to the night—in the 31st inning. The Rochester team has two runs and the Pawtucket team has two runs, and baseball rarely abides a tie ball game. You win or you lose.

Other reasons may wither in the light of day, when morning's logic arrives to temper night's emotions. But right now they include miscommunication; stubbornness; questionable judgment; what appears to be a clerical error made several months earlier, in distant Ohio; and, finally, this: Baseball players play baseball. They hit and catch and throw and chase after a white ball until the call and signal of the final out.

"That'll bring up Dan Logan. Struck out his last time up in the twenty-ninth inning. Singled in the twenty-seventh. Runner at first base. Two away. Here's the pitch to Logan. Misses outside, ball one. . . ."

Among the very few watching the game are several miserable men in the press box, a glorified term for a weathered trailer that appears to be suspended from the old stadium's rafters behind home plate. It has no insulation, no heat, no bathroom, and the wind howling in from the outfield is doing little to fill those inside with the hallelujah joy of the risen Lord. For the last eight hours, a sportswriter from the Pawtucket *Evening Times* has gazed from this vantage; he is underdressed and shivering. Beside him sits his competitor from the *Providence Journal*; he is unimpressed and annoyed. A talented writer who hopes to ascend soon to the big-league *Philadelphia Inquirer*, he has never liked the inferior level of baseball at uninviting McCoy Stadium. Everything is so . . . minor league. A never-ending Pawtucket Red Sox game might as well be sportswriting hell. The coffee is never hot, the editors never stop calling, you can never escape.

Also huddling in the press box are the public-address announcer, who has been calling out the same surnames for nearly eight hours now; a McCoy Stadium aide, who has been playing the same music between the incessant innings and pitching changes; and the official scorer, who has recorded every at bat—around 200 so far, and counting. On the other side of a cheap partition are Bob Drew and Pete Torrez, broadcasting the game for WPXN in Rochester, 1280 on your AM dial. Drew, believe it or not, is the general manager of the Rochester Red Wings. He has fallen so far from favor with his superiors that he is doing the radio play-by-play for this entire road trip: ten games in ten days. Torrez, beside him, is an injured Red Wings relief pitcher of modest talent, whether on the field or in the broadcast booth. He often begins his brief observations with, "I tell ya, Bob."

But Drew has been the one doing the telling. For nearly eight hours now, he has described this game in kinetic bursts of baseball words—"Ground ball, Valdez at shortstop, got it, throw to first base, in time"—that have crackled and carried four hundred miles through the night air, across southern New England, over the Hudson River and into central New York State, to Rochester, a city of 240,000 that has proudly supported its hometown team since the late nineteenth century.

But at three thirty in the morning, Drew wonders: Is anyone listening?

He and Torrez are feeling a fatigue that streams of free coffee can no longer keep at bay, leading to mistakes, exhausted pauses, even brief eruptions of laughter at the absurdity of the mission. It is the 31st inning, with no end in sight.

"Here's the pitch. Ground ball. Back to Hurst. Flips it over to first base, the side is retired, as Logan is out of there, one to three. . . ."

"We started this game at eight o'clock last night," Drew says, trailing off for what seems like hours in radio time. *"Now approaching three forty-five in the morning on Easter Sunday morning. And happy Easter to all of you back there in Rochester. Hope you're enjoying Red Wing baseball.*

"Here in the wee morning, in the wee minutes—or hours—of the

morning on Easter Sunday. If we get a little mixed up you'll have to excuse us a little bit. Bob Drew, along with Pete Torrez."

Another long pause.

"Right, Pete?"

"Yes it has, Bob."

A while back, maybe an hour ago, maybe a month ago, this inning-by-inning standoff in Pawtucket quietly distinguished itself from every other professional baseball game ever played. It is now, officially, the longest in history.

Before tonight, the longest game on record had lasted 29 innings, when the Miami Marlins finally beat the St. Petersburg Cardinals, 4–3, on a balmy June night in 1966, in the low-level Florida State League. The longest major-league game mustered a mere 26 innings: In May 1920, the Brooklyn Robins (a.k.a. Dodgers), now gone from Brooklyn, and the Boston Braves, now gone from Boston, yielded to a misty New England night with the score eternally set in a damnable tie of 1–1. According to the *New York Times,* the home plate umpire "remembered that he had an appointment soon with a succulent beefsteak. He wondered if it wasn't getting dark. He held out one hand as a test and decided in the gloaming it resembled a Virginia ham. He knew it wasn't a Virginia ham and became convinced that it was too dark to play ball."

But no umpire has stepped up to suspend tonight's game. Of the thousands of games played every year, and of the hundreds of thousands played over the last century in ballparks gone and still standing, in Yankee Stadium in the Bronx and City Stadium in St. Joseph, Missouri; in Fenway Park in Boston and Haymarket Park in Lincoln, Nebraska; in Bisbee, Arizona; Paducah, Kentucky; Waterloo, Iowa; Wenatchee, Washington; everywhere and anywhere in North America—of all those many baseball games that came before, no game has lasted as long as this one. A game still unfolding in Pawtucket, Rhode Island, at the Triple-A level of baseball, the last stop before the major leagues. More than any other ever played, this game is testing the imagined charm of two baseball teams playing on and on, forever.

The score is 2–2. Is it 2–2? Yes, that's right: 2–2. Strong and insistent winds blowing in from the outfield have created an invisible wall that even the hardest-hit fly balls cannot penetrate. Sometimes the wind borrows the baseball to juggle in the air for a while, like some magical Easter egg, before losing interest and allowing it to drop. The ballplayers, meanwhile, are feeling the weight of the night in their arms, their legs, even their heads. And so the innings have dribbled like spilled beer into Sunday, with each one some variation of the inning just completed, the 30th.

Rochester: groundout; strikeout; strikeout.

Pawtucket: groundout; groundout; single; fly out.

No television cameras are filming the game, which means that much of what is occurring, or not occurring, will be left to the mercy of memory, that most flawed of recording devices. The rest is preserved in the meticulous baseball cryptography of the official scorer hunched now in the press box, a young lawyer named Bill George. For every play, he marks down in a spiral-bound scorebook some number-letter combination that, when strung together, will allow the future to crack the official code of this baseball game without a hint of its humanity. A fly out to left field in the top of the 1st inning (F7); a strikeout in the bottom of the 13th (K); a groundout to shortstop in the top of the 26th (6–3).

But the official scorebook can only accommodate 12 innings— three beyond the normal nine. This game, though, is now in its *22nd* extra inning. Fear not: Bill George, solemn keeper of the book, is as serious about his charge as any Columban monk illustrating the Book of Kells. So far, he has used three different colors of ink—blue, red, and black—to note the passage of time as measured by innings. With every careful stroke of his pen, his score sheet gradually becomes a work of art: the Book of Pawtucket.

At three thirty, though, do these ballplayers even care that they have broken a record? A record that is less about achievement than it is about frustration? Most of them are too tired, too cold, and too hungry to contemplate the historic import of the night. They stamp their feet. They blow into their hands. They fold into themselves on the narrow dugout benches and gather around fires that lick from a couple of fifty-five-gallon drums, fires fed by broken Louisville Slugger bats, many of them imprinted with the names of athletes freezing here tonight, the someday baseball famous and soon-to-be baseball forgotten.

The Rochester players hope to be summoned someday by the Baltimore Orioles, their parent club—a fitting phrase, given that every swing, catch, and throw by these sons of the minor leagues is meant to shout to front-office daddies: *Look at me, look at me.* And the Pawtucket players, oh, these Pawtucket players, their asses freezing in a shallow dugout along the third-base side, want so badly to be called up to the Boston Red Sox. Called up is another apt phrase, for Boston is forty-five miles to the north, forty-five miles that might as well be four thousand, so otherworldly is the major-league experience from that of the minor leagues. Word has come down that up in the big leagues, your locker overflows with cleats and gloves and other treats, all free. Imagine.

Well, then, the minor leaguer thinks. If freezing my ass off in Pawtucket will deliver me from Pawtucket, and Rochester, and Toledo, and Syracuse, then bring on a blizzard.

Take number 23, for example, the rock-hard first baseman for Pawtucket. According to that Book of Pawtucket, he has gotten one, two, three—four hits tonight, including two doubles. He is 4 for 12 so far, a respectable, even impressive, performance. An adequate fielder, he has some clout, having hit 27 home runs in 1979 and another 13 last year, all for Pawtucket. In fact, he's been playing for Pawtucket for several years now: a few games in '77 and '78, and all of '79 and '80.

His name is Dave Koza, and baseball has been his life's mission since the age of eleven, when some merchants in his Wyoming hometown of Torrington chipped in a total of $175 to send him to a baseball camp in Oklahoma. You can't glimpse his constant worry by looking at him now, a broad-shouldered Marlboro Man in cleats, with a full mustache and a nose that looks like it's been broken a time or two, every part of him aware of being watched by his adoring wife of two months, the lovely Ann, who will stay in this frigid, godforsaken ballpark as long as he does. No, you can't see by looking at him as he stands so at ease with bat in hand, but Dave Koza is trying to suppress his ever-present worries—worries that intensify with each passing game—that he will not make it to the major leagues. He senses that first phantom tug at the back of his uniform, pulling him off the field, away from the game.

As it is, the Boston Red Sox are crowded with first basemen: Carl Yastrzemski, the heart of the Red Sox and a lock for the Hall of Fame; Tony Perez, another veteran and a likely Hall of Famer; Joe Rudi, a former All Star and World Series hero; Dave Stapleton, Koza's former teammate, a good friend. The team's executives are not looking at their roster of twenty-five players and thinking to themselves: We need a *fifth* first baseman, just in case—a fifth first baseman who is a good but not great fielder and who hits for power but not for average.

Dave Koza knows this. All he can do, then, is take his extra swings in the batting cage, try to solve his problem with those vexing curveballs, field more grounders, and practice his footwork around first base; his career depends upon the mastery of these little things. Then, back in Wyoming, he will spend the off-season keeping fit when he's not working construction, squeezing a rubber ball in front of the television, strengthening his wrists, quietly determined to silence all those in Torrington who keep asking when he'll make it to the major leagues. Torrington doesn't understand Single-A, or Double-A, or Triple-A, or injuries, or fickle front offices, or standing in line behind aging stars who can still perform. It only understands the Yankees, the Red Sox, the major leagues.

For all the childhood charms of baseball, for all the grassy frolics and the sandlot puffs of dust and the relief that comes from swinging a bat instead of a pick or sledge, bitter reality intrudes upon the baseball fields of the Triple-A. Take that six-foot-six beanpole pitching now for Rochester, Jim Umbarger. A left-hander with a good mix of pitches, he reached the major leagues fairly quickly several years ago, but hurt his arm, got sick, fell out of the league, and has been trying to pitch his way back up ever since. He hopes that the Orioles just might need another left-hander in their bullpen—less a hope than a dream, given that the Orioles have the strongest pitching staff in baseball.

Still, for almost 9 innings now, ever since the 23rd, Jim Umbarger has been nearly unhittable. He is twenty-eight years old, high on cups of coffee and dips of tobacco, his curveball so sharp you can nearly hear it snap. And when he stands on the mound, waiting for the next batter to settle in, a batter he will no doubt own, do you know what he wishes? He wishes for a baseball scout to be sitting somewhere in the swallowing emptiness of McCoy Stadium. A scout with nothing better to do than spend Easter Sunday's predawn hours at a minor-league ball game in Pawtucket. A scout jotting down two words to convey in the morning to his major-league bosses: Umbarger's back.

But there is no scout here tonight. And if there is no scout watching, is any of this really happening?

Here, in the International League, you have hungry former major leaguers like Jim Umbarger. You have stars of the lower minor leagues, the sluggers who dominated bandboxes, now facing battle-savvy pitchers eager to demonstrate how a big-league curveball, their good friend Uncle Charlie, can reduce a .300 batting average in Double-A to a .200 average in Triple-A. You have athletes who have always been the best in their county, their state, suddenly realizing that the teammate using the adjacent locker has something extra, something nearly imperceptible, that they lack.

You have hard-luck players, the hopelessly misunderstood. No one on the field tonight has surer hands, for example, than the Rochester shortstop, Bobby Bonner, whose jutting ears only enhance an aura that says nothing gets by him. Although not a strong hitter, he has the gift: that extra sense of baseball anticipation that cannot be taught.

A couple of years ago, Bonner turned his life over to Jesus Christ, snuffing out the fire of his hell-raising Texas ways and startling teammates who remembered a guy not unfamiliar with a postgame beer or joint. Before tonight's game, in addition to stretching and throwing, Bonner knelt in the bathroom and prayed: *Lord, just let me see you in the stands tonight; let me play for you.* Where was Jesus, though, when Bonner finally got his big chance last year, and was called up to play for the Baltimore Orioles and its holy terror of a manager, Earl Weaver? Where was Jesus when a certain ball hit the artificial turf in Toronto and skipped past Bonner like a skimming stone—earning him an error, the profane and everlasting wrath of Weaver, and a return to the minors? Was this all part of the Lord's plan?

Another thing Bobby Bonner wonders: Does his brief major-league visit mean that he will be nothing more than a "cup of coffee" guy? Among the strivers and strugglers in the Triple-A, you also have men whose boyhood dreams have been reduced to the near-desperate desire for a mere cameo in the major leagues—as a September call-up, perhaps, when major-league rosters are expanded to rest veterans and assess minor-league talent, or maybe as a temporary replacement for an injured player, whose pulled hamstring or twisted ankle is the answer to certain lower-league prayers.

After they retire, these marginal players will forever describe themselves as having had a cup of coffee in the major leagues, without even time enough to stir in the milk. At their best they were barely adequate, their names destined to become answers to trivia questions almost too trivial to pose. But in this self-description, they send the subtle but proud signal that at least they made it, their names recorded for posterity in the *Baseball Encyclopedia*.

At least they made it. Consider how many of us have played on sandlots and in league games since the formal organization of baseball in 1871; how many of us have conceived of action on imagined fields while following a game on the radio; have watched afternoon World Series games on televisions wheeled into the classrooms of similarly afflicted teachers; have sat so deep in the bleachers that the players are but white blurs moving across a green expanse; have thrown a spongy ball into a box painted on the side of a school building and heard the thump against brick as an umpire's "Strike three!"; have, alone, in the post-supper twilight, thrown a ball into the sun-washed sky, again and again and again, the game-saving catches coming over fences and hedges and hoods of cars now inexplicably parked in the outfield of Yankee Stadium. The crowd goes wild, and a parent inquires what in the world are you up to, and the answer is nothing. To say you want to play in the major leagues someday is to jinx yourself. Hope is an intimate matter.

Imagine, then, how many have dreamed of playing in the major leagues, if only as a backup to the backup catcher in the bullpen. Hundreds of thousands? Millions? Yet by the end of the 1980 season, just twelve thousand men had ever realized that dream. Twelve thousand; their bodies and ghosts would not fill a third of Fenway Park.

So glimpse now over the shoulder of Bill George, the official scorer, at his masterpiece in progress. Stop randomly at any name and try to divine that player's future based on how well he has played on this long, long night. Pause here, for example, to read the string of symbols that tell the game story of Pawtucket's third baseman, Wade Boggs. Four hits in twelve at bats so far, same as Koza, only with one double instead of two. This twenty-two-year-old bundle of superstition, a curious incarnation of a Southern-gentleman jock, is said to be nothing more than a Punch-and-Judy hitter, when what you want from your third baseman is power. Right? And look at the unimpressive performance of Rochester's tall, movie-star-handsome third baseman, with eyes an almost otherworldly blue. True, the Baltimore organization sees this twenty-year-old as the Oriole third baseman of the future. But in tonight's endurance-testing game, does his subpar performance—eleven outs, two walks, and a single—begin to cast doubt on those big plans? Does this ballplayer, this Cal Ripken Jr., have what it takes to play at the Triple-A level, much less in the major leagues?

In the cold-night concentration of balls, strikes, and what will become of us, Jim Umbarger, the Rochester pitcher who has been to the majors and wants to get back, waits for the next batter, Dave Koza, the Pawtucket first baseman who never has been and can only imagine. Here in the lost world of deep extra innings, every at bat is the alpha and the omega: One swing could both end and begin this thing. One out. One swing.

"There's a ground ball that might get through there. Eaton over after it, got it, nice play, throw to first base! In time!"

Batting for the thirteenth time in the game, Dave Koza has just made the second out in the bottom of the 31st inning. To anyone with even a rudimentary understanding of the national pastime, this sentence appears to have at least two typographical errors. Thirteenth at bat? Thirty-first inning? Yet both are true. What's more, there still exists the possibility, even the expectation, that Dave Koza will have another chance.

Could happen. Because something is certainly happening here in Pawtucket. Something wondrously strange.

"Two outs in the thirty-first. Umbarger, the pitch—shot foul in the left field stands. The count goes to oh and two, to Wade Boggs, the third baseman for Pawtucket. . . .

"No balls and two strikes to Boggs. Here's the pitch. There's a fly ball to center field. That should be in there for a base hit. Drops in front of Dallas Williams and the Red Sox have a runner at first."

But the wondrously strange something happening here is in addition to baseball—besides baseball. It is something just beyond the articulation of those few still in the ballpark, as though this modest piece of Pawtucket broke free of time's restraints with the first pitch at eight o'clock last night to become a community apart, afloat, unrelated now to anything beyond the ballpark's lights.

Someone not here tonight could pose quite legitimate questions to the players and fans, questions that would naturally start with why. Why did you keep playing? Why did you stay? At two o'clock in the morning, and then at three o'clock, why didn't you just—leave? The official answer, that some umpire refused to call it a night, would be so lacking in the weight of common sense that it might twirl off like a deflating balloon before the sentence could be finished. But the truer answer might be as unsatisfying to the outsider as it is surprising to these inhabitants of this in-between place, where time's boundaries have blurred.

Why did you keep playing? Why did you stay?

Because we are bound by duty. Because we aspire to greater things. Because we are loyal. Because, in our own secular way, we are celebrating communion, and resurrection, and possibility.

* * *

Here now is the earnest, skinny batboy, nicknamed "Panic," whose single mother, frantic since the turn of midnight, has already driven to the ballpark and demanded that he come home immediately. But his friends, his surrogate fathers, are engaged in something historic, and a small piece of it belongs to him. He retrieves tossed baseball bats with the same implacable sense of duty as everyone else. He will not go.

Here, too, is the home plate umpire, with red hair as fiery as his desire to become a major-league umpire someday. He works in the off-season at any job that will allow him leave in March so that he can earn lousy pay, sleep in plastic-cup motels, and be part of the game until September: a fan without fealty, an arbiter, the last word. He doesn't know it, but his family in Massachusetts has been calling area hospitals and police departments, looking for him and his young nephew, who is struggling to remain awake somewhere in the stands. The two of them should have been home hours ago.

And here, scattered among the stadium's mostly empty pews, are the last straggling congregants, a few of them steeled by champagne and chocolate Easter eggs, courtesy of a fan who left and returned with treats appropriate to the occasion. These are the McCoy regulars, the constant presence, who will still be here in the seasons to come, long after the players on the field have moved on: a father and his nine-year-old son; a young man who came alone; another whose girlfriend left hours ago. When services began nearly eight hours ago, 1,740 sat in attendance; now there are maybe 19—a number that does not include the few police officers who have radioed one another about an early-morning disturbance off South Bend Street, and who are now watching from the edges of the light.

And here, along the third-base line, in a rudimentary VIP box of blue-painted particleboard, sits the stocky owner of the Pawtucket Red Sox, a poor boy from Woonsocket who made a fortune propping up and selling broken textile mills, including one in Pawtucket, not far from here. Four years ago, he bought and rescued this baseball franchise, which had been so poorly run that many in Rhode Island refused to do business with it, let alone bring their families to watch.

The owner is unhappy; he thinks this crazy game should have been suspended hours ago. But there is nothing he can do but brave the wind, take a sip from a bottle of Chivas dug out of a drawer, and pass it on.

On to his general manager. On to his communications director. On to some of the wind-whipped wives of the players. To Ann Koza, the newlywed wife of the Pawtucket first baseman, who has given over a good part of herself to the major-league dreams of her husband, Dave. That dream is their child, sharing their small apartment on Pond Street, not a quarter mile from McCoy Stadium, and buckled into their car as they drive the 1,900 miles back to his hometown of Torrington, Wyoming, at the end of every season. Some 770 miles on Interstate 90, followed by nearly 900 more on Interstate 80, in a silver Oldsmobile Toronado packed with their luggage and that dream, a precious thing growing more fragile by the day. They make the trip every September, because every September the small clutch of Pawtucket players summoned to Boston once again does not include Dave. On these days-long drives home, Dave's brooding silence and wounded expansiveness combine to pose a single plaintive question: Why, Ann? Why?

Ann doesn't know the answer. But she has faith in her husband, and she tells him so. She accompanies him to Torrington, a place many hundreds of miles removed from her childhood home in Pennsylvania coal country, and works in a sugar beet factory, sharpening the knives that slice the beets. Then, at the start of each season, she returns with him to Pawtucket, a place even more foreign than Torrington, and takes whatever job she can find—including a stint in one of the last Pawtucket mills, where she developed a thick callus on her pinkie from the repetitive task of removing the thread that bound big sheets of lace. She is twenty-three, with large, expressive eyes, long blond hair, and a lack of pretense that draws others to her. She roller skates to the ballpark; she drinks beer; she knows what it's like to work in a mill. And she is devoted to her Dave. In letters she writes to his family back in Torrington, and in words she whispers to him at night, Ann Koza reassures: It will be all right.

*   *   *

The errant priest of the night is Joe Morgan, the manager of the Pawtucket Red Sox, technically absent. He was ejected by the home plate
umpire back in the 22nd inning, after arguing a call with glorious in-
vective that resounded through the bare and cavernous stadium like a
profane Gregorian chant.

Morgan's ruddy countenance conveys an almost amused intelligence that seems to say: Yeah, I'm fifty years old and still wearing a
baseball uniform—but I'm happier than you are, pal. He was an infielder and outfielder whose thirteen long years in the minors were interrupted only occasionally by stints in the major leagues. When his
playing days ended, he took up professions that followed the seasons:
coaching and managing in the spring and summer; driving trucks and
plowing snow on the Massachusetts Turnpike in the fall and winter. He
has been managing in Pawtucket for seven years now. Nearly time to
move on.

Fans in the International League's eight cities are quite familiar
with Morgan of Pawtucket. They know, for example, how much he
enjoys theatrical argument. In disputing a close play at second base,
he may very well pause in mid-quarrel, take several steps back, and
slide into second base to illustrate his point. Such antics might leave
some with the impression that he is another Max Patkin, the droopy-
faced baseball clown who travels the minor-league circuit in a sack of
a uniform that features no number on the back—only a huge question
mark. But Joe Morgan is the opposite of a baseball fool. He knows the
game's obscure rules and philosophical intentions, its wise men and
buffoons, its rhythms. He knows, too, who has major-league ability and
who does not. And if asked, he is always candid. *Son, you might want
to start thinking about the next step in life.* This might be interpreted
as ruthless, but Morgan doesn't see it that way. Some players need to
hear aloud what they have been privately thinking and fearing. When
a player has leveled out in Triple-A, he needs to hear the truth. His wife
and young kids need for him to hear the truth. Blunt honesty can free
families from baseball limbo, nudging them on.

Joe Morgan may have been kicked out of tonight's game, but he has
not left. He is monitoring the proceedings through a break in a forest

green plywood divider, a few yards behind home plate. From here he sees all—the players, the umpires, the fans, everyone whose life now centers around a baseball game being played at three thirty on Easter Sunday morning—but does he know all? Does he know what will happen to Dave and Ann Koza? Or whether the home plate umpire will ever make it to the major leagues? Will Bobby Bonner ever be forgiven for that cheap error in Toronto? Does this Ripken have what it takes to last? Does Boggs? How about that father and his son in the stands? And the anxious batboy?

Damn. The wind keeps blowing infield dust through the hole, right into the ejected manager's searching eye.

"There's the pitch. Popped up. On the infield. The shortstop, Bob Bonner, calling for it. It's hung up in the wind! And—Bonner makes the catch for the final out. The wind played tricks with it again, but Bonner was underneath it to make the catch for the final out. For Pawtucket, no runs, one hit, no errors, one runner left on base.

"At the end of thirty-one innings, here in Pawtucket, Rhode Island, this history-making ball game, the longest game ever played in the history of organized baseball, both minor league and major league. At the end of thirty-one innings, it's Rochester two, Pawtucket two.

"Well, we start another inning here in Pawtucket. Inning number thirty-two. . . ."

At last.

A pitcher from Alabama you've probably never heard of, his blue cap struggling to contain his curly brown hair, his five long years in the minors leading him to this throw, the next of thousands more toward the major leagues he will never reach, rocks back, half pirouettes, and surrenders the baseball to the indifferent night. It cuts some sixty feet of Pawtucket, slices past a batter from Oklahoma who already senses being out of his depth, and smacks into the mitt of a catcher from Massachusetts who will someday hit a home run in an unforgettable World Series. The crack of ball hitting leather echoes like a champagne bottle's uncorked pop.

"Strike," the umpire calls at 8:02, and we've got us a game, at last.

We nearly didn't. For a while, the antiquated light towers that stand sentry just beyond McCoy Stadium's outfield wall of pun-riddled advertisements (shop at Anderson-Little for "Clothes That Make A Hit") refused to share their blessings of illumination. The game—one of the night's many expressions of devotion—came perilously close to being postponed for, of all reasons, darkness.

Elsewhere in Pawtucket, people gathered at dinner tables set for the Passover Seder to recall the Exodus from Egypt and to listen, once again, as a child asked why tonight is different from all other nights. Others filed into the dimness of Catholic churches built by their mill-grunt immigrant forebears (St. Joseph for the Irish, St. Maria Goretti for the Italian, St. Jean-Baptiste for the French Canadian) to light the tapers of their modest candles with the paschal flame, signaling the end of solemnity, the beginning of joy. Beneath spires that have long competed with textile mill stacks for the New England sky above and the Pawtucket people below, believers, for the first time in forty days, exhaled hallelujah.

And here, in this more secular house of worship called McCoy, denizens adhered just as rigorously to the ritual of preparation, all for the Holy Saturday event spelled out on white rectangular tickets stamped with the sacred seal of two red socks: a Triple-A baseball game between the Red Wings of Rochester, New York, and the home team, the Red Sox of Pawtucket, Rhode Island. April 18, 1981. Seven thirty p.m.

But those four towers of light initially declined to cooperate. First, left center went dark, then right center, in a kind of baseball SOS that sent one front-office employee searching for maintenance and another scampering up to the press box to explain the delay, the two of them like panicked cathedral sextons. They knew how many people had worked to snatch from the everyday madness the pacifying, mesmerizing wonder that is a baseball game. They knew, too, that 1,740 fans were settled now into their foldout seats, awaiting escape.

Think of it: all the myriad endeavors combining to conjure the illusion that a baseball game just happened to break out one night in Pawtucket. The concession workers along the open-air concourse, heating popcorn in the glass-fronted machines that envelop the giant horseshoe of wooden seats with a buttery perfume, summoning memories of happy childhoods that never were. The ticket-office workers at the stadium's entrance, dispensing ducats in a booth crammed with maintenance equipment reeking of gasoline, where an entire wall is lined with slotted boxes containing $3 reserved tickets for the 72 home games of the 1981 season, along with spools of $2 general-admission tickets hanging from nails. (Feed money into the small mouth beneath the glass window and a ticket appears, like a thrust tongue.) The three Pawtucket police officers, patrolling the open-air concourse for the extra dough that comes from working a McCoy detail, freed by spring's arrival to shed their heavy winter coats for light, Class A uniforms of navy blue, offset by Sam Browne belts with the leather strap running diagonally over their right shoulders. The grounds crew, manicuring the field, kneading the clay around the pitcher's mound into hump perfection, running a taut piece of string from the foul poles to home plate and laying the lines of white lime that distinguish fair from foul. The diamond cutters.

The clubhouse manager, a teenager nicknamed "Hood," doing laundry, preparing the visiting team's postgame dinner, making sure each ballplayer has his Red Man or Levi Garrett or Beech-Nut chewing tobacco waiting for him at his locker, and, most of all, buffing each player's cleats with Kiwi polish, buffing as though these shoes were about to grace ballroom marble and not infield dirt, careful, careful now, not to smudge any of the shoe's white flourishes with black. Some ballplayers go ballistic over less.

The players, ambling into the salve-scented clubhouses, their home away from home away from home, to stretch and tape, to hit and field and loosen their arms with games of catch. The two participants rarely look each other in the eye, rarely talk, choosing instead to communicate through the call-and-answer *thwock* and *thwock* of the ball hitting the pockets of their leather gloves. Now and then, though, the players throw silent jokes designed to break the facial placidity: a chuckling knuckleball, a wisecracking slider.

Some of these ballplayers will laugh with the open-ended abandon of youth. They are twenty, and twenty-one, and twenty-two, and they have made it to Triple-A, the fields of the almost-there. They are unworldly farm boys from the South and just-glad-to-be-here boys from the Midwest and athletic middle-class boys from Southern California and hungry but homesick boys from Latin America. They are young, and gifted, and close, and so they laugh in the quiet, comforting presence of time—as if now could never be then.

Other ballplayers will laugh as well. Not with the same full-throated glee, but with a hesitancy rooted in wondering whether they have finally become the punch line to clubhouse jokes of: There's the door, what's your hurry? They are twenty-six now, and twenty-seven, and even twenty-eight—men, not boys, who have spent a swirl of summers toiling in dirt-and-grass patches in Elmira, New York, and Bristol,

Connecticut, and Bluefield, West Virginia, and Charlotte, North Carolina, slipping work gloves over their hands, swinging bats like axes. Many have wives and children. A few have even made brief appearances in the major leagues. But they cannot go on like this forever. Time, once a quiet comfort, is now impatient, and clearing its throat.

Every one of these players, young and not so, will move on, but Ben Mondor, the seen-it-all owner of the Pawtucket Red Sox, will still be here, taking his position outside the box office, as he did tonight, to thank the fans for their support. At fifty-six, he has the assured bearing of one who grew up Depression poor, saw action in World War II, and worked hard to make his millions; a short man, he seems tall. The rhythm and phrasing of his words telegraph his roots to the Rhode Island ear: Woonsocket, by way of Quebec. Married and with no children of his own, he keeps souvenir trinkets and packs of baseball cards in his pockets for kids who catch his eye, who hide behind their parents, who greet this wounded stadium, so in need of repair, as a palace of wonder. With tinted glasses and a tight mustache, he is the no-nonsense Santa Claus of the tough Blackstone Valley.

On and on down the line, the people at McCoy assumed their roles, all in the service of a ball game. From Mondor's young assistants—general manager Mike Tamburro and communications director Lou Schwechheimer, who, as usual, did everything short of lacing the ballplayers' cleats—down to the batboy, Billy Broadbent, who swept the bits of yesterday's game from the dugout, helped with the laundry, shagged fly balls during batting practice, and played pepper with Pawtucket's ritual-driven third baseman, Wade Boggs.

Billy lives close by, with his mother, his brother, and his father's absence. He is sixteen, and such a trembling reed of boyish anxiety that one of the Pawtucket pitchers has burdened him with the nickname "Panic." Once a goof who loitered at the ballpark's chain-link borders—like some POW of the chaotic world, seeking refuge in baseball's order—he now stands inside the fence, at baseball's employ. Wearing white polyester baseball pants with red-blue-red elastic around the waist, a long-sleeve blue undershirt, and an oversized Red Sox jersey from Doyle's Sporting Goods that hangs from his frame like laundry on a clothesline, he is the guardian of the bats, responsible for arranging them by player—Gedman's bats here, Walker's bats here, Bowen's bats here—at the end of the dugout.

This is a simple, almost mindless duty, yet Billy often stops his appointed rounds to grasp a Louisville Slugger by its tapered handle, where the sticky remnant of pine tar seals hand to wood—now a hard-ash Excalibur of the imagination. The ballplayer's name stamped on each bat seems to give it personality. One day he tests a heavy Dave Koza bat, solid as the first baseman himself, and impossible to imagine swinging fast enough to rocket a 90-mile-an-hour fastball; the next day a lighter Marty Barrett, smart and buoyant, like the crafty second baseman himself. He holds each bat out and down, gives it a shake, as if measuring its worth in the clutch. He takes a half swing, then another, then another, submitting to the spells of a simple piece of wood.

While others at McCoy completed their various pregame rituals, the home plate umpire attended to the anointment of thirty-six fresh Official Wilson International League baseballs that come a dozen to a box. Sitting in front of his navy blue locker in the cubbyhole of an umpire's room, chewing Carefree sugarless gum, he plucked one virgin baseball after another from the paper-tissue nests in which they rested, like Fabergé eggs, then rubbed each ball with a just-so dab of a strange dark salve that ties most every baseball game directly to the American clay. A salve called Lena Blackburne Rubbing Mud.

Russell Aubrey Blackburne, a.k.a. Slats Blackburne, a.k.a. Lena Blackburne, was a smart but inconsistent infielder who played on and off in the major leagues from 1910 to 1919, then returned in 1927 for one at bat—a run-scoring single—and again in 1929 to pitch one-third of an inning. He became a longtime major-league coach and manager who seemed destined to be remembered, if at all, as the Chicago White Sox skipper who engaged in two fistfights with the same player: Art Shires, a talented but truculent character whose nickname "Art the Great" reflected his relationship with modesty. In 1938, though, while coaching third base for the Philadelphia Athletics, Blackburne became intrigued by an umpire's complaint that the applications normally used to remove the gloss from new baseballs—tobacco juice and muddied infield dirt, among them—either failed to cut the sheen or made the balls more susceptible to tampering. Later, while walking along the tributaries of the Delaware River, not far from his South Jersey home, Blackburne came upon the perfect ingredient: the mud along a certain stretch of Pennsauken Creek. A dollop of this muck seemed to dim the shine on a new baseball without compromising its white integrity. Word spread from the Philadelphia clubhouse to other American League teams that Lena had dug something up. Before long he was working the curious side job of providing major-league franchises with coffee cans of his special mud, sometimes called Magic Mud, a silky pudding that to this day enables umpires to discharge one of their many pregame duties, as detailed in the official rules of baseball: to "inspect the ball and remove its gloss."

So this duty-bound umpire, Denny Cregg, sat, plucked, spat, and rubbed. If truth be known, he would have preferred a postponement tonight. Although a devoted baseball lifer, with major-league aspirations of his own, he had spent the day moving his family's belongings out of a rented floor in a triple-decker and into their own house, their new home, in the Massachusetts town of Webster, an hour's drive north. He was exhausted. Instead of standing for three hours in this nose-runny cold, shouting ball, strike, and out, wouldn't it have been nice to cozy up to his pregnant wife and their three-year-old son tonight, enjoy the scent of fresh possibility in rooms awaiting the Cregg imprint, and start Easter Sunday with a nice big breakfast? Wouldn't that have been nice?

But baseball waits for no one. Cregg packed up a ten-year-old nephew, eager for some baseball distraction, and drove down to a job in Pawtucket. His first order of business: preparing these thirty-six game balls. To him, the Lena Blackburne ritual is so solemn a duty that he rarely accepts any offer of help. He likes the feel of it, the control of it, this application of mud without grit, this laying of hands. A chewing-gum spit to the palm. A finger scoop from the plastic bucket of mud. Not too much; not too little; just . . . so. A mixing of mud and spittle, and then a rub. There.

*   *   *

As the stubborn 6:30 sunset withdrew the last of the brightness, the fans waited and waited in the creeping darkness. The supposed game time of 7:30 gave way to 7:40, then 7:50. The public-address system could only share the obvious: delay due to lights in need of repair.

Disrepair at McCoy is common. The old ballpark, a concrete mass of infrastructural aches and bruises, belongs not to the Pawtucket Red Sox but to the financially strapped City of Pawtucket. This is why the stadium often has the feel of a glorified public works garage: here, a duffel bag filled with batting practice balls; there, a malodorous dump truck; and come winter, mounds of sand and salt everywhere, courtesy of the highway department. This is also why Pawtucket Red Sox officials dispatched a couple of city workers, including one nicknamed "Killer," to the Light Room, within the McCoy labyrinth, to coax another night of brightness from those cranky pieces of city property, the stadium lights.

With hidden city workers flicking switches, literally, hopefully, fans could do little more than consider the larger meaning of the lights and shadows confusing the field, or thumb through the ninety-cent official Pawtucket Red Sox program, a jumble of statistics, advertisements, and photographs that provides indisputable proof of the death and burial of 1980, a dismal year in Rhode Island. The team lost fifteen more games than it won to finish in seventh place, and the state backed the losing incumbent, Jimmy Carter, in the presidential election. But this is a new season, a new administration. Forget that outfielder and fan favorite Sam Bowen hit only .229; he'll be back! And forget that first baseman and power hitter Dave Koza hit only 13 home runs; he's again swinging for the fences! If Bowen and Koza reach their potential, and if Boggs at third base has another good year, and if the pitchers—Ojeda and Hurst, Smithson and Parks—stay healthy, who knows what might happen? Maybe the Pawtucket Red Sox will win the International League playoffs to earn the coveted Governors' Cup; maybe some of these Pawtucket ballplayers will emerge as the Boston stars of tomorrow. The next Tiant. The next Yastrzemski. The next—dare we say it—Ted Williams.

If you doubt this possibility, just turn to page 43 in your program to see the posed photograph of five Pawtucket players, hitchhiking in their uniforms, caps, and cleats at the Interstate 95 entrance ramp, their right thumbs pointing north, toward Boston. One of them holds a handwritten sign that reads, "Fenway Park." These ballplayers, Rich Gedman, Chico Walker, Julio Valdez, Luis Aponte, and Keith MacWhorter, played briefly for Boston last season, and are hoping to return to that magical place where someone else carries your luggage.

"On their way to Fenway," the caption reads.

Nearly thirty years later, the photo will come to memorialize for MacWhorter what might have been. Of those five hitchhiking players, he wound up with the shortest major-league career; a six-foot-four right-hander, he appeared in 14 games in 1980 for the Boston Red Sox, gave up 26 earned runs, finished with an 0–3 record, and never returned. "I never won a game," he will say, looming large in his small office in East Providence, where he works as an investment consultant. "That's my bitterness."

But every month, MacWhorter, a Rhode Island boy who readily acknowledges that he was a two-pitch pitcher lacking that career-saving third, will receive a pension check from Major League Baseball for about $85. Every month, then, he will be reminded at least of this: However briefly, Keith MacWhorter is among the very few to have played in the major leagues.

That black-and-white photograph—of five uniformed baseball players looking to hitch a ride north—sums up the Pawtucket Red Sox, the International League, the 1981 season, tonight's game. Buy your lottery tickets at the Li'l Peach convenience store, the program suggests. Bank at the Pawtucket Credit Union. Use the fine writing instruments of Cross. Dine at the Mei-King Restaurant, enjoy Hendrie's ice cream, savor a drink at the Blarney Stone Pub.

Hope.

Finally, at eight o'clock, a half hour late, the umpires determine that the faulty stadium lights are blanketing the field with sufficient brightness. The dedicated switch flipping of Killer and his City of Pawtucket colleagues has succeeded—though the stadium tower in left-center still refuses to release its light.

Please rise.

The twilight's last gleam has vanished, and beyond center field the broad stripes and bright stars blow straight in. An umpire who would rather be home adds two more words to the opening anthem, two commanding words of release that tell a pitcher, who will never know the big leagues, to ready himself on the mound; that sends a catcher, who will play in the big leagues for thirteen years, into a coiled squat; and prompts a hitter in his last baseball spring to dig a fleeting foothold in the batter's box dirt.

Play ball.

Strike one.

Hallelujah.

Now here comes the second pitch of the night from the starting pitcher for the Pawtucket Red Sox, Danny Parks, a devout Christian from Alabama who so hates to fly that he keeps his nose buried in a Bible from takeoff to landing. A sinker-ball pitcher who tries to induce batters into hitting ground balls, he scoffs at the stereotype of born-again ballplayers being as meek as lambs. But he has become the tough-luck anchor of his team, a master at losing ball games by one run. He is twenty-six, married, and in his sixth minor-league year, the doubts about his baseball future intensifying. He begins his economical windup, raising his glove from waist to head, as if offering the ball up to God, then pushes off the mound's rubber hyphen to thrust his six-foot, 185-pound body forward. The pitch.

Waiting for it is the leadoff batter for the Rochester Red Wings, the sure-handed second baseman Tom Eaton. The clump of Red Man chew distending his right cheek is as essential to his at bat as the Louisville Slugger in his hands; he believes that this tug of toxic brown stuff adds extra weight, extra power, to his wiry frame. He, too, is twenty-six, and is now just starting his first year in Triple-A, but already the confidence of the pitchers at this level is doing little for his. In particular, their paralyzing curveballs—often threatening him with bodily harm before changing course at the last moment—haunt his dreams, yet clarify his mind. Although indirect by nature, they tell him to his face that he is a talented minor-league ballplayer, period. Intellectually, he has known this from the moment he signed with the Baltimore Orioles organization four years ago for $1,000, a modest amount that signaled he was less a major-league prospect than a good person to have on a team—a fill-in who allows management to focus on more talented players. Emotionally, though, Tom Eaton has hope. He has been underestimated before. And he has that Red Man tucked in his cheek, an extra something. Who knows.

The pitched ball tails away to hit Eaton on the instep of his right foot. It stings, but he would never let on to his manager. Best to shake it off. Besides, how long can a 9-inning baseball game last? Three hours at most? He hustles gamely to first base, mouth shut. Years later, people will see this errant pitch as a harbinger of what is to follow: a divine message, delivered at the expense of Tom Eaton's right foot, saying that you're in for it now, ladies and gentlemen.

The rest of the half inning suggests the opposite: fly out to left; routine groundout; called third strike. Bang, bang, bang.

From the unheated press box above, Bob Drew, the general manager cum play-by-play announcer for the Red Wings, describes the McCoy scene for his thousands of listeners back in far-off Rochester. He has no Pawtucket counterpart; no radio station carries the PawSox games because, quite frankly, few in Rhode Island care. So his words alone paint the night for those not present, save for the sporadic observations of his sidekick, Pete Torrez, and the steady muttering hum of the modest crowd beneath him, a hum occasionally punctured by the faint calls of roaming vendors with foreign New England accents.

Pawpcawn heah! Pawpcawn. . . .

Drew has read aloud the lineups with all the enthusiasm he could muster, though it still sounds like a recitation of the unimaginative specials from a diner's menu: "Tommy Eaton will lead it off for the Wings; Dallas Williams will bat second; Cal Ripken will bat third; Mark Corey will be the cleanup hitter; Dan Logan will bat fifth; Chris Bourjos will be batting sixth; Drungo Hazewood seventh; Bob Bonner will hit eighth; and Dave Huppert, making his second start of the year, will do the catching. He will bat ninth. . . .

"For Pawtucket, Lee Graham will lead it off; Marty Barrett will be second; Chico Walker will hit third; Russ Laribee will be in as the DH, he'll be the cleanup hitter; Dave Koza will be at first, batting fifth; Wade Boggs, the third baseman, will bat sixth; Sam Bowen, the right fielder, will bat seventh; Rich Gedman, the catcher, will bat eighth; and Julio Valdez, the shortstop, will bat ninth."

If Drew had rattled off the birthplaces of each player, rather than their names, he would have sung an anthem of the Americas. Leading off for Rochester: Tulsa, Oklahoma, followed by Brooklyn, New York; Havre de Grace, Maryland; Tucumcari, New Mexico; Trion, Georgia; Chicago, Illinois; Mobile, Alabama; Uvalde, Texas; South Gate, California; and pitching, Richmond, Virginia. And for Pawtucket, leading off: Summerfield, Florida, followed by Arcadia, California; Jackson, Mississippi; Southington, Connecticut; Norfolk, Virginia; Omaha, Nebraska; Brunswick, Georgia; Worcester, Massachusetts; San Cristobal, Dominican Republic; and pitching, Huntsville, Alabama. From the mill towns of New England to the suburbs of the Pacific Coast; from the housing projects of the Midwest to the sugarcane fields of the Caribbean: a ballad of bus fumes and ambition.

The Rochester team emerges from the dugout to create nine red-and-white disruptions on the dark green field. Among them, the starting pitcher, Larry Jones, once a prince of Florida athletics; he was an All-American wide receiver at Seminole High School who played both football and baseball at Florida State University before deciding to concentrate on pitching. The Baltimore Orioles signed him to a contract for a modest amount in 1977, but the money didn't matter; he would have paid them for the chance. He has not forgotten his first week in rookie ball, in Bluefield, West Virginia, when the manager invited the latest crop of would-be Baltimore stars to take a good look at one another and remember: Less than 3 percent of those who sign professional baseball contracts ever reach the major leagues.

Jones was twenty-two then, tall and powerfully built, with a record of sustained athletic achievement and a fastball that arrived at more than 90 miles an hour; he felt confident that he would be among the chosen few to ascend. But here he is now, four years older, a veteran of minor-league suspicions and doubts. He thinks that his manager is more interested in internal politics than in player development. He thinks that one Baltimore executive in particular is the worst man he has ever met. He thinks—no, he knows—that the meter is running; that athletes don't get better with age. Every spring training, when the best minor-league players vie for those few remaining spots on the major-league roster, he has a brief audience with Earl Weaver, the cranky Baltimore Orioles manager, whose message, in effect, is always the same: You're going back to Triple-A. Keep doing what you're doing. If anybody gets hurt, maybe you'll get a chance.

In other words, Jonesy, be realistic. The Baltimore Orioles have the finest pitching staff in Major League Baseball: Dennis Martinez; Scott McGregor; Mike Flanagan, a Cy Young Award winner; Steve Stone, another Cy Young Award winner; and Jim Palmer, the winner of three Cy Young awards, which means that he was voted the best pitcher in the American League *three* times. Face it, Jonesy. This is a business. You're a living, breathing insurance policy, in case one of these All Stars gets injured.

So what do you think Jones and all his fellow pitchers in Rochester are secretly hoping for, beyond the desire to see their teammates and good buddies get lit up—knocked out of the game—every time they take the mound? It is so awful to think that you don't even want to say it aloud, but this is what they wish: That the elbow on the storied right arm of future Hall of Fame pitcher Jim Palmer swells like a Florida grapefruit. That he gets injured. That the injury leads to an urgent message to pack up and head to Baltimore. That one night, maybe in New York, maybe Kansas City (and that would be all right, too), Weaver will grunt the name of the night's starting pitcher:

Jones.

Now starting. In Pawtucket. Jonesy.

He needs just eleven pitches. Groundout to second; groundout to first; line out to second. Done.

*   *   *

Drew, the Rochester broadcaster, has tried to describe the weather conditions, but his words fall short: *"A cool and windy night here in Pawtucket, Rhode Island, the wind blowing right in from center field. No threat of rain; however, it is a very chilly night. . . ."*

Chilly? Though the thermometer reads 45 degrees, the April night air carries an early December bluster with a January bite. Football weather, for Christ's sake. But a veteran Rochester pitcher who knows a thing or two, a Missouri farm boy named Steve Luebber, has an idea. He has played in the major leagues; in fact, he once came within one pitch—one pitch—of a rare no-hitter. Of course, that near feat means absolutely nothing now, as he finds himself thirty-one years old, back in the minor leagues, and relegated to the open-air visitors' bullpen along the first-base line, where pitchers sit with their hands clenched in warm-up jackets. Still, he has an idea.

On the other side of the chain-link fence, where civilians dwell, kids are begging for any kind of artifact touched by someone who actually plays baseball for a living. All right, all right, Luebber tells them. Let's make a deal. I'll trade you baseballs for any wood you can find.

Wood for baseballs? To the children of Pawtucket, this tall and courtly ballplayer with hangdog eyes must seem like the thickest rube. Before long there comes tumbling over the divide a bonfire's worth of twigs, branches, lumber, even slats from a white picket fence.

From a picket fence? Are these kids ripping apart some old lady's garden? Luebber doesn't ask. He just pays for the delivery with scuffed-up baseballs. Soon he has a fire burning in one of the fifty-five-gallon drums used as garbage cans, fueled by paper, broken bats, and whatever else these Pawtucket kids have culled from their deforestation project. The game has just begun, but already the Rochester pitchers need a fire to warm their precious hands and moods, its flames lighting up a corner of this Depression-era ballpark like some Dead End Kids spud party along New York's East River. *If I had the wings of an angel, over these prison walls I'd fly. . . .*

These earliest innings follow ordinary baseball time, unfolding with a familiar leisure occasionally interrupted by intimations of drama. Glance down at your program, consider the advertised merits of the $3.99 steak special at the East Side Checker Club ("Includes Soup, Salad, Potato, Vegetable and Bread and Butter"), and look up to find that you've misplaced the top half of the 2nd inning: groundout; pop out; fly out. Or become mesmerized by the wink and flicker of light near the visitors' bullpen along the first-base line, wonder whether you see fire coming out of a barrel, say to yourself that yes, yes, that is a fire, then return your gaze to the field, only to see players wearing red caps running in and players wearing blue caps running out, the bottom half of the second done: strikeout, groundout, groundout.

In the bottom of the 3rd inning, two singles allow the Red Sox to move a runner to third base, where he watches two teammates strike out before a third grounds out to end the threat. In the bottom of the 4th inning, Chico Walker, the twenty-three-year-old Red Sox left fielder who hit a home run during his brief first visit to the major leagues last year, something that can never be taken from him, hits a baseball deep, deep to center field. It dies of exhaustion at the warning track. But up in the press box, Mike Scandura, the earnest young reporter for the Pawtucket *Evening Times*, who is dutifully recording every pitch in his C. S. Peterson's Scoremaster simplified Baseball Score Book, considers this hard-hit ball a possible indication of things to come. He jots: "370 drive into the wind."

In the top of the 5th inning, Chris Bourjos, the left fielder for the Red Wings, stands at the ready in the batter's box. He appeared in 13 games with the San Francisco Giants last year, a fact worthy of boast, but the boast will end by the Bay; his major-league career is over, though two more years of standby in the minors await him. He is the nephew, by the way, of Otto "Dutch" Denning, a bit major-league player whose name resonates mostly because of a great story he used to tell about himself. In 1943, while playing subpar baseball for the Cleveland Indians, Denning was summoned by the team's player-manager, Lou Boudreau, a future member of the Hall of Fame.

Boudreau: How'd you like to see Niagara Falls—for free?
Denning: I'd like that.
Boudreau: Good, because we're sending you to Buffalo.

Now the nephew of Otto Denning swings at a 1–2 pitch and sends the ball high, higher, and short, maybe sixty feet from home plate. Parks, the pitcher, knows well enough to get out of the way, as Wade Boggs, the third baseman, and Dave Koza, the first baseman, stutter toward the ball and each other, their heads tilted impossibly back, the two of them similar enough in appearance to be brothers. Both have darkish hair cropping from under their blue Pawtucket caps. Both have full mustaches. Both have powerful builds. Both have Boston hopes.

Tracking that plummeting white dot in the wind, their eyes are so locked on heaven that neither sees the other coming. Two minor-league unknowns, destined to collide.

Dave Koza (11), quarterback for the Whites, is about to kick a 30-yard field goal and score the last three points for his team. . . .

August 30, 1971

The 27–0 score was helped along when Dave Koza intercepted a pass and ran it back for the first touchdown. . . .

September 6, 1971

The ball apparently just can't keep up with speedster Dave Koza, who led his team to victory over the Bulldogs. A 6–1 senior, Koza gunned in 19 points for the Blazers in their 11th victory. . . .

February 28, 1972

Triple winner was Dave Koza, shown above with his discus throw of 148 feet 5 inches for 1st place. He also took first in the triple jump (39 ft. 10 in.) and the long jump (20 ft.). . . .

May 11, 1972

The history of Torrington, Wyoming, turns brittle by the year in the narrow basement of its newspaper, the *Torrington Telegram*. There, stacked against the wall, near some dusty coffee cups and a winter glove missing its right-hand mate, reside bound copies of the newspaper; the years captured within are printed on their spines. The newspapers, browning and drying like late-autumn leaves, reach back a century to tell the bit-by-bit transformation of a nowhere place of a railroad way station, eighty-four miles north of Cheyenne, into a proud and vital agricultural center, with sugar beets, corn, winter wheat, cattle, and fifty-eight hundred residents. By Wyoming standards, a city.

Open any volume from the early 1970s, release that first whiff of the paper-crumbling past, and journey back to the time-frozen stock shows and 4-H competitions, the summer headlines ("First Snake Bite Happens Monday") and great Thanksgiving deals down at Gibson Discount, where Cat Stevens's *Tea for the Tillerman* album can be had for just $3.97. A woman named Julia is writing her gentle "Scoopin 'n' Snoopin" gossip column ("Hello Folks! Have I ever got a 'goodie' for you this time . . ."), and the Hill Top Kar-Vu Drive-In Theatre is doing its best to keep citizens apprised of cultural trends by featuring such fare as *The Young Graduates* ("The 'Hot Pants' Generation is Loose").

And with every turn of a yellowing page, it seems, another story is trumpeting the athletic exploits of the hometown hero, Dave Koza. Here he is, leading the high school football team to an undefeated season as its quarterback, defensive back, and kicker. Here he is, photographed falling backward after scoring 2 of his 21 points in another basketball victory. Here he is, on graduation day, receiving the football award, the basketball award, and the track award. Koza, Koza, Koza, and the only reason he isn't receiving an award for baseball—his best sport—is that the high schools don't play baseball. Blame it on the late spring, or maybe the lack of local interest.

This posed a problem for the family. When Dave Koza was ten years old, his father—an affable retired navy veteran, fond of his drink—moved the family from Florida to his home state of Wyoming. They settled in

Torrington, where young Dave struggled to understand a community that did not offer organized baseball to adolescent boys. He did not shy from informing his parents that he wanted to go back to Florida—back to baseball.

His understanding father, Gene, found a vacant lot beside the Safeway grocery store, planted four poles, unrolled some chicken wire, and laid out a regulation-size Little League field. With that, organized baseball for young boys came to Torrington, allowing Dave to demonstrate his almost preternatural skills for people other than his parents and brothers. One night, while taking in the previews before a show down at the Wyoming movie theater, his parents saw an advertisement for the Chandler Baseball Camp and thought: Dave. After learning that a session at the camp would cost $175—$175 that they did not have—the Kozas asked for help from several merchants in town, many of whom were appreciative of Gene Koza's efforts to start a local Little League program.

Soon, Dave Koza, all of eleven, was traveling eight hundred miles to Chandler, Oklahoma, to a place that so many other boys would only know through the small advertisements that occasionally appeared in the back of *Baseball Digest*:

BASEBALL CAMP
FOR BOYS 8 THRU 18
Three Weeks Intensive Training.
See Our Brochure Before Deciding.
Write, TOM BELCHER, Baseball Camp, Chandler, Okla.

This was a military-style baseball camp; no swimming pool, no tennis courts, no air-conditioning to counter the oppressive Oklahoma heat. For eleven hours a day, these Pee Wees and Midgets, Preps and Minors ran baseball drills; practiced bunts, slides, and hitting the cutoff; played baseball games—and then drilled some more. Before lights out in the stuffy cabins at ten, they gathered in the mess hall to watch film footage of nothing but baseball; black-and-white clips from a World Series one night, an instructional film on fielding the next.

Its founder, Bo Belcher, an irrepressible public relations director for the Oklahoma State Fair, opened the baseball camp in 1958, on rural land that used to be the city dump. By the late 1960s, his son Tom was running the camp, and everyone knew that Tom Belcher had been with the New York Mets—"a stocky right-hander," the camp's brochure said, who had starred as an All-American in high school and college before signing a bonus contract with the Mets right there at the camp. The brochure featured a photograph of Belcher in a Mets uniform, along with these words: "Tom was with the Mets for a short time in 1963."

That Tom Belcher never appeared in a major-league game now seems beside the point. He played an underwhelming three years in the minor leagues, spent "a short time" with the Mets at their spring training camp in 1963, and, eventually, returned to run his father's camp, where he taught these true boys of summer the fundamentals of the game, showed them the benefits of dedication, regaled them with Casey Stengel anecdotes, and loomed before them as the personification of the Possible. When Tom Belcher died in 2006, several years after waning demand forced him to close his baseball paradise, legions of former campers mourned.

But when the camp was in its glory, back in the mid- and late 1960s, a Wyoming boy named Koza thrived. Thanks to a godfather's beneficence, he returned to the camp when he was twelve, then accepted Tom Belcher's offer to work as a camp counselor for a few more summers. He cleaned the cabins, raked the fields, and played baseball, baseball, and more baseball, often while wearing a used wool uniform so itchy and stifling that it must have been intended as preparation for greater things; a toughening up for the leagues to come. When his camp sessions ended, he would return to Torrington to star as a pitcher and outfielder in the Babe Ruth and American Legion games, before football season arrived to offer him another field on which to excel.

By his senior year in high school, Koza had become the official Local Hero, of whom much was expected. He was working in the stockyard directly across from the high school football field, running calves into the chute, clipping their young horns, then powdering the wounds to stem the bleeding. But everyone knew that Dave Koza wasn't long for Torrington.

"He was our All-Everything," says Paul "Cactus" Covello Jr., Koza's classmate and friend. "Groomed from the git-go to play baseball."

Cactus had enviable connections; his family owned a prominent car dealership. So he and Koza would loop the town, "dragging Main," in Cactus's gorgeous car, a 1967 Impala convertible, blue with a white top. They'd prowl Main Street, turn left after the Trail Hotel, hug the railroad tracks, turn into the lot at the Ten Pin Tropics bowling alley—where carhops waited to serve you—and linger a while. Then they'd retrace their path and do it all over again, night after night, with an occasional diversion to the Hill Top drive-in just to shake things up. Cactus was proud to hang around with Koza, in part because everyone in town knew that he'd be famous one day. Not that Koza would ever say that, or even think it. He was just one of the guys, though first among them: big and strong, quick as a cat, and exuding the air of one not to be trifled with.

The Dave Koza baseball odyssey that began with all those day-long trips to the Chandler Baseball Camp continued after high school graduation, when he decided to attend Eastern Oklahoma State College—mostly because the baseball coach at the two-year school was also an instructor at Chandler. He played and pitched well, but if fifty people came to one of his Mountaineers games, thirty of them were scouts following his more talented teammate, Tito Landrum, who would later appear in two World Series. Then, after the end of spring semester, it was on to Colorado Springs, where Koza played semiprofessional ball in exchange for a construction job and a place to live.

In the late spring of 1974, after a night game in Colorado Springs, Koza was invited by a scout to a Denny's Restaurant, a familiar setting for minor-league deals of modest order. The scout, Danny Doyle, had played briefly in the major leagues—13 games in 1943 as a weak-hitting catcher for the war-depleted Red Sox—before gaining some renown within the organization as a gifted scout. He had signed the Red Sox pitching star Jim Lonborg, and would one day sign an even greater star, Roger Clemens, but right now he was locked on Dave Koza. Sign now for $15,000, he said.

Koza was a nineteen-year-old boy. He asked if Doyle would come back to Torrington to meet his parents. But the scout said he was too busy, and needed an answer by midnight, yes or no. After telephoning his parents, the young man reached for the proffered pen and signed his baseball life away to the Boston Red Sox.

"I went home, packed my stuff, and went to Elmira," Koza will later say.

Rookie ball in Elmira, New York, along the Empire State's southern tier, led to Single-A ball in Winter Haven, Florida, which led to Double-A ball in Bristol, Connecticut, which led to Triple-A ball here in Pawtucket, which led to this moment. Seven years of chasing baseballs for a living—a fourth of his lifetime—culminates now in this pop fly at the pitcher's mound. Dave Koza drifts to his right, looking up, ready to catch a ball he believes is his.

Mine, he thinks. Mine.

Wade Boggs is twenty-two years old, with a devoted wife named Debbie and a two-year-old daughter named Meagann—both of whom are at the game tonight, as usual. They live on one floor of a triple-decker a few blocks from McCoy Stadium, but when the season ends, they will return to live with his parents in Florida. They drive a red 1975 Dodge van, bought used. The carpeting on the walls and ceiling suggests that the van once accommodated parties; now its purpose is to transport the belongings of an itinerant baseball family.

Debbie, cute, with round cheeks and blondish hair that curls at her shoulders, grew up poor in Tampa, so poor that, for a while, she dreamed of becoming a nun. It seemed so glamorous; that is, until she learned that the job required you to be Roman Catholic. Still, there was something about watching her Catholic girlfriend don a lace veil for Saturday-night Mass, looking so very much like a princess.

She and Wade began dating at H. B. Plant High School. Though he was nearly three years younger, his mature, chivalrous ways won her heart. She cheered him on at his high school baseball games, often tallying his eye-popping statistics for him (he batted .522 as a junior!). But the competition adjusted to his talents when he was a senior, and his batting average plummeted. His father, an air force master sergeant, hustled to the public library to check out a classic—*The Science of Hitting,* by Ted Williams and John Underwood—and ordered his son to study the master's tips and observations: how to hit to the opposite field; how to coordinate hip and wrist action; most of all, how to hit your pitch—how to swing only at the pitches in your "wheelhouse." The boy's batting average quickly returned to its rarefied level, a level that he thought would justify a first-round selection in baseball's amateur draft.

Instead, the Major League Scouting Bureau rated Boggs a nonprospect; supposedly, he didn't run well enough. The Boston Red Sox drafted him in the seventh round, and then only because one of its scouts, George Digby, argued that hitters this gifted are a handful in a generation. "I was crushed," Boggs will later tell *Sports Illustrated,* but he signed—for just $7,500. "I knew what I wanted," he will tell the magazine article's author, Peter Gammons. "I knew the other scouts were wrong."

In 1976, two days after graduating from high school, Boggs traveled twelve hundred miles north to Elmira, New York, to play in the New York–Penn League. After the end of an unremarkable season, he returned to Florida to marry Debbie in a Baptist church. Their two-day honeymoon in Clearwater began with a romantic night of shared vomiting, courtesy of some microwave cheeseburgers bought at a convenience store.

After Elmira came Winston-Salem, then Bristol—and now, the beginning of a second season in Pawtucket. If you ask Debbie, they are happy, living in a more spacious apartment than, say, that two-room place in Winston-Salem, where their only furniture was intended for lawn use. Wade's job is to play baseball, and Debbie's job is everything else: wife, mother, statistician, you name it. Over the years she has operated a switchboard, managed a beauty salon, swept up at a florist's, tarred and shingled roofs, and worked the overnight shift at a warehouse. Her earnings have helped to finance his baseball education, giving him the time to concentrate, to practice. Without Debbie, there is no Wade.

And who is Wade? He is a man who swears that he wanted to be a major-league baseball player ever since he was eighteen months old; whose father tied his ambidextrous son's left hand behind his back to force him to throw with his right hand, broadening the number of baseball positions he could play; who has not forgotten how high school classmates signed his yearbook with "See you on 'Game of the Week' "; who is so driven by statistics—his own—that his teammates claim he begins recalculating his batting average a nanosecond after hitting a ball into play.

One story. Last year, on the final day of the 1980 season, the PawSox were losing 6–0 in the 9th inning to the Toledo Mud Hens, with Boggs leading Toledo's Dave Engle for the International League batting title by less than a percentage point. If he didn't bat again, the title was his.

But players in the Toledo dugout, possibly equipped with a pocket calculator, determined that if Boggs made one more out, their team-mate would win the batting title. So, with two outs, Toledo's pitcher purposely walked Pawtucket's Ray Boyer, hardly an offensive threat, to force Boggs to come to the plate. Boyer, understanding what was happening, tried to get thrown out. He strolled to second, sauntered to third, and then began a leisurely jaunt toward home. But the Toledo pitcher purposely threw the ball into the backstop, committing Boyer to score and forcing Boggs to remain in the batter's box.

Boggs grounded out to first, lost the batting title by .0007 of a point—and broke down.

Say what you will about Boggs, and some of his teammates clearly do, but he has worked extremely hard to be on the field tonight. Just ask the grounds crew. Or the batboy. Or some of the hangers-on from the neighborhood. They know.

They know that he arrives at the ballpark several hours before a game—before any of his teammates—to prepare. They know that someone has to hit dozens of ground balls to him at third base, and so they swat him ball after ball in an otherwise empty ballpark, helping him to quiet the rumors that he can barely field his position. They also take turns pitching to him as he fine-tunes that godlike hand-eye co-ordination of his, the loss of that batting title ever-present in his mind. It could be a groundskeeper pitching batting practice one day, a mope from the neighborhood the next. Boggs doesn't care if you're a Little Sister of the Poor, taking a break from that home for the indigent el-derly you help to run in Pawtucket; if you, dear sister, can throw strikes consistently, have at it—but be careful. Somewhere around here there is a groundskeeper who floated on air after Boggs told him he had just thrown the best batting practice Boggs could remember. The next time out, so the story goes, the groundskeeper hit Boggs in the helmet with a pitch. *Grab a rake, pal, you're done.*

What these people behold is a captive to ritual. He wakes up at the same time every day, arrives at the ballpark at the same time every day, and essentially fills out a curious checklist of things to do, each one connected to the other, every day. When to dress. When to take his first pinch of smokeless tobacco. When to warm up his arm. When to field grounders, and for how long. When to touch each of the three bases, in order. When to visualize the four at bats before him. When to take batting practice. When to take wind sprints. Everything has to be just so, down to the placement and use of the pine tar, weighted doughnut, and resin in the on-deck circle. But of all his superstitions, the strangest and most off-putting is this: Whether as a joke or in complete sincerity, he refuses to allow any of his bats to touch the bats of his teammates, supposedly out of fear of contracting their bad bat-ting habits.

These daily, time-consuming rituals, eighty or so of them, reflect in part a rigid upbringing in a military household in which you were at the dinner table by 5:30 or you didn't eat. But more than that, they represent Boggs's commitment to preparation; to dividing his day into specific segments of time so that he knows exactly what he ought to be doing—what he *needs* to be doing—at any given moment. This melding of mind and body, then, takes hours to complete, down to the moment that he carves the *chai* sign, the Hebrew symbol for life, in the dirt with his bat before stepping up to the plate. Boggs is not Jewish, but when he was about eleven years old he read in the back of a comic book that the *chai* sign signaled luck. The thought lodged in his Little League mind.

"It's having positive energy and positive karma all around you," he will explain three decades after this game. "I was a firm believer that if you kept the same momentum going, everything follows. I'm not one for spontaneous effort."

But for all the emphasis he places on daily order, there are some things over which the Wade Boggs of 1981 has no control. He cannot prevent the Boston Red Sox from acquiring the gifted third baseman Carney Lansford from the California Angels during the off-season, any more than he could have prevented the Toledo Mud Hens from conspiring to deny him the batting title. Nor can he stop the whispers within the Red Sox organization that he is a powerless hitter; that he is an unremarkable fielder; that he is not a team player. By the end of the 1980 season, after five years in the minors, Boggs had an impressive career batting average of .313, but there was something about him that the Boston front office did not like. The winter before, the Red Sox chose not to protect him from being bought at a nominal price by any of the twenty-five other major-league clubs, but no team considered him worth the cost. And so Boggs returned to Pawtucket, where, it seems, only he realizes how extraordinary he is.

Until he is summoned to the major leagues, what else can Boggs do but follow his rituals, draw ancient Hebrew symbols in the Pawtucket dirt, and wait. Just as he is waiting now for this ball falling like an overripe apple from the sky.

Mine.

Koza and Boggs do not see each other, their heads tilted so far back that Boggs's cap tumbles to the ground. Even as they collide at the mound, even as their upraised arms become entwined, their gloved and bare hands seeming to form two birds, brown and pink, about to take flight, the two men only have eyes for that falling ball.

It plops into Boggs's jostled glove, pops out, and plops for good into Koza's lobster claw of a first baseman's glove. The batter is out. Koza pirouettes to keep the Rochester runner honest at first, then turns back to face Boggs. The teammates speak for a fleeting moment. What do they say? Maybe "That was mine," or "One out," or, simply, "Are you okay?" Neither will remember.

Koza taps Boggs on the chest with the ball. A tender gesture: We're in this together.

A cameraman for WPRI Channel 12 sits behind home plate, on the other side of the billowing netting between fans and field, quietly recording a few scenes for the end of the eleven o'clock news.

The footage captures a small part of one game's incremental, even ordinary, progression: the 5th, 6th, and 7th innings. But the passage of thirty years will strip this B-roll snippet of its deadline urgency, imbuing it instead with an almost meditative, art-film quality. The needs of a late-night newscast in Rhode Island will have long passed, along with the baseball careers of these assembled men, leaving only a few minutes of sounds and images from a strange April night: the ambient lights and music of the ballpark, the cacophonous rumble of murmurs and cheers, come-ons and taunts.

The backstop netting behind home plate sways in and out of focus to lay blurry crosshatches across the unfolding scene, as if to underscore the impenetrable barrier between past and future. Beyond the outfield limits, streetlamps lend the soft romance of the boulevard to drab, industrial Division Street. Out there, past dead center field, a light that brightens a warehouse's loading dock also shines directly into the eyes of catchers, vexing Pawtucket's two backstops, Rich Gedman and Roger LaFrancois. Somewhere behind you, an unseen concessionaire calls out "Ice cream heah," his voice challenging the perceived insanity of a frozen dessert on such a cold night. Over your left shoulder, a few fans huddle in winter coats, their cheeks and noses flush, their legs covered with a green plaid blanket. And on the grass before you, players set aglow by stadium lights perform their quiet tics and habits between the brief and sudden bursts of action. Notice what happens, for example, when a Rochester batter hits a fly ball well foul of the left field line, somewhere in the direction of that bookmaker's place, the

Lily Social Club. Pawtucket's left fielder, Chico Walker, jogs toward the foul line in that exaggerated trot known to all outfielders: an act of feigned hustle, perhaps, but also of faint distrust—of double-checking that the foul ball is indeed foul; that it's not some trick of the eye. He returns then to his position in the dark, verdant grass, which seems to nearly swallow him.

Watch Rochester's Tom Eaton after he is thrown out trying to steal second base, possibly because the pitch that hit him on the right foot back in the 1st inning stole a step or two. He rises from the ground after receiving the shortstop's thumping tag, on his injured foot no less, with his uniform dirty and his red helmet off his head, his pride spilled before him in the dirt. He cannot stay; he must leave. He picks up his helmet and trots off, chastened.

Other little baseball moments reveal themselves. After each play, for example, Koza turns to remind the outfielders of the number of outs, raising two fingers in the top of the 6th inning, no matter that the scoreboard immediately behind them brightly trumpets the same information. Infielders are taught to do this in childhood as a way to keep everyone alert, on the fairly good chance that one of the Little League outfielders has been daydreaming again about that girl he likes in the fifth grade. One finger raised for one out, two fingers for two outs, and a closed fist for no outs—or, rather, *still* no outs.

Rochester's young third baseman, Cal Ripken Jr., approaches home plate with an unmistakable air of purpose. Standing six feet four, with a slender body destined to fill out, he rakes the dirt smooth with a sweep of his right cleat and then his left, cleats with Oriole-orange highlights that may well have been a gift from the Oriole hero Frank Robinson, a family friend. He peers at the pitcher with shoulders slightly hunched, suggesting mild curiosity about what comes next, then raises his thirty-five-inch-long bat, the fingers of his white-gloved left hand fluttering along the handle. Tonight he has warmed his bats by that fire in the barrel, in the belief that he can reduce the sting that follows bat-on-ball contact on a cold night. In his mind, he even sees his bat bending during his swing—having snap.

He waits, a study in confidence rooted both in his undeniable talent and in the endless hours he has given to learning the game. "Singularly focused," one of his Rochester teammates, John Hale, will later say. "He was at the ballpark all the time. He made no bones about it: 'This is my existence. This is all I care about.'"

There is also his bloodline. His father is Cal Ripken Sr., the intense third-base coach for the Baltimore Orioles and an experienced Schlitz-and–Lucky Strike traveler of the county roads of the minor leagues, both as a player and as a manager. The young man standing in the batter's box is just twenty years old, but in many ways he, too, is a minor-league veteran, with a connection to major-league royalty that is evident in the cleats he wears. He spent many childhood summers trailing his dad, fielding grounders, shagging flies, and absorbing the levels of the game in ballparks up and down the Eastern Seaboard—in Miami, and Asheville, and Memorial Stadium in Baltimore. Not long ago, Earl Weaver, the Orioles manager, watched young Ripken take fielding practice and thought: Baltimore's next third baseman, or maybe, just maybe, its shortstop. The kid reminds Weaver of Marty Marion, the tall, gifted shortstop of the St. Louis Cardinals of the 1940s. At ease onstage; baseball mature.

Ripken's teammates know how determined he is to improve; how he studies opposing pitchers and hitters for any wink of information that might give an edge; how he wants to succeed so completely that his diminishing nickname of "J.R."—a twinned reference to being the son of Cal and to the *Dallas* television show—slips from usage. Jim Umbarger, a Red Wings teammate and a former major-league pitcher, marvels at Ripken's ability to wait on a pitch longer than anyone he has ever seen. His finger-snap reflexes grant him the extra millisecond to determine what kind of pitch is coming at him, adjust, and drive it to left, center, or right.

His teammates believe that Ripken already knows he is destined for major-league glory, though their own destinies are nowhere near as certain. They gather around Floyd Rayford, the doughy catcher and infielder nicknamed "Sugar Bear," like children at a campfire to hear his thrilling and somewhat unnerving tales of what it's like up there, in the bigs. Last year, Sugar Bear got called up and had 4 singles and

5 strikeouts in 18 at bats (hell, he's already assured mention in the *Baseball Encyclopedia*!). Now, amid the lull of the clubhouse or the hum of the bus, Rayford will tell his Rochester teammates how there's no grace period. How it seems as though every game is 2–1, the scary manager Weaver is screaming again, and you're just hoping the ball isn't hit to you. Sugar Bear at least has been to the mountain. The others wonder whether they, too, will one day ascend. As for Ripken, he *grew up* on the mountain. He clearly has no doubt, his teammates think. He knows he'll make it.

Cal Ripken's teammates are wrong, though—hoodwinked by his talent, his workaholic ways, his focus at the plate. He hopes to make the major leagues, but he would never describe himself as certain of it. In fact, he remains in awe of the prospect, no matter that he grew up on the fields of minor-league baseball, and knows the likes of Robinson and Weaver. Many years later, he will say that he found "no comfort in knowing what it's all about."

Just consider all the anxieties the young man has had to contend with in the last two months alone. A few weeks earlier, at the beginning of Baltimore's spring training, Bryant Gumbel interviewed the two Cal Ripkens, senior and junior, for a segment of the *Today* show. Then, after performing well during spring training, the younger Ripken was among the first players cut from the major-league squad. After that, while taking extra batting practice just before leaving to join the Triple-A team, he popped something in his right shoulder. The trainers ordered him not to swing or throw for a few days to allow the injury to heal, leading some teammates to whisper that the Chosen One had pulled an "attitude muscle," and was fabricating an injury to express his displeasure at having been cut from the big-league camp. He soon corrected this misinterpretation—an indignity he will not forget—by gutting his way around being placed on the disabled list. And even when he did things exactly right, some humbling moment always followed, some reminder not to get ahead of himself. On Opening Day in Rochester, for example, he hit a home run, only to be removed for a pinch hitter later in the game. Something else he will not forget.

The wintry weather of Rochester in April has cut into opportunities for the batting practice that Ripken thinks he desperately needs. He doesn't feel comfortable at the plate yet, even when facing the batting practice pitches of Rochester's middle-aged manager, Doc Edwards. So he and Sugar Bear Rayford have been arriving early to the ballpark, taking turns pitching to each other, taking as many as a hundred swings in a row, drilling line drives into the Rochester outfield's frozen expanse. It seems to be helping.

Consider all these pressures, uncertainties, and mixed messages. The truth is, Cal Ripken is just a big kid, still struggling to manage the competing feelings of elation, anger, and insecurity. In fact, the boyish exuberance that he couples with his strong competitive streak can sometimes wear thin. He loves to wrestle and to play pranks, but Tom Eaton, who is nearly six years his senior, is growing tired of being pinned to the floor and shoved into lockers. It's not dignified, Eaton will tell him, though with big-brother affection. At the same time, Ripken's white-hot desire to win, always, leaves little allowance for the inevitability of failure. He is quick to lose his temper—usually, but not always, with himself. A couple of years from now, after Ripken will have emerged as an up-and-coming major-league star, a veteran teammate, Ken Singleton, will show him a videotape of yet another Ripken fit; something thrown, something slammed. Embarrassed, Ripken will work hard from then on to contain his temper, to be a model of restrained passion, the message imparted by Singleton finding hold somewhere deep in his temporal lobe: "We don't do that here."

But right now, as he waits for what comes next in Pawtucket, Cal Ripken Jr.—still learning to be something other than J.R.—has cleared his mind of everything but this at bat. Nothing else matters: not the cold, not the Baltimore Orioles, not the pinch-hitting slight from a couple of weeks ago, nothing but this at bat. He is not one to reassure himself that he is simply working through a slump; that he has to be patient; that he has time. No. He is hungry. Now.

"Every at bat was the seventh game of the World Series to me," Ripken will later say. "It seems that it was all about *this* moment."

After working the count to 3 and 2, Ripken sends a sharp grounder toward third base, where Boggs plays the violent hop so deftly that a sportswriter up in the press box circles the play. He rifles a throw to Dave Koza for the third out and the end to Rochester's half of the inning. Ripken is out by three steps.

As the Pawtucket players run off the field, Ripken halfheartedly rounds first base and stops at the infield's outer lip, defeated. He yanks his red helmet off and, with the helmet still in the grip of one hand, slams it hard to the ground. Then he flips the helmet toward the visitors' dugout in a gesture that signals complete disgust. Was he fooled by the pitch? Did he not follow through with the proper mechanics of his swing? Did his bat hit the pitch he dreams of a quarter inch too high, sending it chopping down into the grass, rather than rocketing into the outfield? Did Boggs rob him of a hit? It is just one out, one out in the 6th inning of a Triple-A game in Pawtucket, in the very beginning of the 1981 season. He is extraordinarily talented. He comes from royal baseball stock, Baltimore black and orange. Two innings from now, he will have another at bat.

No matter. He's not Cal Ripken Jr., not yet. He's just J.R., he is twenty years old, and he has grounded out.

Anywhere else but here, walks are recommended, both for the heart and for the alleviation of stress. In baseball, though, the sages know better. With gnarled fists jammed into warm-up jacket pockets, and bony asses somehow finding comfort on splintery wooden benches, these hoary diamond prophets will pause from spitting out another toothlike shell of a sunflower seed to growl again the game's stay-off-the-moors equivalent:

It's the walks that kill you.

The 7th inning has arrived, and Danny Parks has just walked Rochester's leadoff batter, Mark Corey, which has led to another walk: that of Parks's manager, Joe Morgan, now strolling toward the mound, and not for his health, or to take in the air. Time-out for a chat.

Morgan, head down as if prepared to hear confession, runs a cleat over the mound. Parks, head bowed in contrition, then sweeps a cleat over what Morgan has just swept. Back and forth they go, gardening, muttering, engaged in a slow, self-conscious dance in which partners try not to look each other in the eye. Is Morgan thinking of pulling Parks from the game? Is Parks begging to stay in?

The catcher and chaperone, Rich Gedman, stands nearby, the stadium lights glinting off his dark blue helmet. The third-base umpire, Jack Lietz, has his hands in his pockets to ward against the night's cold. Somewhere a concessionaire inadvertently highlights the pivotal moment by yelping, "Heah! Heah!"

Morgan walks without urgency back to the dugout, perhaps to buy a little more time for the relief pitcher, Luis Aponte, who is warming up in the half-light along the left-field sideline. Parks stays in the game. And the very next pitch he throws is smacked past him for a single into center field.

Now, with runners on first and second, Chris Bourjos, the nephew of Otto "How'd you like to see Niagara Falls?" Denning, lines a single into left field, prompting a ghostly chorus of growling diamond prophets to sing it again: It's the walks that kill you. The runner taking off from second base is the strong and speedy Mark Corey, whose image has appeared for the third year in a row on a Topps baseball card touting the "future stars" and "prospects" of the Baltimore Orioles. In truth, his major-league career is all but done. He has played in 49 games for Baltimore over the last two years, and has just 10 more big-league games left in his future. After this season, he will play four more years in the minor leagues, becoming a have-glove-will-travel guy who will set his suitcase down in Charlotte, North Carolina, and in El Paso, Texas; in Evansville, Indiana, and in Vancouver, British Columbia; in Jacksonville, Florida, and in Portland, Oregon, never to fulfill the promise conveyed on small rectangles of cardboard hoarded by children. Right now, though, he is still a cardboard prospect, and he is racing toward third base, two hundred pounds of determination, bound for home.

The Pawtucket left fielder, Chico Walker, dashes to his left. He is powerful, compact, and, in many ways, an odd baseball fit. A young man from Chicago's South Side, by way of Jackson, Mississippi, he grew up worshipping Stan the Man—not Stan Musial, the Baseball Hall of Fame star of the St. Louis Cardinals, but Stan Mikita, the Hockey Hall of Fame center for the Chicago Blackhawks. What's more, he is a second baseman by nature, but this season the Red Sox moved him to the outfield to make room for the franchise's second baseman of the future, Marty Barrett. Walker cannot say he is happy with the change, but if playing the outfield will get him back to the major leagues, just point him to left, center, or right.

Last year he played for the Boston Red Sox as a September call-up, just long enough to convince him that he belongs in the major leagues, not in Pawtucket. Even so, he will never find complete welcome in Boston, and never know the reasons why. He will wonder whether he was so good at playing both the infield and the outfield that he was considered not quite good enough at either. He will wonder whether, as an African American, he was bumping up against an unspoken quota imposed by a Red Sox front office not known for its courage in matters of race. How could he not wonder these things as, for several years to come, he will bounce up to Boston and down to Pawtucket, up to Boston, down to Pawtucket. He will move up and down so often that a real estate company in Pawtucket will specialize in finding him apartments on sudden notice, as in 1984, when he will be the last player cut on the last day of Boston's spring training camp. "It got frustrating after a while," Walker will later say. "I'm going back to Pawtucket for what? I'm eligible to be the mayor of Pawtucket."

Walker will be accused in some quarters of allowing his discouragement to affect his play, just as the Red Sox will be accused in some quarters of not giving him a fair chance. But he will get his mind straight; he will prevail. His major-league career as a fill-in player will last well into the 1990s, after most of the men around him tonight have retired and gone soft. As for playing the outfield, Chico Walker is a natural, as he demonstrates on this very play. He receives the ball on its first hop, a few yards in front of a billboard ad for Miller Beer asking if you've got the time, but he does not. Though his momentum pulls him toward center field, he manages to plant his left foot and hurl the ball toward home in an act counter to physical intuition. Morgan will later declare it to be "the best throw from left field I've ever seen in this stadium."

Some 250 feet away, at home plate, Walker's target looms: the Pawtucket catcher Rich Gedman, wearing glasses that he has no fear of breaking. He is thick-bodied, tough, and, at twenty-one, precociously gifted in coaxing the best performances from his pitchers. To find where Gedman comes from, just follow the nearby Blackstone River northwestward for forty miles, against its natural flow, through Pawtucket and past Woonsocket, past Whitinsville, past all the communities that for nearly two centuries used the Blackstone as a power source and industrial sewer. The textile mills would reward the river for its muscle by discharging dyes into its waters; the woodworking plants did the same with solvents and paints; the metalworking shops, heavy metals. Follow this tainted river to its origins, to Worcester, and there you will find Gedman's working-class hometown. His father drove a brewery truck and his mother worked in a factory, but he played baseball well enough to escape similar drudgery, and, at seventeen, was drafted by the Red Sox.

Last September, he was called up to Boston and in nine games batted a measly .208. He is back now in Pawtucket, eager to prove himself of major-league worth and acutely aware of the opportunity created by an off-season gaffe of historic measure, in which the Red Sox front office allowed their star catcher, Carlton Fisk, to slip into free agency and onto the payroll of the Chicago White Sox. But he is mature enough to know that he must block thoughts of the possible future from his mind, and focus on the now. He follows the advice that he will share with his own players, decades from now, as the manager of his hometown minor-league team, the Worcester Tornadoes: "One pitch. One out. One inning."

One play. Mark Corey rounds third base and charges toward home, intent on outracing the baseball sailing in fast from somewhere behind his left shoulder. Gedman plants his feet at the front of home plate, eyes on the approaching ball, yet fully aware of the man coming toward him at full speed. He must resist the natural impulse to face this threat, because right now the ball matters more than his own physical well-being. Corey begins his slide about six feet from the plate, his head and torso back, his left leg up and pointed out; he has become a human arrow.

The ball bounces once to beat him to home, but it arrives three feet to the right, forcing Gedman to reach for the ball and swing his mitt back across the plate, just as the blur of Corey's body sweeps past.

With expressions nearly childlike in their naked search for approval, the two men look to the umpire, Denny Cregg, a square block of blue, who quickly extends his arms parallel to the ground, then jabs a finger at the plate, pointing to the phantom evidence of the truth he is about to share.

Safe!

The denizens of McCoy Stadium, less than 1,700 now, and filling fewer than a third of the seats, release a collective cry of "Naaaaaah!" at the realization of Rochester taking a 1–0 lead. Amid the unintelligible expressions of outrage that follow, one man's call rises clearly above the rest, taking advantage of the acoustics created by the stadium's many uninhabited quarters to offer the umpire this Holy Saturday blessing:

"You stink! Yeah, you! You stink!"

Parks rushes up to invade Cregg's personal space, his face distorted in fury, the peace he finds in the Lord momentarily set aside. He walks away, comes back to argue some more, walks away and comes back again, enraged but defeated. He knows that he is done for the night. Here comes Morgan, and soon after, the relief pitcher, Luis Aponte.

Danny Parks flips the ball to Aponte, jogs off the mound, shares one more thought with the umpire that does not appear to be "And a pleasant good night to you, sir," tugs at the bill of his cap, and disappears into the dugout. After next year, he will disappear from professional baseball altogether, convinced, former teammates say in agreement, that the Red Sox organization never gave him the big-league opportunity he had earned. In the years to come, the Pawtucket Red Sox will send word down to the Huntsville, Alabama, area that it would like its hard-luck workhorse back for this reunion or that celebration. No response will ever come.

Now for the 7th-inning stretch, that strange custom in which fans at a ball game rise as one, as though simultaneously struck with the desire to use the facilities, shake off the pins and needles, sing "Take

Me Out to the Ball Game," and look at one another with expressions of mild surprise that say: Can you believe that we do this? To remain seated would breach a civic bond among strangers that is sealed by an admixture of mustard and beer. The custom's origins are lost to generations of kicked-up infield dirt, which is perhaps as it should be. The preferred lore holds that during an Opening Day game in 1910, between the Philadelphia Athletics and the Washington Senators, the president best remembered as the heaviest, William Howard Taft, took pity on his seat and stood up in the 7th inning. Those around him rose as well, thinking that the country's leader was preparing to leave. A few minutes later, though, Mr. Taft rescinded his presidential pardon of a seat, sat back down, and, supposedly, gave birth to a baseball ritual. Not true. The custom dates at least to 1869, when the baseball pioneer Harry Wright, the center fielder, manager, and organizer of what is considered to be the first truly professional baseball team, the Cincinnati Red Stockings, recorded in a letter the odd behavior that he had noticed by the fans: "The spectators all arise between halves of the seventh inning, extend their legs and arms and sometimes walk about. In so doing they enjoy the relief afforded by relaxation from a long posture upon hard benches."

More than a century after bewhiskered Harry Wright chronicled the need of fans to find relief from protracted relaxation, McCoy's shivering hundreds rise, their numbers shrinking by the dozens with each passing inning, to share a collective stretch and yawn before the sleep they expect will soon come. After all, it's the 7th inning; just 2 innings to go.

Gary Levin, nineteen, stands behind the visitors' dugout on the first-base side with his girlfriend Lisa, the two of them fresh from a Seder at his aunt's house on Pawtucket's Fowler Avenue, close to the Seekonk River. His relationship with Lisa won't last, but his memories of this night will: honoring his Jewish faith with shank bone and matzo ball soup in a carpeted basement, then breaking Passover with hot dogs and hot chocolate at a concrete ballpark.

Meanwhile, somewhere among the right-field seats there stands Bob Brex, twenty-nine, a communications specialist for the state energy office. Since he does not attend church with any regularity, his Easter ceremony tomorrow will be at the Barrington home of his Italian grandmother, a retired bridal gown maker (She did Paul Anka's wedding!) who, every year, thrives on serving as the hostess of an Easter Sunday feast: breaded veal cutlets; homemade ravioli with turkey-and-herb filling; and that delicious custard, made with Marsala wine, called zabaglione. Brex will arrive early to perform the chore that has become his Easter ritual, the ceremonial pounding of the veal strips before they are breaded, and then he will join other family members for a meal of generational love. But this night is his alone; he stands and surrenders all responsibility to the ritual and stretch of the 7th inning.

And many rows down, in front of Brex, stand Ron and Danny Card, father-and-son season ticket holders who are as at home at McCoy as they are in their rented first-floor apartment on Providence's East Side. Ron, of proud Pawtucket stock, is a self-employed computer programmer in his mid-thirties, with dark brown hair, a mustache, and a bit of a gut. He wears a flannel shirt under a sleeveless winter vest and has a cigarette burning, another cigarette, always another cigarette. Danny, his skinny, PawSox–obsessed son, has sandy hair flopping over his forehead, and is wearing sneakers, dungarees, and a jacket too thin for the night. Triple-A baseball enthralls Danny. Yes, his father is sort of a McCoy mucky-muck, a first among fans who chats regularly with the guys in Pawtucket's front office—*Hey, Ben!*—and then imparts the inside information he has gleaned to those seated around him: *So-and-so might get called up to Boston.* But Danny cares less about those who make it to the major leagues than those who haven't yet, or won't. Even at the age of nine, he appreciates the long odds playing out before him; he even has a used Dave Koza glove. And before every game, he joins other kids who place pens and papers inside the carved-out bellies of their plastic milk jugs, tie strings around the handles, and bob them before the dugout like lures of promised fame, in hopes of a bite.

Danny knows that he should go to bed early tonight; tomorrow is Easter. But a nascent sense of obligation—of honoring the unspoken contract between player and true fan—has convinced him that he and his father should never leave a ball game until the last out is recorded. In fact, the two Cards recently agreed on a pact for all baseball games, beginning with tonight's: We stay until the end.

So they rise: father and son and hundreds of others, as the April winds blow and the barrel fires burn and a baseball game takes pause. They rise and look about this place called McCoy. With the drab gray rafters above their heads complementing the drab gray concrete at their feet, the stadium has the permanent feel of a natural formation, carved by time from the industrial-residential landscape of Pawtucket. And yet, especially under these lights, the place also seems dreamlike, transitory—a mirage that fans and players have overtaken somehow and now share with its ghosts:

Standing at the very back of section 1, on the first-base side, watching from the concourse, Depression-hardened men in battered cloth caps and mud-flecked overalls shaking their heads in disbelief that the thing ever got built. Standing in the blue general-admission seats, in section 12 along the third-base side, ballplayers in woolen uniforms with red-and-navy piping and the word "Slaters" scripted across the chests, itching to snag the next foul ball to show they still have what it takes. And standing before the best box seat in the house, white hair crisply parted and bristle-short on the sides, wearing a dark suit offset by a shamrock-patterned tie and a red rose in the left lapel: Himself. The Prince of Pawtucket. Mayor Thomas P. McCoy. Dead since 1945, but looking out upon his handiwork, all aglow, and sniffing:

"McCoy's Folly, indeed."

There was a time when all of this was water. In the mid-1830s, a man named Samuel Hammond dammed up Bucklin's Brook to create a reservoir that soon became a favored recreation area. Smartly dressed women took afternoon boat rides with mustachioed suitors. People swam in its cool waters, picnicked at its shores, skated upon its frozen, glasslike surface. The surrounding streets received names that suggested connection to the water: Lake, and Lakeview, and Pond. By the early 1900s, though, the man-made reservoir had become more of a forbidding swamp than an inviting hole, a muck-bottomed pool that parents warned children to avoid, which only emboldened those children to toe its murky edges, catching frogs, tempting the brown waters. Back then, everyone seemed to know someone who knew someone whose neighbor lost a child to Hammond Pond.

A large textile concern offered to give the pond to the city so that it could be filled in and used for recreation. But the city's engineers opposed the generous proposal, having not forgotten their struggles in laying a sewer line in the vicinity. Everything beneath the ground was either quicksand or water-bearing silt; the engineers could not exactly agree on which. The *Providence Journal* tried to explain: "They reported that workers did not seem to sink as rapidly as men usually do in quicksand, but that if a man stayed very long in one spot he would sink."

Over the years, city elders considered turning the pond into a racetrack, or maybe an airfield. But the municipal dithering stopped when Pawtucket became the fief of Thomas P. McCoy: an Irish gamecock, one historian called him, and the overseer of a Tammany Hall in New England miniature, as pure an American political boss as Croker of New York or Curley of Boston.

He had some ideas for the property.

McCoy, one of seven children of Irish immigrants, was born in Pawtucket in 1883, two years before the incorporation of the city. His childhood effectively ended in the eighth grade, when, he later wrote, "a turn in the fortune of my family compelled me to go to work." He held a series of jobs through his teen years before becoming a railway conductor, which required him to rise every morning at four o'clock. This work shift not only allowed him to take evening high school classes and courses at Brown University, it freed him to pitch for the Street Carmen Union's baseball team, where his proficiency at throwing a spitball might have been a harbinger of things to come.

He rose to become a popular union leader whose easy charm and oratorical ability intrigued the city's Democratic political machine, now in the control of ascendant Irish Catholic leaders of mill-worker lineage who had displaced the old-guard Protestants of mill-owner connections. After paying his dues in politics and populist causes—for a time he was president of the St. Mary's Total Abstinence and Benevolence Society—McCoy was elected to the state legislature in 1920, where he became known as a progressive Democrat and champion of immigrants, with cutthroat backroom skills. By 1930 he had risen to become the Democratic candidate for lieutenant governor, although his ticket lost amid allegations of fifteen thousand tampered ballots, which ensured the state remained in the control of the Republican Brahmins. In terms of Rhode Island, then, a routine election.

To maintain his position as a state powerbroker, McCoy redoubled his efforts in Pawtucket, becoming city auditor, city comptroller, and the kingpin of a political operation so tight-knit that the councilman overseeing his discharge of fiscal duties was his brother Ambrose. His landslide election as mayor in 1936 merely provided him with the title to the position he already effectively possessed. Not only was McCoy now the mayor, *and* the auditor, *and* the comptroller, but he was also the chairman of the Sinking Fund, chairman of the Purchasing Board, and clerk of the city council. Oh—and the city's Weigher of Merchandise.

McCoy controlled Pawtucket so completely that the line blurred between man and city. Some of his fiscal decisions, including a restructuring of the tax base, enabled Pawtucket to tough out the Depression's devastating effects on the textile industry. He also increased the budget of the relief rolls, improved health services, modernized the city's public safety programs, and took full advantage of the Roosevelt administration's many funding programs, including the New Deal, to build a new city hall and other much-needed public facilities. On the other hand, he and his cronies often dipped into city coffers for unauthorized expenditures; routinely tossed reporters out of city hall; used city funds to create a newspaper that—surprise!—wholeheartedly supported the administration; and played a role in the travesty of the 1938 election, in which one in eight ballots cast in Pawtucket were later deemed to be irregular.

But the mayor had the touch. He seemed to know every one of the city's seventy-five thousand residents by name. One day a teenage boy, looking for a job during the Christmas break, was summoned to the mayor's office. The boy was not connected in the classic Rhode Island sense. His immigrant parents had settled in Pawtucket more by chance than by design. His Scottish father, a good mechanic, had first landed a job as the driver for a local affluent family, and was now working as a woodworking teacher in the public schools, while his Northern Irish mother, accustomed to the cultural sophistication of London, wondered how she came to be living on Oswald Street in Pawtucket, Rhode Island. Their older son demonstrated only passing interest in school, but their younger boy, who would later describe himself as "shy to the point of mutinous," was so academically oriented that a friend from church had arranged for him and his brother to attend a private boarding school in Massachusetts. Now this boy needed a job over the Christmas break, and he timidly entered the office of the great fixer, the mayor of Pawtucket.

Galway, how are you? Mayor McCoy called out to young Galway Kinnell. *Of course, I'll get you a job. At the post office! Sorting mail! We need that at Christmas! Give your mother and father my best!*

Galway Kinnell, of course, went on to become one of the greatest American poets of the twentieth century, the winner of the Pulitzer Prize and a National Book Award. In later years, he will talk with great wonder and affection about the Pawtucket of his youth: the trolley car rides, the hours whiled away at the Pawtucket Boys' Club, the summer job at a textile mill dedicated to the war effort. He will remember coming across a book of poetry by Edgar Allan Poe—"It was many and many a year ago, In a kingdom by the sea"—that opened his mind and ears to a musicality in language that he never found in the Rhode Island voice.

And he will recall, with great affection, his brief encounter with the omnipotent, omniscient Mayor McCoy, who once called a painfully timid boy by his first name. "He was really good about it," Galway Kinnell will say. "He made me feel good that I had a real job. Even though I didn't, really."

At the height of his power, with the huzzahs drowning out the charges of corruption, Mayor McCoy decided to build a baseball park somewhere in Pawtucket. The old spitballer cherished his younger days as an athlete, and often regaled his entourage of gofers and hacks with tales of his physical exploits. How dazzling he was at left halfback; how gifted at tennis, at swimming, at checkers. How he once knocked out "Irish Pat" Brennan in two rounds. "Then he would get out the record books to top that with 16 straight wins as the pitcher on the Carmen's team, with a batting average, during the season when they won the pennant, of .632," one of his loyalists later wrote. "Any wonder, his friends ask, that he insisted on completion of Pawtucket Stadium—against the pressure of EVERY ONE in his Democratic city organization—so there might be football and baseball for the people of Pawtucket."

To his credit, McCoy understood baseball's integral role in Pawtucket and in the Blackstone Valley. By the twentieth century, the Rhode Island System had evolved into what the historian Doug Reynolds called a "moral economy." Workers agreed to lower pay in exchange for various considerations, including cheaper rents in company-owned mill housing, available care at company-controlled hospitals, and access to various company-sponsored diversions. Diversions like baseball, often with company teams chock-full of ringers and competing in industrial leagues. The game was thought to boost morale; to help "Americanize" immigrant workers; to underscore central ideals in life and in business. Teamwork. Allegiance. Pride.

As a Pawtucket mill executive, cited by Reynolds, put it: "Let the worker get outdoors (either as participant or observer) . . . and when the whistle blows he will return refreshed both mentally and physically . . . adding to the life of the worker and to his period of productivity. Both the worker and the company benefit."

Considering McCoy's past as a union leader, his baseball park plan was intended less for mill owners than for mill workers, thousands of whom were now without employment. Beyond the entertainment and community pride to be created, the building of a ballpark meant jobs. After receiving assurances of federal funding from Washington, the mayor announced that a ballpark and a recreational field would be built in the city of Pawtucket—on the sinkhole site now occupied by Hammond Pond.

Work began in the summer of 1938, with shifts of men toiling knee-deep in muck, by the sunlight of day and the floodlights of night, round the clock, six days a week. Their first task was to drain the swampy pond, but the project wound up swallowing time, manpower, money, and more, thanks to the underground springs. The pond seemed to have an insatiable appetite for the hundreds of concrete and wood pilings being driven into its maw to create a semblance of solid ground. Stories of vehicles and construction equipment disappearing into the ground overnight became part of Pawtucket lore. A retired detective captain in the Pawtucket Police Department named Ted Dolan will remember how his father, a city laborer who went by the name of "Cozy" Dolan—after a turn-of-the-century ballplayer for the Boston Beaneaters—swore until his death that a city truck sank so deep into the ground at the ballpark's construction site that workers just left it to become another awkwardly shaped piece of piling. Jerry Sherlock, who also grew up in Pawtucket, will recall visiting the site and watching four or five trucks pour the cement for the stanchions that were needed to hold up the stadium. "And we'd go back the next day, we can't find any sign of the four or five trucks of concrete," he will say. "They were gone! They just sunk in the pond!" To hear the locals of Pawtucket tell it, the site all but swallowed a parking lot of vehicles.

As the years passed, and those pilings continued to vanish into the earth, the project came to be called "McCoy's Folly." The federal government's Works Progress Administration suspended its financial support until the city could provide assurances that "a safely constructed stadium could be built at a reasonable cost." The workers nicknamed the site "Alcatraz." The original cost estimate of $600,000 ballooned to well over $1 million, even as the project was scaled back from a planned fifteen thousand seats to fewer than six thousand. Still, Mayor McCoy stood firm. The protracted construction of the stadium helped to feed many Pawtucket families, including the Pappas family, two parents and eight children crammed into a third-floor rear apartment in a six-unit triple-decker up on East Avenue, in the Greek neighborhood. The immigrant father, Andrew, was a bartender when he could find work, but he gladly traded his white apron for overalls to work down at the sinkhole. He would come home, roll another one of his cigarettes, and tell tales of filling the pond with cement, tons and tons of cement.

In the middle of construction, Andrew Pappas was struck by a car on East Avenue, injuring his back and legs and putting in jeopardy his slot down at the stadium project. The family had no choice but to send his son Billy in his stead, even though Billy had been born with a bone infection that impeded his ability to walk. "They couldn't lose that money coming in," Mike Pappas, another of Andrew's sons, will later say. "So Billy stood for him."

Andrew Pappas returned to the mire after a couple of months. Back then, if you were fortunate enough to get a job, you made damned sure you kept it. Eventually, those rolled-up cigarettes caught up with him; he died at sixty-three, of lung cancer. But his son Mike, who would later become a public-address announcer at the stadium his father helped build, never forgot this Greek immigrant coming home from work in his worn clothes, bone-weary, spattered with the mud of baseball promise.

Thanks to Andrew Pappas, and Cozy Dolan, and hundreds of other forgotten laborers, truck drivers, and engineers, the Hammond Pond ground finally took hold. Mayor McCoy came out on a Sunday afternoon in November 1940, two days before the municipal elections, to lay the cornerstone of the ballpark in the presence of a small crowd of city workers and their families. He buried a sealed box that contained, among other items, a letter that dedicated the stadium "to the health, happiness and enjoyment of the people of Pawtucket for all eternity." He also seized the chance to address those who had doubted his perseverance:

"As for those carping critics, let me say to them this stadium will bring pleasure and happiness to the people of this city long after they have returned to the dust whence they came."

In July 1942, the City of Pawtucket threw a celebration for the completion of the stadium that its mayor had all but willed into existence. No matter that the project had cost $1.5 million—more than the construction of Notre Dame's considerably larger football stadium; more than the assessed value of Fenway Park. No matter that its steel fencing and other finishing touches were installed in apparent violation of a federal ban against using vital war materials for "nonessential" projects like baseball parks. No matter that it had the feel of floating on an invisible swamp, rather than being nestled into the earth; the dugouts, for example, were not dug out, but built into the grandstands, so that the first row of seats began several feet above the field.

No matter. With admission free if you bought a twenty-five-cent defense stamp to help the war effort, a crush of patriotic fans overwhelmed the box office. Entertainers who were famous in Providence sang, the local fife-and-drum corps played martial tunes, and somebody read words of congratulation sent by President Roosevelt. Before long, a semiprofessional team from Pawtucket christened the ground by beating a team from Lynn, Massachusetts, 4–2.

Three years later, as the rest of the country rejoiced over the war-ending surrender of Japan, Mayor Thomas P. McCoy returned to dust, well in advance of most of his carping critics; he was sixty-two. The following spring, the city he once ruled held a lavish dedication ceremony at the stadium, home now to a new professional team called the Pawtucket Slaters—after Samuel Slater, the textile industrialist who started it all. Young schoolchildren performed every ethnic dance imaginable, Irish and Russian, Chinese and Dutch, and older students conducted a Pageant of Nations, and the Boys and Girls Glee Club sang "The Bells of St. Mary's," and the governor of Rhode Island, among other dignitaries, prattled on. But the long morning ended with the stadium being named after Himself: McCoy. As it should be.

Now the mud-covered workmen in section 1 find their seats, and the Pawtucket Slaters do the same in section 12, and Mayor McCoy settles into the box seat forever reserved for him. The 7th-inning stretch ends and the baseball game resumes, in a ballpark that is said to be settling, still.

Bottom of the 7th: Groundout; fly out; groundout.

Top of the 8th: Walk; sacrifice bunt; strikeout; strikeout.

Bottom of the 8th: Groundout; infield single; double play.

Top of the 9th: Strikeout; walk; pickoff; strikeout.

With Easter maybe an hour away, everything is set. The Rochester

Red Wings are ahead, 1–0, in the bottom of the 9th inning, and in the visitors' clubhouse, the postgame meal is nearly ready to be served. The clubhouse manager, the young man called Hood, has anticipated everything. As soon as the game ends, any minute now, the Rochester players will come tromping in, cleats scraping the concrete and carpet, their hands cold, their bodies aching, and he'll have a buffet feast waiting for them. Not the routine clubhouse fare of cold-cut sandwiches, but a hot meal of chicken with pasta, a big bowl of salad, and plenty of beer and soda. These ballplayers will leave happy tonight, filled with good food and the knowledge that the International League's best clubby had taken care of them once again.

Hood is just nineteen, but he has been working at McCoy Stadium longer than any Pawtucket player or front-office guy; hell, he predates the owner, Ben Mondor. That sweep of brown bangs only enhances his golly-gee look, but that dimpled half smile of his, just this side of a smirk, suggests there's no joke he hasn't heard, no con he hasn't been in on. After all, his rise within the McCoy organization has basically followed the *Our Gang* model of business success. Back in 1974, years before Mondor bought the team and applied a sense of order and charm to the ballpark, not much attention was being paid to the little things: the laundry, the meals, the minor amenities. Somehow, whether by mistake or by penny-pinching design, these responsibilities fell to a group of wily neighborhood kids. For a while, in fact, it seemed that Pawtucket urchins were running some of the essential operations of a Triple-A baseball franchise, applying a system rooted in a reverence for baseball, but financed entirely by tips.

Back then, Hood was a twelve-year-old spit, the son of a city councilman, living on the third floor of a triple-decker and answering to his altar-boy name of Michael Kinch. He had a friend from Pond Street named Killer, whose first job at McCoy was to change the numbers by hand on the scoreboard in left field. (For no pay; Killer did it for the prestige.) One day an upheaval in the strange clubhouse hierarchy at McCoy led to Killer's ascension to batboy in the home team's dugout, which opened up a batboy position in the visitors' dugout that Killer offered to his little friend from the neighborhood, Michael. Before long, all the Pawtucket players were calling this innocent but ever-present boy by the name of "Hood." Does this kid have a home to go to, or does he live here year-round, in the locker room? What's up with this kid, this hood?

McCoy had no washer or dryer, so Hood and the others in the crew would begin every morning by piling duffel bags of laundry—all the uniforms and undershirts, the socks and towels—into several shopping carts that had been, um, borrowed from a local supermarket. With dimes and quarters jingling in their pockets, they'd wheel these malodorous carts in a caravan up Pond Street. Turn right at Kepler, then left onto Meadow, passing a few of the triple-deckers that make up nearly half the city's housing stock, hovering at curbside, reminding everyone of the cheek-by-jowl days of mills and factories. Then right onto Summit Street, where they'd wash, dry, and fold the game-day uniforms at a coin-operated Laundromat that would someday become a place for the cleansing of soul and spirit: the Iglesia Metodista Luz y Esperanza, the Light and Hope Methodist Church.

Then, a couple of hours before game time, Hood and another boy would hop on a bicycle and wheel through the same cluttered array of triple-deckers, bars, and quotidian businesses, weaving the quarter-mile path to their personal paradise, the House of Pizza, on Division Street, across from the Rainbow Bar. After collecting their order, Hood would balance himself on the handlebars while holding a dozen hot pizza boxes, and the two would return to the ballpark, rolling through the neighborhood like an act in search of a circus.

And every three or four days, Killer's mother would drive a couple of the kids to the Star Market, on Newport Avenue, to buy food for the postgame meals, and to Russo Brothers wholesalers, on Mineral Spring Avenue, to stock up on the little things that maintain an ordered exuberance on the ball field; in other words, the sugar and tobacco craved by the ballplayers. The Hershey bars and Snickers bars and Milky Way bars and lots and lots of Bazooka gum. The Copenhagen, and the Skoal dip; the Red Man, Levi Garrett, and Beech-Nut chew. Some ballplayers liked to work up some Bazooka, stretch it out, wrap it around a ball of tobacco, then pop it back into their mouths. Hood, Killer, and the others knew every ballplayer's favorite brand of chocolate and chew, and would have these treats waiting for them at their respective lockers, just above their freshly polished cleats.

Hood was still a boy, of course. After all his postgame chores, which sometimes occupied him until well past midnight, he would run up Pond Street, through the sprawling and night-spooky grounds of Memorial Hospital—established, naturally, through the beneficence of some turn-of-the-century textile industrialist—and emerge on Prospect Street to see his mother watching from a top window of the triple-decker they lived in, waiting for her son. Not Hood; Michael.

But you cannot immerse an impressionable boy with a latent wiseass streak into the rowdy locker-room universe of young men and not expect him to be transformed. The ballplayers tested Hood, taunted him, teased him about his Rhode Island accent, an accent that is not quite the same as Boston's; it is harsher somehow, inflected with a faint hint of New England otherness. But these ballplayers from Elsewhere, many of them nowhere near as sophisticated as they fancied themselves to be, didn't know any better, so they'd deliver payback for generations of hick jokes by constantly telling him to pahk his cah in Hahvahd Yahd.

Before long, here was Hood, Pawtucket through and through, speaking with a mint-and-julep southern drawl that magically lifted at the end of every baseball season. Here he was, fourteen years old, sitting in the locker room with cheek distended by some Red Man tobacco, spitting into a cup. Here he was, wisecracking with the ballplayers, giving it back to them, playing the occasional prank, often at some peril. He once gave such a hard time to Jim Rice, now starring in left field for Boston, that the muscular ballplayer bound him to a baseball bat with duct tape and dunked him in the hot tub, the way you might primitively parboil a chicken before putting it on the rotisserie spit. (As a kind of bookend to that story, one night a few years later, Hood forgot to defrost the poultry he needed for the postgame repast, so he simply improvised—to the alarm of a visiting ballplayer who found whole chickens bobbing in the clubhouse hot tub.)

Seven years have passed. His family has moved into a single-family home of their own. His father will soon be elected mayor. And here is

Hood, still, essential to McCoy's operations, working yet another game between the Rochester Red Wings and the Pawtucket Red Sox. He arrived at eight this morning to tackle his never-ending checklist of subservience. Doing the laundry (they have two washers and two dryers at McCoy now). Scraping the dirt from cleats with a wire brush and then polishing them. Mopping the floor. Laying out towels at every locker. Stocking up on candy, gum, tobacco, soda, and beer. Running to the supermarket to buy eight whole chickens to cut into sixty-four pieces. Cooking the postgame meal in the narrow new kitchen that shares space in the boiler room. Making sure to time his food preparation by the inning. After all, baseball measures time not by the second, but by the out.

The chicken, seasoned with Shake 'n Bake, went into the oven at 400 degrees right around the 3rd inning. The Aunt Millie's marinara sauce went onto the stove at a low flame in the seventh. The big vat of pasta started cooking in the eighth. Maybe now he can pause for a moment.

Hood has seen and done as much as can be seen and done at an old ballpark in Pawtucket. But. And he knows this sounds crazy, but: This dream job of his—of working at a baseball stadium all day, befriending the future stars of Major League Baseball, earning decent tips—has grown tiresome. His teenage years are nearly gone, and when he does the math of his past, he realizes that he has missed proms, summers at the beach, and endless hours of blank childhood, all in the service of ballplayers who, honestly, can sometimes be insufferable, spoiled jerks. At nineteen, he is about the same age as some of these athletes who expect him to pick up their towels from the clubhouse floor. Maybe the time has come to set aside Hood, and return to being Michael.

It will take this young man a couple of years, but he will find his niche in his home state of Rhode Island, where most everyone sounds just like him. He will leave the McCoy fold and flirt with careers in nursing and business before becoming a police officer in the Blackstone Valley town of Cumberland, a few miles north of Pawtucket. The kid once called Hood will one day become Deputy Police Chief Michael Kinch.

Right now, though, he has to set the table with paper plates and plastic cutlery. Dig out the bottles of Wishbone salad dressings, French, Italian, and Blue Cheese. Then check on the pasta. These Rochester ballplayers are going to be walking in any minute, and they'll be hungry, too.

In the bottom of the 9th inning, with the visiting team up by one run, anything can happen. This is what we tell one another, because we are creatures wired to run toward the light, no matter how dim. The game's vital signs might well be fading by the pitch, but even those who would wish flat-lining to this cold and spent game—all the Rochester players, the three umpires, and perhaps even a few Pawtucket players—understand that anything can happen. They know that, theoretically, just one at bat could last forever, with foul ball after foul ball spinning into infinity, like the never-ending decimal measure of pi.

Yes, anything can happen. But it usually doesn't. According to the baseball historian and researcher David W. Smith, a lead carried by a team into the 9th inning holds up 95 percent of the time.

Three more outs and everyone can call it a night. The home plate umpire, Denny Cregg, can sleep for the first time in his new home up in Webster. Those Pawtucket players so inclined can go to My Brother's Pub and greet the resurrection with a cold one. The Rochester players can eat some of Hood's buffet offerings and grab a quick beer in the bar at the Howard Johnson motor lodge. But no one's going to get too crazy. The teams have another game to play, early tomorrow afternoon.

Marty Barrett leads off in the bottom of the ninth. He has played all of two weeks in Triple-A, but already he has impressed his teammates with his competitive disposition and high baseball IQ—meaning, of course, that he will forever be labeled "scrappy," which also connotes shortness, no matter that he is listed at five feet ten. All right, maybe he's five feet nine. A right-handed hitter, he scans the field for those barely perceptible clues that might provide advantage. How the pitcher, Larry Jones, holds the ball before beginning his windup, for example; he might be tipping the kind of pitch he's about to throw. Or whether the infielders are shading left or right, in anticipation of the pitch they know is about to come. If the second baseman is cheating toward center field, it might mean fastball. Marty Barrett notices these things.

Less than three hours ago, he was so cold that he was practically sending telepathic messages to those malfunctioning stadium lights, willing them to remain broken so that the game would be postponed. Now he fights for this dying game's continuance. His thirty-three-inch bat is at the ready, his eyes hunting.

Barrett swings at the first pitch, sending a ground ball to the second baseman. He runs because you never know; anything can happen.

Anything doesn't. One out.

With opportunity diminished by a third, the pressure of preserving life falls to Chico Walker, easygoing, card-playing, and anxious to get the hell out of Pawtucket. Unlike most of his teammates, he harbors no uncertainty: he *knows* that he is major-league material. And if anyone doubts this, well then, here: a double driven into deep center field. The sudden and faint possibility of Chico, the team's most popular player, stirs the thousand or so remaining fans.

The Rochester manager, Doc Edwards, emerges from the dugout and starts for the mound, where he plans to have a little chat with his pitcher, Jonesy. In some ways, every step that draws them closer only widens the gulf between them. Here is Experience, a forty-three-year-old former backup catcher who could afford to lose a few pounds, coming to explain the world to Expectation, a twenty-five-year-old fastball pitcher who often gets teased about his likeness to Jim Palmer. If only he had a modicum of Palmer's control.

Still, Edwards knows some things. He grew up in the coal country of West Virginia, where his father promised to break his legs if he followed him into the mines. The old man played catcher in the local amateur and semipro leagues, and the son noticed how his father seemed to be the captain of the field, yelling it up, positioning players, having a good time. Sensing a way out of rural Appalachia, the boy reached for a catcher's mitt that almost immediately defined who and what he was—a catcher. After serving as a navy corpsman in the marines, an experience that earned him his nickname, he played professional baseball in places like North Platte, Nebraska, and Selma, Alabama, before landing with the Cleveland Indians in 1962. He bounced around long enough to play for the New York Yankees during that once-great team's inglorious swoon in 1965, but a .190 batting average ensured his return to the minor leagues, where the pride in knowing Mickey Mantle did little to ease the grind of seasons in the backwaters.

He may have a bit of a belly now, and his hair may be flecked with gray, but Edwards is quite familiar with the insecurities that nag his players. He hasn't forgotten those night whispers of doubt. Just fourteen years ago, for example, in 1967, he sat in the lobby of a players' dormitory in Cocoa, Florida, just hoping to land a job with the Houston Astros. At twenty-nine, he was a good-fielding catcher with a low batting average who needed just one more year in the major leagues to be eligible for a pension. He was working construction in the offseason, one of his four children had a hip problem that might require surgery—and he just needed the job. "I know I can handle the glove," he told the reporter from the *Sporting News* sitting beside him. "I feel like I'm as good as or better than any receiver in camp."

He did not get the job. Back down to the minors, to the Oklahoma City 89ers.

Three years later, though, Edwards received a godsend of a baseball gift. He was in his early thirties, done as a player, and minding his own business as a bullpen coach for the Philadelphia Phillies. One day the team's two catchers broke their hands in the same game. Then their two replacements got hurt. Suddenly, the Phillies had no choice but to promote their all but retired bullpen catcher to the big leagues. Old Doc Edwards responded with 21 hits and a .269 batting average in 35 blessed, unexpected games.

So this man approaching the mound, a former major-league player who has caught the likes of Whitey Ford and Jim Bunning, a baseball lifer who hasn't even reached the halfway point of a career that will last more than a half century, knows some things. And he's coming to impart some of his hard-earned wisdom.

But the pitcher, Jonesy, thinks he knows a few things, too. He thinks that Doc is a cover-your-ass manager who favors veteran ballplayers and doesn't work hard enough to develop and promote the younger players. Jonesy isn't alone in his assessment. Similar sentiments have found their way into the Rochester newspapers, which has irked Edwards, not least because the public airing of dissatisfaction violates old-school clubhouse protocol.

Edwards wants to manage in the major leagues someday. Jones wants to pitch in the major leagues someday; someday soon. Theirs is not a father-and-son relationship. Now they are standing together on the mound, discussing how to end this cold and miserable night that possesses them both.

Edwards tells his young pitcher: With the way the wind is blowing in, the only thing that can hurt us is if you screw up somehow. Then he walks off the mound. And on the next pitch, Jonesy bounces a curve-ball past the catcher, allowing Walker to take third.

Russ Laribee, the pride of Southington, Connecticut, and the designated hitter for the Pawtucket Red Sox, waits with heavy bat in hand. A large man, with a retro mustache that conjures the dead-ball era and muscular legs that give him what he calls light-tower power, he stands in the center of a night so difficult for him that this one game will come to define his professional baseball career. He went 0 for 11? And struck out how many times? Seven? In one game? How is that even possible?

No single day characterizes a person; no single game defines an athlete. But if such a false measure is applied, the entirety of this night must be considered: the before, the after, and this at bat, now.

As with so many men on the field, baseball has provided Laribee with a way to help his parents envision a better life for their son. His father is a retired corrections officer; his mother is a secretary at a state school for juvenile delinquents. And Russell works as a baseball player, always has, often to the detriment of his social development. In high school, for example, he was the three-sport star athlete who dreamed of becoming a meteorologist and who did not attend his senior prom. He likes to say that he was so devoted to baseball that he couldn't be bothered with girls, but in truth he was so shy that being in close proximity to the opposite sex rendered him mute.

A powerful hitter with a strong arm and good speed, he excelled at every step up the ladder: Southington High School, the University of Connecticut, the Cape Cod League, all the way up to the Boston Red Sox organization's Double-A team in Bristol, Connecticut, where, for two years, he enjoyed the elevated status of the homer-launching home-town hero. Laribee strongly suspects that Red Sox officials no longer see him as a prospect, though, and he resents what he imagines they say about him: subpar outfielder with occasional hitting clout—a designated hitter. He loves Ben Mondor and the other guys in the front office, but he has no rapport with his manager, Joe Morgan, whom he regards as a savvy baseball man with little interest in player development—a familiar minor-league lament. He likes many of his teammates, but he is taken aback by the team's lack of cohesiveness. At times it seems to be less a team than a collection of cliques. The Feeling Sorry for Themselves Clique. The Drinking and Partying at the Expense of Their Talent Clique. The Clique That Mistakes Cruelty for Humor, intent on finding a teammate's psychic weakness and picking at it, picking at it, until the teammate crumbles in a heap. Russ Laribee is beginning to wonder whether he belongs here.

One morning three months from now, sometime before dawn, Laribee will telephone Joe Morgan at home to break the news that he would not be taking the team bus for the airport, where the PawSox were to catch a flight for Tidewater, Virginia. The very idea of giving up a baseball career will stun Morgan. He will urge his designated hitter to stick out the rest of the season (there's only a month left!), attempt to understand the young man's explanations, then slam the phone down. But Laribee, aware of his many strikeouts yet confident that he can hit major-league pitching, will have his reasons. Nearly twenty-five years old, and clearly not a Red Sox prospect. Time for a time-out to decide whether it's time.

After a fantastic year of playing baseball in Italy, where he will be hailed as the Babe Ruth of Nettuno, Russ Laribee will end his career and become a door-to-door salesman of Electrolux vacuums. His analytical mind, which once had teammates saying he thought too much about each at bat, coupled with his improved social skills, will serve him well in management and sales. Eventually, he will become a sports handicapper, working from his home in southern Connecticut. "Mr. East," he will call himself. Thirty years after losing his gamble to play major-league baseball, he will advise paying clients on how to make smarter bets on the game: *There are twenty-two of thirty teams that average more runs scored per game versus righties than lefties. Overall thru May 11, that has led to the unders prevailing to a 157–122 mark if at least 1 left-hand pitcher starts the game, or 56.3 percent of the time, a decided winning advantage. . . .*

The thirty-six-ounce bat in Russ Laribee's hands may be the heaviest in the team's rack, but he feeds off its intimations of power. He likes to envision the precise mechanical crush of all that weight propelling the ball, just as he likes to imagine the luck granted to him by the argyle socks he wears to the ballpark (Barrett, his roommate on the road, always asks him, "You got those diamondbacks on, baby?"). His other private tic: taking an uneven number of practice swings between pitches—one, or three, or five—so that any swing at a live pitch equals an even number of swings. Don't ask why; he cannot explain.

Now, as the pitcher raises his left leg to begin the delivery of the next pitch, Laribee's analytical mind is whirring: *Stay away from any sinker ball. Forget the wind blowing in. Drive the ball up in the air and into the outfield. Make contact.*

Contact. Laribee sends a fly ball deep enough to left field for Walker on third base to tag up and score. The official scorer up in the press box makes two blue-ink entries beside Laribee's name: SF7 for sacrifice fly to left field, and RBI for run batted in. The score, in the bottom of the ninth, is now Rochester 1, Pawtucket 1.

In the future, whenever this long night is revisited, Laribee's humbling statistics (no hits, eleven outs, seven strikeouts) will invariably be brought up with there-but-for-the-grace-of-God glee. But Mr. East, the pride of Southington, Connecticut, will get to say this: "I tied the game."

With two outs and the game tied in the bottom of the 9th inning, the Pawtucket Red Sox take a sudden interest in offense. Dave Koza hits a single, Wade Boggs walks, Sam Bowen walks—and Larry Jones leaves the game, having given up a few inconsequential hits and just one run in 8⅔ innings. He has pitched extremely well. But not good enough. It never will be.

Nearly thirty years from now, he will sit in the living room of his high-rise apartment, the marina lights of Sarasota, Florida, winking below. As he watches a video clip of himself pitching in this game, so fluid, so young, he will say the names of the teammates who float in and out of the frame: "Dallas Williams. Eaton. Bonner. There's Logan." Then, in explaining the proper grip of a two-seam fastball, he will dig out an old baseball he just happens to have tucked in a baseball glove, tucked in a bag, tucked away in a closet. The ball will be dated like a document to stipulate that on June 18, 1979, in the Double-A Southern League, Charlotte beat Nashville, 3–0.

Winning pitcher: Jonesy.

The two managers adjust. Doc Edwards chooses Jeff Schneider, a left-handed short reliever who throws bullets, to pitch. Joe Morgan decides to remove his starting catcher, Gedman, from the game for a right-handed pinch hitter named Mike Ongarato, a clubhouse cutup of twenty-five whose career is nearly over. He is a gifted athlete, able to play almost any position, but his batting average has dropped in direct relation to his ascension through the minor-league system. He has found other ways to contribute to the team, though: filling players' cleats with shaving cream; mastering the classic hot foot; wearing a fake nose and glasses around the batting cage to look like Groucho Marx in uniform. All silly stuff, but the pressure of conflicting dreams can build up in a clubhouse; sometimes you need a guy like Ongarato to provide release.

This is not one of those times. Ongarato is thinking *bases loaded, two outs, a base hit, we win*; that is all he is thinking. But Schneider is throwing hard and high, and Ongarato often falls for that joke of a pitch. Before he knows it, he has two strikes on him and here comes another one, high and hard. He swings and misses.

Strike three.

Third out.

Extra innings.

Hundreds of fans head for the warmth of their cars. Players in both dugouts throw more wood onto their barrel fires. Hood, in the visitors' clubhouse, scurries to save the chicken and pasta he has so carefully timed to be served at this moment. Easter approaches.

And Mike Ongarato returns to the dugout, dejected, not yet aware of the historic distinction his cameo appearance will grant him. Someday, though, he will all but boast of his failure, describing his strikeout as the necessary plot device in the story of a historic night.

"If I get a hit," he will say, "it's just another game."

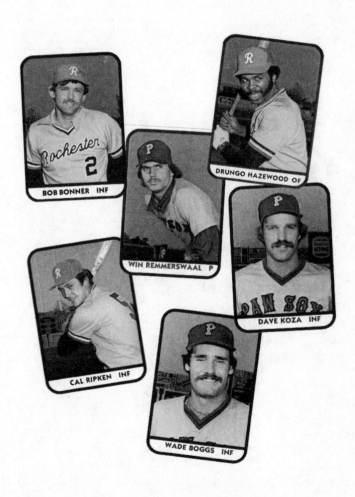

Like a boat slipped off its mooring, a baseball game in Pawtucket floats away upon the open waters of the night. The accepted length of 9 innings, established in 1857 by the Rules and Regulations Committee of the National Association of Base Ball Players, has provided no winner, no anchor of resolution. The players and fans have been cut loose by the swing and the miss of a clubhouse prankster, and are feeling the first stirrings of extra-inning excitement jumbled with extra-inning dread. They begin to wonder where this game will take them.

The two pitchers in the game, Jeff Schneider for Rochester, Luis Aponte for Pawtucket, seem determined not to provide the answer; or, rather, not to be part of the final say. Schneider will pitch $5\frac{1}{3}$ innings and strike out eight batters. Aponte will pitch four innings and strike out nine, confounding Rochester batters with his herky-jerky delivery and nasty forkball, which is held as though Curly has wedged a baseball between the index and middle fingers of the pitcher—call him Moe— before Moe's execution of a double eye-poke. When thrown with a snap of the wrist, the ball moves with deceptive speed before dropping at the plate like a shot bird. It is a fitting pitch for Aponte, whose craftiness on the mound seems born of decades of experience and tribulation. Five years ago he was pitching so poorly that he voluntarily left the Red Sox organization to spend three years in the baseball wilderness, where he developed a repertoire of deception—a forkball, a sinker, a slider, and what some say is a spitball. His hard work culminated last year in a late-season ascension to the major leagues, where he pitched in four games for the Boston Red Sox and kept everyone guessing about his age—perhaps to thwart the age discrimination so prevalent in the game. "He was about twenty-eight years old then," his teammate, Roger LaFrancois, will later say. "But he was really around forty."

At the end of this season, Aponte will rejoin the Boston Red Sox, and begin to build a modest major-league career that will grant him lifetime man-of-importance distinction when he returns to live in Venezuela—where, according to teammates who have played winter ball there, he is a national hero, popular enough to be president. He will work for many years as a scout in Latin America for the Cleveland Indians, then devote his energy to growing the type of fruit you want to pitch as much as eat: oranges and tangerines, lemons and mangoes. At the moment, though, the domain of this presidential pitcher extends no farther than a patch of Rhode Island grass and dirt, where batter after batter cowers before him. In the 10th inning, he retires the last hitter to face him with what else but a third strike, completing what he will always consider to be the apex of his baseball career.

Aponte returns to the clubhouse and huddles into a jacket, satisfied, but eager, too, to return home to the warm Pawtucket apartment he shares with his wife and two boys. This is not Venezuela weather.

He is replaced by Manny Sarmiento, his fellow Venezuelan, roommate on the road, friend, and occasional adversary. Before season's end, the two will engage in a brutal fight, supposedly over a card game, and supposedly including a Sarmiento bite to Aponte's stomach.

Quiet and withdrawn, Sarmiento seems to be the darkness to Aponte's light, though this may be because he doesn't really know anyone in the organization, and hasn't detected an opportunity to open up—to demonstrate, for example, his lovely singing voice. Traded to Boston by the Seattle Mariners just a couple of weeks ago, he was immediately sent down to this someplace, this Pawtucket, where the air of the exotic that envelops him is intensified by his proud but foreign Cincinnati Reds pedigree. Nearly a decade ago, Dave Concepcion, the All Star shortstop for the Reds, saw the gangly sixteen-year-old Sarmiento dominate a game in the boy's hometown of Cagua, and made note; within four years, the boy was pitching for the 1976 World Champion Reds. Now, at twenty-five, Sarmiento has nearly five years of major-league experience, and he is working on a forkball, Aponte's pitch, to find his way back—eventually to Pittsburgh, where one day, before a game, he will sing the national anthem.

With one out in the bottom of the 11th inning, Dave Koza—the hero of that boy sitting on the third-base side, Danny Card, who is cold but resolved to honor that pact with his father to stay until the end—wants, again, to finish this game with a single swing, maybe with a shot that clears the army advertisement in right field that urges everyone to be all that they can be. Strange to think of it this way, but Koza tries to hit home runs for a living. At this point in his career, some of what he exhibits at the plate is muscle memory, but much of it remains his mind instructing his body. Smoothing the batter's box dirt with his cleats. Planting himself perpendicular to the plate. Taking a slight step back in the box if the pitcher throws hard—and Rochester's Jeff Schneider does. Trying not to be obvious in any adjustments; the catcher might spot the overcompensation and call for a pitch accordingly. Resting his wide-barreled bat on his right shoulder, then raising it up as the pitcher prepares to throw. Keeping the grip on the handle loose, trying to hold the bat with the fingertips, left pinkie resting on the knob. Keeping the hands in and the bat close to the chest. Telling himself to throw the head of the bat out toward the ball. Remembering what Ted Williams always says. Ted Williams, the greatest pure hitter who ever lived, wandering foulmouthed and single-minded through spring training in Winter Haven, perhaps taking comfort once again in seeing no one his equal among the latest crop of mewling man-children.

Williams: Hips ahead of hands; hips ahead of hands.

The outfield wall: Be all you can be.

The pitch: Screw you.

Koza hits the ball high and deep to right field, toward the outfield billboards for the Regina Pizzeria restaurant, and the North Kingstown Shell station, and the army's come-on. But the Rochester right fielder circles beneath, waiting. He possesses this game's most distinctive name and most impressive physique: Drungo Hazewood, six feet three and a lean, rock-hard 210 pounds. He is twenty-one years old, as fast as Mercury, with explosive throwing ability—but, in terms of major-league baseball, he is through.

One evening nearly thirty years from now, in Sacramento, California, a knock on the dark screen door of a possibly vacant house will summon a large silhouette into view, the only brightness coming from the soft blink of a Bluetooth in his ear. *Drungo Hazewood*, the figure will say, and he will welcome the visitor inside, apologizing for the lack of furniture in the living room—the result of a relationship's fresh breakup. He will sit at a kitchen table, fifty years old now and wearing a bathrobe, but formidable still. He will tell his baseball story.

His mother, Catherine, was a housewife who gave her life to raising ten children and helping to rear who knows how many grandchildren. With her ninth about to be born, Catherine announced a dare: Whoever wins a foot race to the hospital gets to name the baby. Her son Aubrey won the challenge, and he had a good friend whose last name was Drungo. So Drungo Hazewood it was.

His father, Leonard, was a welder and sandblaster who never missed a day of work at the old McClellan Air Force Base. If he didn't feel well in the morning, he'd drink some strange Deep South concoction, sit there sweating for five minutes, then go out to earn another day's pay. Leonard was not one for idleness. Shortly before he died, he told Drungo to join the military.

But, Dad, Drungo answered, I'm fifteen.

The boy found another path. A baseball standout and a football All-American at Sacramento High School, he was preparing to play football at the University of Southern California when the Baltimore Orioles chose him as their first-round draft pick in 1977, offering him $50,000 to play the game he loved more. His mother had to sign the binding contract for him because he was only seventeen. The next thing this black kid from Sacramento knew, he was playing rookie baseball in Bluefield, West Virginia, where part of his training was outrunning dogs. But he struggled in rookie ball, batting .184, averaging a strikeout every third at bat, and underachieving for the first time in his young athletic career. Still, he was promoted in 1978 to Baltimore's Single-A team in Miami, where he hit a little better, and then to its Double-A team in Charlotte, North Carolina, where he hit 49 home runs in two years.

In his autobiography, *The Only Way I Know*, Cal Ripken Jr. described his teammate Hazewood as the Olympian ideal, a breathtaking blur of muscle when scoring from first base on a double, and someone you did not want to anger. He recalled an infield brawl with the Memphis Chicks that ended with the ejection of several ballplayers, including Ripken and Hazewood. Though others managed to laugh off the incident, Hazewood could not calm down. He changed into street clothes without showering, grabbed a baseball bat, and, according to Ripken, snapped it in half. "I saw it happen, but don't ask me *how* it happened," Ripken wrote. "I've seen replays of guys snapping the bat over their knee, but Drungo didn't snap this bat *across* anything, and he didn't hit it *against* anything. He just *twisted* and it snapped like a toothpick." With the bat's broken barrel tucked into his pants, Hazewood ran down to the Memphis clubhouse and began pounding on the door, demanding to finish the brawl. His manager had to drag him away and lock him in an office until he settled down.

Now, calm in his kitchen, Hazewood will smile at the suggestion that he could snap a bat in two with his hands. "Bat could have been cracked," he will say. "Don't make it sound like I'm Hercules."

According to Ripken, he and Hazewood were considered essential to Baltimore's future at the time, along with the outfielder John Shelby, the pitcher Mike Boddicker, and the shortstop Bobby Bonner. "As much talent in one human being that's ever played the game," Doc Edwards will say of Hazewood, and Baltimore clearly agreed. At the end of Charlotte's 1980 season, the Orioles summoned Hazewood to show what he could do in the major leagues. It did not go well. In the one game he started, he batted four times and struck out four times. For the last strikeout, in what would be the last at bat of his major-league career, he held his bat in check as the ball zipped past for a called third strike.

The problem: Drungo Hazewood, a number-one draft pick for the

Baltimore Orioles, could not hit a curveball. All the "if" clichés of baseball applied: He couldn't hit a curveball if he knew it was coming; if his life depended on it; if it was gift-wrapped; if you put it on a golf tee for him; if he had a tennis racket, an ironing board, a car door. Hazewood recalls one spring training in which two coaches threw him nothing but curveballs: Here's Uncle Charlie, and another Uncle Charlie, and another, and another. It did not take. Hazewood might have been able to compensate for this weakness in Double-A, where many pitchers lack the confidence and ability to throw curveballs for strikes. "But once you go from Double-A to Triple-A, there are pitchers who played in the major leagues and know now how to pitch," Edwards will say. "They can throw a curveball for a strike anytime they want. And you get a steady diet of pitchers who are taught to throw what you can't hit."

Tonight, one that he will remember as being so frigid "that when you opened your eyes, the insides of your eyes got cold," Hazewood is demonstrating what he cannot do. In this strange game against Pawtucket, a place he has never even heard of, he is in the midst of going 0 for 4, with three strikeouts. Back in the 7th inning, against wicked Aponte, he tried lamely to bunt his way out of his curveball embarrassment. Then, with the count 2–2, he lunged at another curveball, missing so badly that his momentum carried him across home plate and, appropriately, toward the dugout. He trudged away, glancing briefly at right field as if seeking an answer, the bat held by the barrel in his large hand looking like—well, as Ripken would have it, looking like a toothpick, and about as useful.

Not long after the night is up, Hazewood will be sent back down to the Double-A team in Charlotte. He will play in the minor leagues for two more years, take a break from baseball when his beloved mother becomes sick with breast cancer, and never return. His mother will die, he will quickly have two children, and, he will say, "The next thing I know I'm working construction."

Hazewood will turn bitter. He will come to believe that the Baltimore organization gave up on him prematurely. "I should have been in the big leagues by nineteen," he will say. "I never would have been a

.300 hitter, but home runs, RBIs, stolen bases, runs scored. If I get on base . . ." His voice will trail off to the quiet place of what-if.

So the Drungo Hazewood of baseball will disappear. His former teams and teammates will not be able to track him down for the occasional reunion. And if a fan's Drungo Hazewood baseball card somehow reaches him by mail, with the standard request to please autograph and return in the stamped and self-addressed envelope enclosed, he will just keep the card. In the hothouse environment of Baltimore Orioles fandom, people will adopt his name as their online handle, or invoke it whenever they want to discuss failed prospects, or say it out loud just to be funny: Drungo Hazewood. Rumors will circulate that the butt of this joke is homeless, or dead.

All the while, the Drungo Hazewood of Leonard and Catherine will be working, anonymously, like the rest of us. For a while he will load and unload the belongings of others for a moving company, traveling across the country, passing through the hometowns of ballplayers he once knew. Then he will get his commercial trucking license and begin making deliveries for the Sara Lee Baking Group. He will rumble and jostle his way to Fresno and Reno, to Carson City and Yuba City, passing the interstate hours by thinking about his children, his grandchildren, and the best time of his life: the days he spent playing baseball on nights like this, as cold as it is, with got-your-back teammates close by, and the Baltimore organization invested in his future, and Koza's fly ball coming to him as if it had found him. So easy to catch.

The night swells. The wind blows in from center field and whips through the stands, where fewer and fewer fans are subject to its snap. The souvenir stands along the empty concourse have been shut down, which sends one of the teenage concessionaires, Kenny Laflamme, clambering up to the press box to ask his stepfather, the scoreboard operator, for the keys to the car. He is fifteen, with shaggy blond hair and a small build, on the cusp of a growth spurt. He is also so shy that he began the season as a soda vendor—at his parents' behest—but simply could not bring himself to say "Soda here" in such a public arena; the thought nauseates him. But the accommodating front office found a place for him at one of the souvenir stands, where he sells pennants and T-shirts and PawSox yearbooks filled with pictures and promises. He closed his stand hours ago, has watched more than his fair share of this interminable game, and now all he wants to do is stretch out somewhere and rest. The cozy solitude of his stepfather's black 1978 Ford Pinto in the parking lot seems much more inviting than this press box, which is basically a mobile home, circa 1942, suspended in air without heat or air-conditioning, and with windows that, even when hooked shut, do not keep out the cold. A part of the stadium's original construction, the press box is furnished with foldout chairs and tables, a refrigerator stocked with drinks and cold cuts (for some reason, the availability of olive loaf will linger in the memory of its denizens), and men in various emotional states.

For example, Kenny's stepfather, Richard Courtens, thirty-four, is a Rhode Island social worker who earns five bucks a game, plus free admission, to man the scoreboard. But because the scoreboard allows for only 10 innings, he is busily trying to trick the small console in front of him into "turning the corner"—that is, to begin a second game, basically, while maintaining the totals of hits, runs, and errors from the "first," which the system is inclined to erase. So there he is, fiddling with the damn thing.

He's not the only one with problems. Before the game went into extra innings, Bill George, also thirty-four, a North Providence lawyer by day and Pawtucket's official scorer by night, only had to remember his wife's parting plea to stop at Dunkin' Donuts on his way home and pick up some chocolate-covered Easter treats for their two young children. But now, with zeroes adding up like so many eggs, he has to figure out what to do if the game lasts much longer. His scorebook allows for only 12 innings—a reflection, like the scoreboard, of the game's own expectations—so he, too, must improvise. George decides to switch from a blue pen to a red pen, and finds what room is left in the book's diamond-shaped boxes, already crammed with his cryptic symbols of the game's progression (that F9, for example, represents Dave Koza's recent fly out to right fielder Drungo Hazewood). From now on, the little boxes reserved, say, for the happenings of the 3rd inning will also contain information from the 13th, with the different ink providing the necessary distinction. The plan makes the head ache, but there you have it. It might just work.

And what about poor Bill McCourt? The young accountant is the glorified gofer of the press box. He provides its creatures with the starting lineups and statistics, makes sure they have enough drink and food (More olive loaf, anyone?), and keeps an eye on the "ticker"—a gray box, about the size of a toaster, that slowly spits out a stream of inch-wide yellow paper with the latest developments from major-league games around the country, all in capital letters, AND. WITH. EVERY. WORD. SEPARATED. BY. A. PERIOD. Every so often, McCourt tears off the tape in the midst of an ellipsis and rushes the strip of baseball information to the public-address announcer, the reporters, and the two radio guys from Rochester. In addition to overseeing all this, he is also providing music to the entire stadium through a small cassette player wired into a sound system— a cassette player that the shy boy Kenny might have gotten for his fifteenth birthday. He is pushing buttons, fast-forwarding and rewinding to send forth a giddy symphony of game-appropriate sounds and songs: the national anthem to start the game; "Take Me Out to the Ball Game" for the 7th-inning stretch; frenetic music, worthy of Benny Hill, for when the grounds crew rakes the field; and maybe a half dozen songs that play over and over as the game drags on. What he wants to play is the song that resounds through McCoy after every PawSox victory: "Celebration," by Kool and the Gang, the selection of which encourages fans to file quickly out to the Pawtucket streets. What he wouldn't mind playing at this point is the anthem from *Annie* that follows every loss: *The sun'll come out tomorrow, bet your bottom dollar that tomorrow, there'll be sun. . . .* What he must play, until the game's resolution saves him, is a never-ending loop of inoffensive treacle. Even the most ardent fan of Sammy Davis Jr. can only take so much of "The Candy Man." *Who can take a sunrise, sprinkle it with dew, cover it with chocolate and a miracle or two? The Candy Man, oh the Candy Man can . . .*

Here in the press box is the public-address announcer, Bob Guthrie, making sure to pronounce every name correctly—LOO-iss A-PON-teee—because Pawtucket's front-office guys are sticklers for that. Here are the two radio guys from Rochester, Bob Drew and Peter Torrez, providing the New York metropolis known as both the Flour City and the Flower City with a slow-tempo baseball serenade. And here are the two newspaper reporters, neither of them quite sure what to do as this game all but yawns and curls up before them. Mike Scandura, of the Pawtucket *Evening Times*, is thirty-five, from upstate New York, and a devoted Yankees fan who forgot to wear enough layers of clothing. Since the *Times* does not publish on Sundays, he is at McCoy tonight out of love more than obligation—recording every play down to the pitch in his maroon C. S. Peterson scorebook—though he plans to make extra money by writing a freelance game story for a Rochester newspaper. Sitting beside him is Angelo Cataldi, the *Providence Journal* reporter, who is also a Yankees fan, but there the similarity ends. Even though he was born and raised in nearby Providence, Cataldi hates it here. He does not belong here. Get him the hell out of here.

Cataldi, thirty, has a helmet of black hair and a knack for witty negativity. When he graduated from the Columbia Graduate School of Journalism, he thought his prestigious degree would open a hundred doors. It opened just one, the door to the newspaper back home, a door he did not want to enter. He has toiled at the *Providence Journal* in what he considers to be the minor leagues of journalism for four years now, doing everything from fielding the "Sears screwed me" complaints for the Action Line feature to covering the travails of the Boston Red Sox. But his work has lately attracted the interest of a major-league newspaper, the *Philadelphia Inquirer*. Moving his growing family from its home state to Pennsylvania would be an upheaval, of course, but one thing would be wonderfully certain: Angelo Cataldi would never have to cover a Pawtucket Red Sox game again.

He hates covering PawSox games. Has he mentioned how much he hates covering PawSox games? You have no idea. Especially on Saturday nights like this, when the games last beyond his first dead-line, at 10:15 or so, usually because they're so poorly played, and what can he do, he's at a minor-league ballpark that is basically a landfill under lights, and he's sitting in a cold, barren press box that looks as though it was tacked up at the very end of the stadium's construction, as though the builders suddenly said *Oh shit, we don't have a press box*—and there goes his deadline for the next edition. And as much as he despises being at McCoy on a Saturday night, this night is the worst, the absolute worst, because a half hour has already been lost to the earlier malfunction of the stadium lights, which means he wants to kill somebody, and his impatient editor will be calling any minute, and now the wind is blowing right into his face, blowing through the cheap windows of this lousy press box, in this hellhole of a ballpark, this Pawtucket dump.

"Like I said," Angelo Cataldi will say years later, from Philadelphia, where he will become the famously bilious host of a morning radio sports show. "I worked from a negative perspective a lot of the time."

So you can see why Kenny Laflamme, a teenage boy so shy it makes his stomach hurt, would prefer not to spend the rest of the night with Angelo and the boys in a mobile home suspended in the air. His stepfather hands him the keys. He exits the stadium, climbs into the Ford Pinto, locks the doors, stretches out—and falls fast asleep.

Midnight at the ballpark. And in the midst of its baseball blur, perhaps in the 13th inning, perhaps between the fly out to left by Rochester's Dallas Williams and the fly out to right by Pawtucket's Marty Barrett, though no one will remember for sure, a humble wish resounds through McCoy Stadium:

On behalf of the Pawtucket Red Sox—happy Easter.

Have the Pawtucket Red Sox ballplayers really paused, in mid-rumination of another gob of chewing tobacco wrapped in bubble gum, to wish a happy Easter to the few hundred fans crazy or lonely enough to still be here? As they mutter among themselves about the goddamn wind and the goddamn cold, and this being a goddamn pitcher's night, and we're never going to get home at this rate, goddamnit, are these ballplayers really considering the joy to be found in an empty tomb?

No.

This call for a brief time-out from all the "Now batting" pronouncements and "Candy Man" nonsense, this call to say, simply, Happy Easter, take hope, hallelujah, and now back to "Now batting," comes from the front office—which means that it comes directly from the team's owner, Ben Mondor. The hard-nosed soft touch. The salty savior of Pawtucket. Good luck finding someone to say a bad word about him; in fact, good luck finding someone who won't choke up while speaking of his kindness. Bob Ojeda, one of the Pawtucket pitchers huddled in the dugout, possessed of a hunger that will surely take him places, borrowed $500 from Mondor last year to pay for a cross-country flight for his father, a furniture upholsterer in California, so that he could see his son's major-league debut in Boston. Ojeda tried to repay the loan when he got sent back down to Pawtucket, but Mondor refused. And Hood, down there in the visitors' clubhouse, fretting over his postgame pasta turning to mush, hasn't forgotten how, after he sprained his ankle playing junior high school basketball a few years ago, Mondor would pick him up at his home, drive him to McCoy for proper whirlpool treatment of his injury, and then give him a ride back. Hood will describe his younger self as just a knucklehead kid from the neighborhood, and here was Mondor—the *owner* of the Pawtucket Red Sawx!—chauffeuring him around like he was Richie Rich.

But the more you hear of Mondor's many kindnesses—the gifts, the "loans," the Christmas cards sent to anyone who ever played for him in Pawtucket—the more you wonder: What's this guy doing in the cruel business that he pronounces as "bazeball"? With his fireplug build and those large tinted glasses, he looks too avuncular, too much like the friendly butcher down at the Star Market, until you notice how meticulously his gray-white mustache is trimmed. It reflects fastidiousness; an orderly mind; a dedicated focus on every detail. Every hair.

Tonight he is wearing a pea jacket over two sweaters, but his feet feel as though they are encased in ice, and he is finding little protection against the elements in his owner's box, a flattering term for a particle-

board partition that is furnished with a few chairs and covered over-
head by a stretch of sections 10 and 11.

A nearby alley leads deeper into the stadium's maze, below the
grandstand, where the ball club still shares space with its landlord,
the City of Pawtucket. That is why lawn mowers sit in the ticket office,
infusing the air with the hint of gasoline, and why city dump trucks
are sometimes parked on the third-base side, infusing the air with
the hint of garbage. But amid this public-works bazaar, amid all the
grass-tinted blades and street-scraped plows scattered about, Mondor
has managed to carve out an office, fastidiously appointed, of course,
and just a short walk from his so-called owner's box. The bookcases
in the corner were purchased with S&H Green Stamps, the couch is a
hand-me-down from a ballplayer dispatched a couple of years ago to
Double-A, the chair and desk were found at a secondhand store—and
the occupant is a multimillionaire who is asking himself, once again,
why he disrupted sweet retirement to try and save a doomed baseball
team.

George Bernard Mondor never played much baseball as a boy; his
career statistics would reflect one half inning during a pickup game in
grammar school. He is not a man, then, who interprets life in terms of
baseball, whose guiding principles are peppered with its familiar met-
aphors. Instead, he interprets baseball through the terms of life—his
own. Through his personal victories and losses, he understands what
it means to face an overpowering pitcher; to stay in the box; to hit it
where they ain't; to lay down an exquisite sacrifice bunt. He recognizes
the game's gift of escape. Born in a small Quebec outpost, about sixty
miles north of Montreal, in 1925, he was the tenth and last child of a
skilled carpenter and a woman who took in boarders. Two of his siblings died before he was born, including an infant named Bernard, so
baby George became Bernard, or Ben, in his dead brother's honor. A
few years later, just in time for the Depression, the family left Canada
in search of opportunity, but found little in Mount Vernon, New York,
and even less in northern Rhode Island, in the Blackstone Valley mill
city of Woonsocket, where, at the very least, many people conversed in

French. The father reluctantly went on relief, and took whatever pick-and-shovel work he could find.

A sense of the young boy's Woonsocket world can be found in the story of a neighbor. The Mondors lived in a double-decker on Providence Street, not far from the home of Little Rose Ferron, a bedridden young woman who was said to be a mystic and stigmatic in direct communication with Jesus and the Virgin Mary. When she died at thirty-three in 1936, thousands crowded the streets of Mondor's neighborhood to pay their respects. Some of her followers campaigned for Little Rose's beatification, and even managed to have her body exhumed—twice—to be examined for evidence of the supernatural; incorruption of the body, that is. The exhumations, though, suggested an entirely routine return to the clay, and church officials were never persuaded by various claims to the miraculous. The prayers for beatification went unanswered. But people still visit her grave in Woonsocket's Precious Blood Cemetery, some convinced that they detect the distinct perfume of roses.

Though Mondor was never much of a believer in the holy story of his neighbor—a nice enough girl, but that was about it—the discipline and mysteries of French-Canadian Catholicism helped to mold the man he would become. He was taught by the Sisters of the Religious of Jesus and Mary at the Holy Family parochial school, and then by the Brothers of the Sacred Heart at Mount Saint Charles Academy, where he was accepted as a charity case because his family could not afford the tuition. He met his future wife, Madeleine Valois, in a pew at Holy Family Church. His courtship would require playing croquet with a few of the nuns who ran the all-women's Catholic college she attended in Connecticut, and making room for one of them when he took Madeleine for a thoroughly unromantic boat ride. But these were the rules, and faith mattered to him.

Mondor joined the navy right out of high school and spent the better part of four years as a navigator aboard the USS *Willmarth*, a destroyer escort that found itself in various hot spots throughout the Pacific theater; for example, he and his shipmates spent Easter Sunday 1945, thirty-six years ago tonight, at the Battle of Okinawa. After the war, he returned to the States, only to be told that he had served in the military illegally because he was not an American citizen, and therefore not eligible for free college tuition or any other benefits under the G.I. Bill of Rights—an injustice he never forgot. When he was finally sworn in as a citizen several years later, the judge shook his hand and apologized for the American government's ingratitude. By this point, though, free college was almost beside the point. Mondor was educating himself, reading Shakespeare by night and working by day in the accounting office at a Woonsocket mill, where he took note of the nepotistic, money-wasting business practices that would lead to its closing a few years later.

By the early 1960s, Mondor had developed his own plan for survival in the threatened textile industry of New England. He and two partners bought an old mill in Pawtucket and began producing women's wear fabrics. His partners dropped out, but Mondor kept plugging, selling the business and reinvesting the considerable profit into bankrupt textile operations from Massachusetts to Pennsylvania, always with an eye toward salvaging the company and selling it at a gain. He applied his eye for detail to each company's books, studying the margins, assessing the risks and possibilities. He became so successful that by 1974 he could retire at the age of forty-eight. He and Madeleine did not have any children, a source of sadness for both, but they did have many nieces, nephews, and godchildren, and a lovely colonial in Lincoln, and lots and lots of money, and each other. There were rosebushes and an art collection to tend to, and a chance to see the world by more agreeable means than a navy ship.

All the while, as Mondor scrimped and hustled his way to success, through the postwar years, the 1950s, the 1960s, and into the 1970s, that concrete gem of Pawtucket, McCoy Stadium, slipped gradually into disrepair. It became a hulking symbol of the fading fortunes of a city whose essential textile mills were moving south or closing up, one by one. In some ways, the stadium was very much like a closed mill, an empty place echoing faintly of toil and striving, yearning to hum again.

After the death of Thomas P. McCoy in 1945, the ballpark named in his honor served as the home field for the Pawtucket Slaters, a minor-league affiliate of the Boston Braves. But the team and its league folded after a few years, and by the 1950s the stadium's nearly six thousand seats were rarely occupied. Its concourse became a haven for pigeons and vandals, its field a dusty plain used for high school games and Babe Ruth games and Little League games and beer-league softball games and good old sandlot games. Park security was usually provided by an overweight watchman who would sit in a chair, beer in hand, outside the bar that would become the Lily Social Club, rising now and then whenever he sensed mischief afoot. "He'd chase the kids away," remembers Ted Dolan, who grew up across the street from McCoy. "Of course, he couldn't catch you."

By 1961, the stadium was all but abandoned, entrances and ticket windows boarded up, walls defaced with graffiti that said, in effect, no game today. Vandals had busted the lights, damaged the sound system, and punched holes in the ceiling to expose girders and steel rods to the elements. Rust covered the grandstand's seats and railings. The stadium had become headquarters for the city's highway department: a storage facility, really, for trucks and heavy equipment, piles of paving blocks and mounds and mounds of salt and sand. Just twenty years after the city proudly held a "Laying of Cornerstone" ceremony, where a band played, and people cheered, and the mayor read aloud a letter dedicating this playland to the enjoyment of Pawtucket "for all eternity," the stadium had become, in the estimation of the Pawtucket *Evening Times*, a "shameful eyesore."

Still, in fits and starts, professional baseball returned to McCoy, as though willed by the mayoral specter sitting in his box seat, waiting to throw out the first phantom pitch. In the mid-1960s, a Double-A team for the Cleveland Indians called the Pawtucket Indians briefly played before small crowds more interested in the future stars of the Boston Red Sox than in those of an American League rival. Of what little is remembered from those two Indians years, there lingers the story of a Pawtucket player sliding into second base and mysteriously slicing his leg. After the game, he and his teammates returned to the infield to investigate, and there, near second base, they unearthed the culprit: an old hubcap—a remnant, perhaps, of one of the vehicles supposedly swallowed by the swamp decades earlier.

Then, in 1970, a team called the Pawtucket Red Sox was created. A Double-A franchise at first, it joined the Triple-A International League in 1973. Its owner, Joe Buzas, the acknowledged king of minor-league baseball, had saved dozens of teams across the country, sometimes buying and flipping them like so much real estate. A former major-league shortstop (30 games with the 1945 New York Yankees), he routinely introduced himself with a feigned jab, as if to test your boxing mettle. He was a crusty, bighearted adherent to the old school, which meant that he was legendarily tight, and would have saved the shells of shucked peanuts if he could find a use for them. Whenever his Pawtucket team ended a home stand, for example, he would pack up the unsold boxes of popcorn into his car and drive 120 miles to sell them at the home stand of the team he owned in Bristol, Connecticut. And after every game, he had that kid who was always hanging around, that Hood, gather up the used baseballs and feed them into a strange, octagonal box filled with erasers that, with turns of a crank, would scrub the balls almost clean, so that they could be recycled as "new" for the next game.

In 1975, after two years of losing money, Buzas sold the team to Phil Anez, an ambitious advertising executive from Woonsocket with a rock-star haircut and a fondness for the track. Using a $10,000 loan from his grandfather and a much larger loan from the Small Business Administration, he bet all he had on the Pawtucket Red Sox, and talked excitedly of his many ideas for making the team profitable. But such naïve exuberance can be skeptically received in a hard-knock, insecure place like Pawtucket. When Anez was introduced as the team's new owner to the mayor of Pawtucket, His Honor's first question was not a pleasant how-do-you-do, but a distrusting: "When are you moving the team out of Pawtucket?" Anez insisted that he had no such plans, thus providing the first public indication that he may not have entirely known what he was getting into. The second came when he shared with New England the news that he was, at heart, a New York Yankees fan.

Anez improved the concession stands at McCoy, launched a blitz of special nights and promotions, bought "Charlie Finley type multi-colored uniforms" of scarlet and blue for the ballplayers, and hired usherettes to, as he put it, "give a little glamour and beauty to the ballpark." He also named a sixteen-year-old girl from Lincoln as Miss Pawtucket Red Sox, whose duties, according to the *Providence Journal*, were to "sweep the bases, bring refreshments to the umpires and provide a general focus of attention." However off-putting it might have been to use a teenage girl as a "focus of attention" on a baseball diamond, Anez was at least correct in sensing a need for distraction from the poor quality of the baseball being played. The Pawtucket team lost 87 games and won just 53 that season, an appalling record that was punctuated by one last public-relations gaffe. With only a few games left to play, the team's two batboys—Eddy, thirteen, and Larry, fourteen, both being raised by single mothers—quit after learning that they would not be compensated for their season's work. By the time Anez agreed to pay the boys a couple of hundred dollars each, on advice of counsel and the state Department of Labor, he had become the villain in a national story line worthy of Horatio Alger: *The Fatherless Batboys of Pawtucket.*

Anez began to panic. City Hall refused to help repair the broken stadium, and the talent he wanted from the Red Sox organization to fill its seats never came. Believing that he could broaden his fan base with a change in nomenclature, Anez rechristened the team the Rhode Island Red Sox—the RISox—"in honor of the many fans who made 1975 the tremendous success it was." But by removing "Pawtucket" from the name, of course, he effectively separated the team from its home, alienating everyone from the mayor in city hall to the maintenance crew raking the field. He also capitalized on the bicentennial year by selling season tickets at $19 for children and $76 for adults, and trotted out every gimmick and come-on in the worn playbook of struggling minor-league franchises. A safecracking contest. Another visit from Max Patkin, the Baseball Clown. Ten-cent Beer Night ("Wasn't pretty," Hood will recall). Win A Jalopy Night, in which some lucky fan won an old heap in need of a new motor. Win A Pony Night, in which the sight of a miniature pony being trotted onto the field had every parent in the stadium praying not to be in possession of the winning ticket. (Joe Morgan, the manager, will remember the time "a little girl won it, and her old man didn't want her to take it, naturally, and she was crying. . . .") Each promotion signaled the desperation of a cash-strapped operation in search of an identity. Sometimes, it seemed that McCoy had devolved into the place to go if you wanted to throw food, drink to excess, and take your life's frustrations out on the players and umpires on the field, thus saving money you might otherwise have spent on psychotherapy.

The ballplayers could sense that things were not quite right. Jack Baker, the team's powerful first baseman, whose nickname—"Home Run"—pretty much says it all, will remember two off-field moments above all others. That time in Charleston, West Virginia, when deputy sheriffs effectively impounded the bus *and* the team by preventing them from driving away—apparently because the team hadn't paid its Charleston hotel bill in many months. And the time when the team participated in "Rhode Island Red Sox Night" at the dog track in Lincoln, and Baker and a dozen other players were paraded onto the track between races, as if the Black Sox scandal of 1919 had never happened, as if baseball and gambling went together like apple pie and ice cream.

The bicentennial season ended in another losing season, both in the standings and at the box office, and the Pawtucket Red Sox—make that the Rhode Island Red Sox—seemed on the verge of folding up or leaving town, like so many of the mills once within walking distance of its ticket window. After revealing that he had lost money and could not stomach any more jalopy and pony giveaways, Anez announced plans to move the franchise to Jersey City, which did not seem particularly interested in receiving it. Meanwhile, the International League was demanding that he pay several outstanding bills for bats and balls and other baseball supplies. He asked for more time, but made it clear that he wasn't going to throw good money after bad. Fed up, the International League stripped Anez of the franchise. He would leave the stadium, for the last time, in tears.

Although Anez always felt forsaken by the Boston Red Sox and the City of Pawtucket, he would tell anyone who listened that he accepted responsibility for his failure, citing as his biggest mistake the decision to remove "Pawtucket" from the team's name. He would file for bankruptcy. His marriage would break up. He would avoid any circumstance in which he might hear or see the phrase "Pawtucket Red Sox," going so far as to cancel his subscription to the *Providence Journal*. And he would never again set foot in McCoy Stadium: too painful.

More than thirty years later, Phil Anez will say, with voice breaking: "I still think about it every single day."

After banishing Anez, the International League awarded the franchise to a Massachusetts businessman, who instantly compounded problems by announcing plans to move the team to Worcester. No, you're not, the drama-weary league said, and ended the negotiations. Now it was January 1977, and both the International League and the Boston Red Sox were in a bind; with Opening Day just three months away, they had no one in charge in Pawtucket. But a man with ties to both worlds, a Pawtucket bank executive and former Red Sox pitcher named Chet Nichols, knew someone who might solve all their worries, a real character with deep pockets named Ben Mondor. It was a hard sell, though. His first of many conversations with Mondor on the subject began this way.

Nichols: So, how would you like to buy a baseball team?

Mondor: How would you like to go play in traffic?

In truth, the thought rather intrigued the retired, somewhat bored millionaire. While he had not forgotten his impressions of McCoy upon attending a PawSox game a couple of years earlier—*What a dump*—Mondor was drawn to the challenge, to the potential story line of: Once-poor kid from Woonsocket saves the game of baseball. Several meetings with Red Sox executives in Boston went smoothly enough, but when Mondor asked to see the books, as a good businessman should, he discovered that the Pawtucket Red Sox franchise was in hock for hundreds of thousands of dollars to the beer distributors, the food vendors, the newspapers, the telephone company. Having no desire to inherit someone else's debt, Mondor said no, thank you, gentlemen, and the best of luck to you.

Desperate to win him over, baseball executives concocted an elaborate, smoke-and-mirrors swap on paper that effectively sent the debt-ridden Pawtucket franchise to the Canadian hinterlands, never to be found, and replaced it with a clean, unencumbered franchise that could be presented to Mondor as a virginal enterprise. After some additional haggling, he accepted the terms, and the challenge. His first order of business: Hire an assistant who knew the ins and outs of the baseball business, because he sure as hell didn't.

On an icy, late-January day in 1977, Mondor arranged to have lunch with Mike Tamburro, a tall, earnest young man with a curl of brown hair that looped over the center of his forehead. Tamburro was only twenty-four, but he had already served two years as the general manager of Boston's Single-A team in Elmira, in western New York. He had a reputation for working as long as it took to get things done, an ethic he developed as a boy, peeling potatoes and washing dishes at his family's Italian restaurant outside Worcester. The Red Sox front office thought highly of him, and knew of his strong desire to return to New England, made clear by his constant inquiries into the travails of the Pawtucket franchise.

The two men met at the To Kalon Club, an august, white-linen Pawtucket establishment that Mondor had chosen to impress the young man. For decades the TK Club—whose Greek name means "the beautiful"—had been the preferred social refuge of mill owners, bankers, and other masters of the Blackstone Valley universe. Local lore had it that to understand the power endowed in the club, you need only take a drive on Interstate 95, just outside its doors. The highway follows a relatively straight line from Florida to Maine, save for the dangerous shimmy it performs in Pawtucket, swerving this way and that as if to avoid plowing right through the almighty TK. But now, with textile businesses closing and a disturbing pall settling over the downtown, the club was losing the beauty promised in its name and maintained by money. A musty scent was creeping into its pool room, its bowling alley, into the hand-painted scenes of country squires on horseback that adorned some of its walls. Still, surrounded by these remnants of privilege not known to their immigrant forebears, Mondor and Tamburro found common ground: on the importance of the Catholic faith in their lives; in the embrace of hard work;

and in the recognition that the success of the Pawtucket Red Sox hinged on returning to McCoy Stadium a sense of wholesome respect for baseball. No more base-sweeping usherettes. No more ponies. And forget this Rhode Island Red Sox nonsense. We're in Pawtucket, so the Pawtucket Red Sox it is.

Even before the check for lunch arrived, the two men knew that they would soon be spending a lot of time with each other. They took the short ride to their new workplace, walking up to the stadium's open concourse, and immediately felt the panic of doubt. The stadium was like a concrete refuse bin, with cups and paper and garbage from the last game of last season, five months ago, strewn everywhere. Silenced by the scene, and with the echoing click-clack of their shoes the only noise, the men passed the Kentucky Fried Chicken concession stand, where chicken bones were frozen into the ice puddles on the floor. Mondor slipped on the mess and slammed to the ground, flat on his back. As Tamburro rushed over, the millionaire looked up at his only employee and said: Son, every businessman makes a classic mistake in his life. This better not be mine.

Mondor got up off the floor, with only his pride hurt. Then the two men walked down to the office area, which, of course, had been cleaned out. Not even a paper clip.

With Opening Day just two months away, the new owner and his enthusiastic aide had to build a baseball enterprise from nearly nothing, a challenge made doubly difficult by his predecessor's parting gift of assorted unpaid bills. In New England, the phrase "Red Sox" is the not-so-secret password to everything; it opens doors, ensures certain considerations, spreads goodwill. But Mondor and Tamburro soon learned that the mere addition of one word, "Pawtucket," changed the magical phrase into a door-slamming epithet. Mondor tried to explain to the team's traditional vendors that he had no connection to the old franchise. Though he was not responsible for its debts, he was a self-made multimillionaire, honorable, a good risk. But many businesses did not care. One day, Mondor and Tamburro went shopping at the E. L. Freeman stationery store on Newport Avenue for pens, pads, and other essential office supplies. They wheeled their cart to the checkout line and asked to set up a long-term account. But when the manager learned that they were from the Pawtucket Red Sox, he asked them to leave the store—the team owed him $2,500, and he had no desire to do any further business with them. The millionaire and his assistant left their crammed shopping cart at the counter and walked out.

It seemed that every affected business saw only the red in Pawtucket Red Sox. When Mondor placed a routine order for International League baseballs with the sports-equipment vendor, for example, he was refused. Once the vendor found out that the Syracuse Chiefs were thinking of supplying enough balls to tide Pawtucket over, it threatened to cut off Syracuse as well. In the end, Mondor was forced to threaten court action in order to secure the God-given right to buy baseballs.

The two men promised dozens of irate fans that they would make good on all the tickets that the previous owner sold in advance for playoff games never played, as well as all those two-year season ticket packages for which the new owners never saw a dime. They mollified their vendors by paying their bills in advance of the season, with Mondor writing large checks to create pay-as-you-go accounts with the popcorn supplier, the peanut supplier, the supplier of souvenirs and trinkets. They received dozens of slightly used Red Sox uniforms from Boston to replace the Pawtucket uniforms that were nowhere to be found in the clubhouse, and arranged with a manufacturer in North Carolina to have a shipment of baseball caps sent two weeks before Opening Day.

Two weeks before Opening Day: no caps.

One week before: no caps.

The night before: no caps.

Seeing no other choice, a frantic Tamburro raced to the Sears department store on North Main Street and bought up its complement of cheap Boston Red Sox hats. Of course, the next day, on the afternoon of Opening Day, April 15, 1977, a few hours before game time, the shipment of baseball caps arrived, by bus. Of course.

The new management assigned a regiment of ushers, Pawtucket police officers, and Pinkerton guards to bum-rush to South Bend

Street anyone under the misapprehension that McCoy Stadium still tolerated drunks pelting people with mustard and relish. Those who were thrown out for rowdy behavior—over the weekend, several dozen would be shown the door—could have saved themselves some embarrassment had they spent fifty cents to buy the official 1977 Pawtucket Red Sox program before engaging in their clownishness. For there, on the first page, appeared an open letter from the team president, Ben Mondor. It was a contract, really, stipulating an end to thirty-five years of uncertainty and embarrassment, hooligans and beer fests, ponies and jalopies and silliness.

"Welcome!" the letter began. "The circus tent at McCoy Stadium has come down one last time."

Now, four years after Mondor wrote that Opening Day manifesto, few in Rhode Island dispute that he has kept his word. With the help of Mike Tamburro and Lou Schwechheimer, another tireless young addition to the front office, he has gradually turned an all-but-bankrupt team, playing in an all-but-abandoned ballpark, into a southern New England attraction that is, dare they say it, profitable. The men have stuck to a plan that embraces the surrounding working-class milieu: keep the prices low, make the stadium safe and family-friendly, and emphasize that the Pawtucket players on the field are the Boston Red Sox stars of tomorrow. The place should be about baseball at its diverting, aspiring best—and the fans apparently agreed. In 1977, Mondor's first year as the owner, the Pawtucket Red Sox had a paid attendance of 111,000 fans; by last year, in 1980, the team had nearly doubled that figure.

Unlike Anez, Mondor has had the financial wherewithal to buy peace with the many vendors who had lost money and trust in the Pawtucket Red Sox. He has rewarded those who believed in him, and punished those who did not, none more famously than McLaughlin and Moran, the dominant distributor of Anheuser-Busch products in Rhode Island—including that beer of the masses, Budweiser. The specifics of the falling-out will blur with time. The beer distributor will claim that Mondor refused to pay an outstanding bill left behind by the team's previous owner. Pawtucket officials will say that the distributor saw the Pawtucket Red Sox as a lost cause, and decided to exercise its *droit de seigneur*—in the name of the King of Beers—to stop delivering precious Budweiser to the ballpark.

No one disputes Mondor's message to McLaughlin and Moran when the deliveries of Bud stopped. To wit: Fuck you.

The patrons of McCoy did not want for refreshment, however. Like so many other vendors, the Miller distributor had also been stiffed for several thousand dollars, but, in an act of faith that Mondor never forgot, it accepted his cash-up-front terms and continued its deliveries. A few years later, of course, with the Pawtucket Red Sox now a popular and profitable enterprise, a McLaughlin and Moran representative visited the stadium to deliver the good news that Budweiser could again be made available to PawSox fans. Isn't that wonderful?

You can just see Ben Mondor, can't you? Sitting at his secondhand desk, smile stretching beneath his trimmed mustache, eyes squinting behind those shaded glasses, entirely amused by the gross misunderstanding of what matters to him. He reminded his visitor that when he needed McLaughlin and Moran, it had forsaken him. Miller, though, had stuck by him, and so he will stick by Miller. In other words, the King of Beers can kiss his French-Canadian ass.

This will become a kind of annual tradition. Every year, a representative from McLaughlin and Moran will pay a visit to McCoy, asking Mondor for forgiveness, begging for reconsideration. Often that representative will be Terry Moran, a son of one of the company's co-founders and well aware of McCoy Stadium's status as a yawning hold of lost potential—Anheuser-Busch's largest "unsold" in the Northeast. Moran will know from marketing studies that McCoy's fans actually wanted a choice in the selection of beers at the stadium, and he will weary of constantly being asked wherever he goes in Rhode Island: "How come I can't get a Bud at McCoy? How come I can't get a Bud at McCoy?"

"It killed me," Moran will later say. "It absolutely killed me. And Ben wouldn't give a shit. Loyalty outweighed everything."

Even so, Moran will dutifully make his pilgrimage to Pawtucket, join Mondor for lunch at the TK Club, enjoy the older man's colorful stories, hear again how the Miller distributor had stuck by the PawSox when Budweiser would not, and wait for the right moment to apologize profusely, again, for the sins of his beer-selling elders. And Ben will always say, politely: Sorry.

The rejection will both wound and impress Moran. What loyalty.

By 2003, a quarter-century after the fallout, the beer-selling landscape of Rhode Island will have changed, and the Miller executives who stuck by Mondor will have died. Moran will try again—only this time Mondor will extend his hand to shake on the deal. "I'm telling you," Moran will say, "it brought tears to my eyes."

Mondor and his two aides had more than relationships to repair. After nearly four decades of neglect, McCoy Stadium had become a large-scale handyman's special. Step by step, though, the new management team made capital improvements. Renovations in the clubhouses. New concession stands. A new washer and dryer, so that Hood and his little rascals didn't have to wheel shopping carts of dirty uniforms up to a coin laundry. Better plumbing, so that the manager, Joe Morgan, didn't get scalded in the shower every time someone flushed a toilet. Mondor also struck upon the idea of painting murals of all Pawtucket Red Sox players who had made it to Boston for at least a year. Not only would the portraits underscore the minor-league team's "future stars" message (Look! The great Carlton Fisk played here once! And Fred Lynn! And Jim Rice!), they would draw the fans' eyes away from the rusted ceiling and other parts of the stadium so in need of repair.

One day a student at the Rhode Island School of Design answered a job posting at the Providence institution that read: *Painter wanted for murals. Please contact the Pawtucket Red Sox.* She sat for an interview with an enthusiastic Mondor and an unenthusiastic Tamburro, whose doubts about the murals did not lift when he learned that the candidate, Tayo Heuser, the daughter of a diplomat, had grown up mostly in Africa, and therefore had almost no understanding of baseball. But Mondor was the boss. Soon, in the freezing months before the next Opening Day, the work crew at McCoy included this earnest RISD student, standing on a ladder in the whipping cold, painting four-by-eight murals of men she had never heard of on the rough concrete walls—and learning on the job that a baseball bat can be one of the most difficult objects to render precisely.

Her first portrait was of the powerfully built Jim Rice, and he looked diminished somehow: un-Rice-like. Her second was of the graceful Fred Lynn, and he looked . . . awkward. "Some of them were really funny-looking," Heuser will say decades later. "They looked like ballet dancers."

In the years to come, as the stadium undergoes renovations, Heuser will have the chance to improve these "Pawtucket Hall of Fame" murals. They will become an identifiable attraction at McCoy for a while, an essential part of every child's game-day experience. But in the late 1970s, you could argue that the original murals were more than a bit odd, and that Mondor had become too fond of them. At one point, for example, he handed Heuser several photographs of various men and assigned her to paint their likenesses in the men's room. She did as she was told, although someone came in while she was mixing paint in a hidden corner of the bathroom. What could she do but remain quiet and still until the visitor finished his business and left. And when she had completed her own business in this sink-and-toilet studio, a group portrait of McCoy denizens adorned the bathroom wall. Here, right above the urinals, were the front-office guys, some maintenance workers, a few of the reporters who routinely covered the team—and the team's owner himself, holding the round white object of his newfound passion. The artist had provided a description, written in Mondor-speak.

"Bazeball," it said.

The oil drums in the dugouts burn on. More spectators rise to leave, punch-drunk tired. At least two children sleep—Meagann Boggs, two, in the arms of her mother, and Kenny Laflamme, fifteen, in his stepfather's Ford Pinto—while a third, David Cregg, ten, the home plate umpire's nephew, fights off the drowsiness and the cold in the desolate stands, and a fourth, Danny Card, nine, honors that to-the-end covenant with his father. The first-base umpire, Tony Maners, notices that his crew chief and counterpart at third base, Jack Lietz, seems to be in discomfort. During a break in the 15th inning, he hustles over to find that his colleague's hands are nearly blue from the cold. Maners gives Lietz his gloves, and jokingly says, "If this thing goes another fifteen innings, give them back to me." Meanwhile, fresh combatants enter the game: two pitchers, the younger one eager to reach the major leagues, the older one struggling to get back. They are separated in age by just five years—a generational gap, though, as far as baseball is concerned.

Pawtucket's new pitcher, Mike Smithson, twenty-six, has spent the night ensconced in scarves, coats, long johns—he'd wear the tarp if he could. Now he is unwrapped and looming from the mound, a six-foot-eight right-hander with the prerequisite mustache who feels the heightened pressure of entering a game in relief; one mistake and it's over. He is from Centerville, Tennessee, a Mayberry-like place about sixty miles southwest of Nashville that takes pride in being the birthplace of the Grand Ole Opry comedian Minnie "Howd-ee! I'm just so proud to be here!" Pearl. Yes, Pawtucket is a long, long way from home—though it shares with Centerville a similar pain. Major businesses in Smithson's hometown, including the Genesco shoe factory, where his father works, will shutter, like so many textile mills. Not that this subtle connection means anything to the clubhouse wags in Pawtucket, who have taken joy in discovering Smithson's college nickname: Snuffy.

Starting his second year in Pawtucket, Smithson feels misused by his manager and the Boston Red Sox. When he signed with Boston in 1976 for $12,000, he banked half and spent half on a new Monte Carlo, brown with a cream-colored landau roof, that he could drive into his bright future. A couple of weeks ago, five years after that purchase, he and his wife, Jenny, drove that same Monte Carlo up from spring training, in Winter Haven, Florida, only to stop again in Pawtucket, some forty miles short of Boston. During that long ride, he flirted with quitting the game and returning to the University of Tennessee to complete the coursework he had interrupted to play ball. It seemed that the Red Sox couldn't decide whether he was a starter or a reliever, and he was tired of it. Tired of watching Aponte get the call before him. Tired of watching Morgan going with his gut, riding the hot hand, and allowing some of his pitchers—Mike Smithson, for example—to sit idle for two weeks at a time.

The Red Sox see Smithson as a talented pitcher whose precision in the bullpen did not always carry into the game, and will abruptly trade him in the spring of 1982 to the Texas Rangers organization—but only after he and his wife have driven their Monte Carlo, once again, some twenty-four hours from Winter Haven to Pawtucket. Checking into their hotel room late on a Saturday night, they will see the phone's message light blinking, and soon learn that he was scheduled to pitch on Tuesday—in Denver. What could they do but sleep, pack up what had just been unpacked, and start driving to Colorado, in their continuing pursuit of the indefinite. Later that year, Smithson will reach the major leagues and stay for eight seasons, including his last two with the Boston Red Sox. He will temper his opinion of Joe Morgan—whom he once saw shimmy up a foul pole to protest a ball that should have been called a home run—and come to recognize in this unusual man a desire to prepare younger ballplayers for the rigors of the major leagues. And whenever he looks back on his major-league career, Smithson will have to admit that he was prepared, thanks in part to Morgan.

Right now, though, in the 15th inning, Mike Smithson offers a sampling of his complicated case as a major-league prospect, as he slings the ball from the side, his body so tall and his arms so long that he practically slaps right-handed batters upon release.

Strikeout.

Single.

Strikeout.

Walk.

Strikeout.

In the bottom of the inning, Red Wings manager Doc Edwards sends in Steve Luebber, the veteran pitcher who, several hours ago, struck a deal with the neighborhood scamps to swap used baseballs for branches, picket fences, and anything else that would fuel a fire in an oil drum. A minor-league geriatric at thirty-one, with sad eyes that support an aura of having seen it all, Luebber serves as a kind of player-coach, which annoys some of the younger pitchers. On the one hand, he seems to be trying to help you along; on the other hand, he's in direct competition with you for the very limited opportunities in Baltimore. But anyone who takes a deep breath and reasonably considers the situation would agree: This guy deserves another shot.

Nearly thirty years after this night, Steve Luebber will find himself in a McDonald's restaurant in Frederick, Maryland, eleven hundred miles from his home in Joplin, Missouri, wearing a golf shirt with another baseball team's logo, eating another cheap lunch, and waiting for another night's minor-league game to begin—this time as the pitching coach for the Blue Rocks of Wilmington, Delaware. At sixty, he will have dedicated more than four decades to baseball, playing and coaching for a couple of dozen teams, from Syracuse, New York, to Tacoma, Washington. A bang-around pitcher who could throw a fastball, a curve, a slider, and a changeup, he played in parts of five seasons in the major leagues, including an appearance in just one inning in 1979 for the Toronto Blue Jays, when he faced three batters and gave up two doubles and a walk. Because he failed to get anyone out, his earned run average—the average number of earned runs he would give up in a 9-inning game—is recorded for the 1979 season as infinity.

In no way does this suggest that Steve Luebber will become some kind of baseball sad sack. For one thing, he will return to the major leagues a couple of months after this game in Pawtucket, if only briefly. For another, he will have won six games in the major leagues by the time his career ends, which is six more than most of us will ever win. He will go on to become a much-admired pitching coach, earning a steady income in a pursuit that he loves. And, sitting at a plastic table in this McDonald's, a line of hungry customers curling around him, he will demonstrate his abiding love by recalling the strengths and weaknesses in that long-ago Pawtucket lineup. Barrett, so pesky at the plate: pitch him in; Gedman, strong low-ball hitter: pitch him away; Koza, weak on breaking pitches: throw him sliders; Boggs, always fouling balls off until he found a pitch he liked: down and away, down and away.

Luebber will be gracious and thoughtful, too, when the inevitable subject of a certain Saturday night in Arlington, Texas, comes up: August 7, 1976. He was the journeyman nobody, transformed into the unhittable starting pitcher for the Minnesota Twins, throwing high and hard for 6, then 7, then 8 innings of no-hit ball, responding in his own way to the "Who the hell is Steve Luebber?" chants running through the Texas stands. Then came the 9th inning, with who-in-the-hell Luebber just three outs from throwing a no-hitter. Now two outs away. Now one out away. A quick strike, and then another, against Roy Howell, a future All Star. Just one more strike, and Luebber will have achieved one of the rarest feats in baseball.

A ball. A ball. A ball. The count is 3 and 2. Just one more strike. A foul ball. Another foul ball. A third foul ball. Just one more out.

Here, in this crowded McDonald's in Frederick, Maryland, where no one will know who the hell he is, Steve Luebber will raise the invisible baseball that he holds forever in his large right hand. With his forefinger and middle finger extended up, as if about to grant a priestly blessing, he will motion downward, throwing that fastball again to Roy Howell, still standing there at the plate three decades later, bat in hand, ready.

A clean, unimpeachable single up the middle will rocket past Luebber and into the McDonald's parking lot. The ball will roll through the legs of his gifted, fated center fielder, Lyman Bostock (shot to death two years later over a misunderstanding), for a two-base error, and the next batter, the dangerous Mike Hargrove, so deliberate in his at-bat preparations that he was known as "the Human Rain Delay," will drive in Howell with a single. No no-hitter. No shutout. Now, from behind the stainless-steel counter at McDonald's, will come the Minnesota Twins manager, Gene Mauch, to collect the baseball, shake his hand, and say, "Super job."

Luebber will smile a smile well short of ruefulness. He will agree that honor is found in having come so close. Still, he will suggest. Still. It would have been nice. Now about that game back in Pawtucket, on the mound in the 15th inning. . . .

Infield hit.

Force-out at second base.

Double play.

*　　　　*　　　　*

Rarely can we point to a specific tick in the time continuum and say: Here. Here, exactly, is where reason took a holiday. But the misbegotten night is blessed at least in this respect, for the exact moment when things fell apart shines brighter than any stadium light. It is about 12:45 in the morning, and for two hours now, knowledgeable players and fans have taken comfort in the baseball standard known as a curfew—a built-in time-out, really, that manages to preserve a game's eternal potential, yet grants those beholden to it the chance to sleep. The understanding is that we will all be able to go home tonight, and someday, maybe tomorrow, we will pick up the game where we left off. After all, according to the International League bylaws and rules that apply to nights like this, no inning shall begin after 12:50 a.m.

Between innings, the three umpires confer with Mondor and Tamburro at the blue-painted lip of the owner's box, along the third-base side. The Pawtucket executives are under the impression that this will be a brief, gut-check conversation, confirming that everyone is on the same page about no inning starting after 12:50. But their isn't-this-night-crazy chat stops short when Jack Lietz, the chief umpire, whose hands a moment ago were blue from the cold, says: Sorry, gentlemen, but the game will continue.

Forgive us, the Pawtucket executives say. The wind and cold seem to be affecting our hearing. Maybe it's our chattering teeth. Could you repeat that?

Lietz says again that the game will continue. He and his brother umpires have no choice. They are literalists of the first order, solemnly bound by the language contained in their bible—the 1981 "International League Instructions for Umpires, Managers and Players"—which makes no mention of such a wise and compassionate option as a league curfew. Previous and future editions of the "International League Instructions for Umpires, Managers and Players" have all said and will say something along the lines of: *A curfew will be in effect during the regular season. No inning shall start after 12:50 a.m. Time will be either Standard or Daylight, whichever is in effect in the city where the game is played.* But no trace of that paragraph appears in the guide's edition for this season, 1981. It seems to have somehow fallen out of the webbing of the text, a dropped ball of suddenly vital words.

The future will provide no definitive explanation for how a boilerplate paragraph vanished from a guidebook essential to the multi-million-dollar operations of a professional baseball league. The most plausible theory is that in the deadline blur of hastily typing, photocopying, mimeographing, cutting, and pasting together the 1981 instruction manual, an employee back at the International League's modest office in Grove City, Ohio, overlooked or misplaced or forgot to include the paragraph, effectively dropping the ball of words onto the floor, where it rolled under a cabinet to be forgotten. Forgotten by everyone, that is, save for International League umpires like Jack Lietz, professional sticklers. "I knew there wasn't anything about a curfew in here," Lietz will later say, "because I read this front to back to pick up the changes that are made every year."

But what about the International League's complementary document, its constitution, a collection of bylaws and rules, which clearly states that on a routine night like this, with no scheduling pressures for travel or playoffs, a curfew must be imposed at 12:50 in the morning? Flabbergasted by the decision to keep playing, Mike Tamburro disappears into the McCoy sanctum, returns with a copy of the constitution, and ceremoniously points out the wording that says, in effect, let's all go home. But even if Tamburro had received these league commandments from Moses himself, beside a burning bush—or a burning barrel—they still would have had no bearing on Lietz, who is guided solely by the aforementioned 1981 "International League Instructions for Umpires, Managers and Players." And Lietz says as much, in words that will stay with Tamburro for decades after:

Those bylaws don't mean shit to me.

With that, another half inning begins, as managers and front-office executives curse and mutter in frustration. "No one was happy, I know that," Denny Cregg, the home plate umpire, will recall. Mike Tamburro is so unhappy that he places a long-distance and late-late-night telephone call to Grove City, Ohio—to the home of one Harold Cooper, the president of the International League. *The* Harold Cooper, whose name

is inscribed on every baseball used in the league; who single-handedly
saved minor-league baseball in Columbus, Ohio; hard-drinking,
forward-thinking, profanity-spewing, irritating, intimidating, and
often endearing Harold Cooper, who at fifty-eight has forgotten more
about the business of baseball than you'll ever know. He was raised by
baseball, all but born in a bat bag and weaned on tobacco spit and spilled
beer. Harold was eight years old when his father was murdered, the body
found sprawled on a couch in an abandoned house. Then his mother
split for New Orleans. Then his grandmother, who was helping to care
for him, got sick and died. Soon young Harold was running wild on a
rough side of Depression-racked Columbus, taunting cops and sneaking
into the brand-new Red Bird Stadium, where he found succor. Before
long the urchin had ingratiated himself with the president of the Columbus Red Birds, who gave him various odd jobs to do, among them:
wiping down the moldy hot dogs with a vinegar rag. Soon he was polishing cleats, working as the clubhouse manager, growing so close to
the ballplayers that many of them attended his high school graduation.
After that, apart from time in the military, college, and a few unrelated
jobs, he has spent his life in minor-league baseball—especially in Columbus. In the mid-1950s, he put together a syndicate of investors to
save the Columbus Jets. Then, in the mid-1970s, as a Franklin County
commissioner, he led the charge to refurbish the stadium and attract a
Triple-A franchise, the Columbus Clippers. Maybe you don't like Harold
Cooper. Maybe he's bitten your head off one too many times, or drunk
you under the table during baseball's winter convention, or told you too
often about cleaning the mold off hot dogs, or shown too much favorit-
ism to his home team, the Clippers. But you respect Harold Cooper. You
respect him enough to fear what he might say to someone calling him at
home at one o'clock on Easter Sunday morning.

No answer. Somewhere in the bowels of an old and nearly empty
stadium, Tamburro hangs up the telephone, wondering all the while:
It's after midnight on Easter Sunday. How can you *not* be home?

So it continues, deeper and deeper into a holy Sunday, a baseball game
wanting to end but unable to find the way. The players and the manag-

ers and the coaches and the journalists and the batboys and so many others cannot leave. They are rooted by the gravitational pull of duty, a magnetizing force too powerful to overcome. They cannot leave.

Single, foul out, strikeout, fly out.

Groundout, strikeout, single, fly out.

Groundout, pop out, pop out.

The game surrenders to the rhythms of the pitchers, empowered by the wind at their backs.

Strikeout, strikeout, error, single, walk, and Pawtucket mounts an anemic, bases-loaded attempt to end the game in the 17th inning, only to have Chico Walker ground out to second.

Groundout, walk, strikeout, walk, walk, and Rochester outdoes Pawtucket by posing a bases-loaded threat in the top of the 18th without so much as hitting the ball. But Bobby Bonner slaps a ground ball to Boggs, who punctures Rochester's hopes with a toe tap on third.

In the bottom of the 18th, Dave Koza approaches the plate for the eighth time in this game. He has 3 hits in 7 at bats so far, and do you know who knows this minor but encouraging statistic better than the official scorer, up there in the drafty press box? Do you know who knows this better than Koza himself? A young woman sitting and faintly shivering in the lonely stands on the third-base side, despite the blanket in her lap, her long blond hair parted in the middle, her large eyes conveying not so much a naïve wonder as an openness to what comes next: his new wife, Ann Koza. And do you know what she is thinking? Of course you do.

Come on, Dave. End this.

Strange how we wind up where we do. All it takes sometimes is a chance encounter, something seen in a pair of eyes, an openness to change. Two years ago, Ann was dating a nice guy in her isolated hometown in northeastern Pennsylvania. And now here she is, at twenty-three, married to the strapping first baseman for the Pawtucket Red Sox, imagining a major-league life, experiencing every game with him, every pitch, celebrating when he celebrates but not despairing when he despairs; she does that alone. And tonight, she freezes as he freezes.

Come on, Dave.

Ann grew up in Tunkhannock, a small working-class town about thirty miles northwest of Wilkes-Barre. Her mother worked as a nurse at a state mental hospital, her father—well, her father worked when he worked, giving piano lessons, doing odd jobs, often on the barter system. They raised Ann to be independent and tough. A good swimmer in high school, she was also a gifted baseball player with no interest in girls' softball. She tried out for the boys' varsity team and was taken seriously by the coach, who told her that she was good enough to make the team, but there were rules against girls playing on a boys' team. She became the manager instead.

After high school, during a spring vacation in 1979, she and her boyfriend stopped in Winter Haven to visit a friend of his, Burke Suter, a pitcher in the Red Sox organization. He introduced them to his handsome roommate, Dave Koza, and that was that. When Ann returned to Pennsylvania, she conducted some International League research, saw that Pawtucket would soon be playing in Syracuse—just 130 miles from Tunkhannock!—and called up Suter to ask for tickets. Koza answered the telephone.

Ann got a speeding ticket on her rush to Syracuse.

Around a minor-league team's schedule, a long-distance romance developed. Ann would drive to Dave's games in Rochester and Syracuse, and, occasionally, all the way to Pawtucket, staying with Dave and his PawSox roommates in the double-wide they rented in a trailer park, beside the old Narragansett Park racetrack, that was owned by an old mob associate (Welcome to Rhode Island!). When the season ended, and the Boston Red Sox had again not included Dave in their September call-ups, Dave asked Ann whether she would join him on his trip back to Torrington, Wyoming.

Yes.

Dave and Ann loaded up his black Chevy Blazer and took the first of their many cross-country rides together, shedding the cheek-by-jowl crowdedness of gritty Pawtucket and the confining hills of Tunkhannock for a flat terrain on the other side of the country, where Dave Koza walked about like a shy giant (*Oh, Dave's back! Dave's back in town!*). They moved in with Dave's friend Cactus, who was now working at his family's car dealership and living in a house in a desirable part of town "up on the hill." Dave always brought back a huge bag of Red Man chewing tobacco for his buddies, courtesy of the Pawtucket Red Sox clubhouse. A Torrington celebrity, he rarely had to pay for a beer.

Dave got a job working construction with friends, who teased him about his fear of scaffolding, while Ann worked at the Holly Sugar Factory when she wasn't on call as a respiratory therapist at Community Hospital. Cactus gave Dave a good deal on a silver Oldsmobile Toronado, a two-door coupe that looked especially fine with Ann riding shotgun. They all went hunting for pheasant and then for elk, camping out in snow-packed mountains, far from Pawtucket, where the very idea of elk was so foreign that Joe Morgan's nickname for Dave was "Elkman."

Then, right after Christmas, Dave got back into baseball shape. Not that he was ever out of it; he kept fit. But come the New Year, he'd get the itch, and want to start throwing to someone. So he'd pack up his glove, his bat, and a few baseballs, and drive across a piece of the Torrington tundra to the old Willi gymnasium, where, on so many boyhood nights, he led his high school basketball team to victory. Now, alone, with no cheering crowds, he'd run up and down the stairs a few times, swing his bat at a series of phantom pitches, then induce Ann to throw him ground balls and line drives and pop flies. If Ann wasn't around, he'd get Cactus to do it. And if Cactus wasn't around, Dave would throw a ball against the wall, *whop, whop, whop*, again and again, like Steve McQueen in *The Great Escape*, imagining himself someplace else.

Every once in a while, Dave, Ann, Cactus, and a couple of others would head down Main Street to drink beer and shoot pool at the Broncho Bar, beneath the indifferent gaze of the mounted elk, whose glassy eyes had watched Cactus and Dave come through the door so many times over the years. Cactus never forgot the night that some knucklehead started giving Dave a hard time, riding him, looking to settle some perceived slight. The two men squared off beside the pool table, the aggressor made his first move, and—bam—Dave laid him out with a cat-quick left to the jaw. Then, typical Dave: He went to follow up, but saw the man was out cold, and left it at that. No second punch; no blood thirst.

Cactus knew better than to ask Dave how it was going, "it" being the man's major-league struggle, and Ann knew all there was to know, except the answer to why. But neither of them could protect Dave from the hounding inquiries of good friends and passing acquaintances. To his credit, Dave never got angry, no matter how many times he heard how he'd be the first person from Wyoming to play in the major leagues (not true, actually, but he would have been among the very, very few). He'd gently explain how hard it is to reach the big leagues, how he still has hopes of making it, and yes, yes, he's met Carl Yastrzemski—and even Ted Williams. Many years later, Cactus will look back on those nights at the Broncho and realize that, for Dave, Torrington was not always the land of escape that it seemed to be. Ignorance about the business of baseball was greater, expectations higher, Cactus will say. "The pressure must have been phenomenal."

A few months ago, Dave and Ann took a short road trip, driving his hot Toronado across the state of Wyoming, 460 miles, through Wheatland, and Douglas, and Cody, all because he said that she simply had to see Yellowstone National Park. Once there, Dave pulled up to a scenic overlook called Inspiration Point, with its breathtaking view of the canyon and the rushing Yellowstone River below. He walked Ann to a suitably romantic spot, reached for the ring he had in his pocket, the one he had bought from Cactus's uncle, a jeweler, and—a station wagon pulled up and disgorged a bunch of mood-ruining kids. Dave and Ann got back in the car and drove around until he found another spot, cleared his throat, and—a troop of Girl Scouts marched into view. Finally, he took Ann to Old Faithful, determined to present the ring to her when the geyser erupted. He waited, and he waited—it was getting a little awkward—and then . . .

Yes.

On February 5, 1981, Ann Creeden, of Tunkhannock, Pennsylvania, and David Koza, of Torrington, Wyoming, were married in the chapel at St. Joseph's Children's Home, a former orphanage in Torrington now used as a facility to help poor and emotionally damaged children. The Koza family held a reception at the golf course and country club. Then the newlyweds aimed the Toronado east and drove the 1,650 miles to Tunkhannock, where the Creeden family held another wedding reception at a little bar called the Inn Between. After that, it was 1,150 miles south, to Winter Haven. Not because that is where Dave and Ann first met, but because it was spring training, and time to try again.

And here Dave is now, at the plate, trying again. And here is his new wife, Ann, wrapped in a blanket in the stands but very much beside him in the batter's box. She doesn't just want him to end the game. She wants him to be the one everyone talks about the next day. The One.

Come on, Dave. End it.

Koza hits a ground ball that the second baseman, Tom Eaton, boots for an error. Then Wade Boggs slaps another grounder back to the pitcher for a quick double play. And what all this amounts to, all the practice and the heartache and the touching aspirations of two newlyweds, is just the 19th inning.

The moon is nearly full. Make of this what you will.

In the Rochester dugout, the pitcher Jim Umbarger sits wrapped in a winter jacket, thick ski gloves and a red ski hat, an outfit so inappropriate that another Rochester pitcher slouched on the bench, Mike Boddicker, calls him the Cat in the Hat, which prompts another pitcher, Don Welchel, to ask whether Umbarger is going to treat everyone to green eggs and ham after the game. Clearly, a Seussian air of giddiness now commingles with the raw cold. Rochester's young catcher, Dave Huppert, notices that some of the ballplayers are so tired and uncomfortable that they are losing what he will call "their mental look."

And in the Pawtucket dugout, the pitcher Luis Aponte, who left the game after the, what was it, oh, yes, the 10th inning, has received permission to go home from his manager, Joe Morgan, who figures that, hell, the forkballer might be needed in the next game, which is less than twelve hours away. So Mike Smithson, who has just been removed from the game, drives Aponte in his signing-bonus Monte Carlo a few blocks to the Pawtucket apartment that the Venezuelan—so popular he could be president!—shares with his wife, Xiomara, and two sons. Like a patient father, Smithson waits for Aponte to make it inside before pulling away. But something is wrong. Aponte is knocking and knocking, but getting no answer. Wait. Okay. He is talking to his wife. He is talking, and she is talking, but the door between them is not opening in welcome. Now there is a lot of yelling in Spanish, the rough translation of which is:

Where have you been?

At the ballpark! The game is still going on!

You lie!

A few minutes later, a dejected Aponte returns to Smithson's car. His wife, he explains, does not believe that grown men are still playing baseball in the dark of an Easter Sunday morning. She thinks instead that he has greeted this holy day by drinking and chasing women. Aponte has nowhere else to go but back, back to McCoy Stadium, the Alcatraz of baseball, the concrete fortress from which you cannot escape.

But if this game is to reach its full-moon otherness, it requires an appearance by the Pawtucket relief pitcher Win Remmerswaal. Without Remmerswaal, you have at best a waxing gibbous moon; with him, you have lunar completeness. And here he is, standing on the mound, six feet two and weighing a measly 160 pounds, averse to warming up, yet able to throw a baseball well over 90 miles an hour. With playful blue eyes, and longish brown hair flowing from under his cap, he conveys an easy intelligence that suggests a subtle, killer mentality, as if he is not emotionally invested in the task before him; as if this is all a lark—baseball, Pawtucket, life. For Win Remmerswaal, maybe it is.

In the top of the 19th, he induces Rochester's leadoff hitter, Dave Huppert, to pound a ground ball to second base. One out.

Remmerswaal is from the Netherlands, which may explain why baseball seems to be more of a hobby for him than a national pastime, and why he seems to abide a foreign code. For example, it made no sense to him that a promotion in the Red Sox minor-league system meant that you went from Single-A, in balmy and beautiful Winter Haven, to Triple-A, in—Pawtucket. Shouldn't it be the other way around?

Remmerswaal does not seem to accept basic social customs, such as adherence to the law, or the value of currency. When he first came to Pawtucket, he spent a few hundred dollars on an old Ford that soon developed a rattle: the sound of Heineken bottles rolling on the floor whenever he came to a stop. The car's license plate was a piece of cardboard with a few meaningless numbers scribbled on it, and its glove compartment became one of many repositories for the paychecks he never seemed to cash. Even now, on road trips, Morgan tries to rouse his ballplayers from bed by telling them that if they want their meal money for the day, they have to meet him in the hotel lobby by 10:00 a.m. But the gambit never works with Remmerswaal, so Morgan just slips the money to him when he sees him, and hopes the Dutchman spends it on food.

Remmerswaal surrenders a cheap infield hit to Tom Eaton.

One time, at the end of a long road trip that included air travel, team officials realized they had lost something in transit—not a piece of luggage, but a pitcher. Remmerswaal. When he finally wandered into the clubhouse several days later, he was greeted with the expected, *Where the hell have you been?* He calmly explained that during a brief layover in Washington, D.C., he realized that he had never seen the nation's capital, and might never again have the chance. He had left the airport and gone sightseeing for a few days: the Smithsonian, the Lincoln Memorial.

Remmerswaal gets the next batter, Dallas Williams, to hit a ground ball to his shortstop, Julio Valdez, who steps on second base and throws to first for a double play that retires the side.

A couple of years ago, on a hot August morning, the front office in Boston called Pawtucket with orders to send Remmerswaal up to the parent team immediately. Lou Schwechheimer, a fresh intern and the most earnest member of the McCoy operation, was dispatched to inform Remmerswaal of the good news: He was about to become the first major league player born and raised in the Netherlands! But Schwechheimer could not find the pitcher, either at his East Providence apartment or at any of the several bars and restaurants that the pitcher was known to frequent. Hours passed. Every time Schwechheimer called McCoy to say he couldn't find Remmerswaal, he was told, Keep looking. Finally, late that afternoon, the intern managed to get into the apartment when Remmerswaal's roommate showed up with a key. Hustling into the bedroom, he spotted two thin, pale legs, both covered with black socks up to mid-calf, protruding from a swirl of bedsheets and laundry.

Remmerswaal.

Schwechheimer started shouting that he had been knocking on the door for several hours. Don't you understand? You're getting called up! Boston wants you right away! Boston! The big leagues!

With an air of serenity, Remmerswaal said: They can wait.

The next year, 1980, Remmerswaal was again called up by Boston, as was the left-handed pitcher Bruce Hurst. During a game in Cleveland, Remmerswaal somehow arranged for a food delivery to the bullpen. As Hurst will remember it, the bullpen pitchers devoured pizza and ice cream, oblivious to the television camera recording their late-game feast. Boston management was not amused.

In the top of the 20th inning, Remmerswaal gets Cal Ripken Jr. to swing at the first pitch. A fly out to right field.

The thing about Remmerswaal: He is smart, almost too smart. "He could talk academically about the physics of an airplane in flight, or why a curveball works the way it does," Hurst would later say. "But if you told him the bus left at eight o'clock, that confused him."

Remmerswaal loves to argue. Not necessarily because he believes passionately in what he is arguing about, but because argument passes the time, stimulates the brain, can be a sport all its own. One time, Ben Mondor was summoned in the middle of a game to address a clubhouse emergency. He hustled into the room to find Win Remmerswaal and another ballplayer about to come to blows. Over what? An intellectual argument about the properties of electricity. Jeee-sus Christ.

Remmerswaal persuades the second batter, Floyd Rayford, to swing at the first pitch as well. A fly out to left field.

What will become of Win Remmerswaal, funny, unpredictable Win Remmerswaal, now peering down from the mound at Rochester's next batter, the impossibly tall first baseman Dan Logan? For one thing, his major-league career, a study in blown opportunity and wasted talent, is behind him: twenty-two games, three wins, one loss, and a reputation for not taking baseball seriously. For another, his life will never be as happy or as carefree as it is here in Pawtucket, where an intern might pitch apples to him for batting practice in the club-house; where Hood makes sure there's plenty of beer available after the last inning; where life is a game, and the game is life. After this season, his professional baseball career in the United States will end. He will play in Italy, marry, divorce, and return to the Netherlands, where his superb pitching for the national team once made him a Dutch hero and attracted the notice of American scouts. He will slip into alcoholism, live rough, and become so sick with double pneu-monia and pleurisy that he will lapse into a coma, only to awaken a few weeks later with brain damage. By the age of forty-two, he will be housed in an assisted-living facility, bound to a wheelchair, clear-headed one moment, talking about traveling by space shuttle the next.

Mondor will always consider Remmerswaal to be his favorite ball-player. There was something about the pitcher's resistance to structure that appealed to his own rigid sense of order. He will never forget to send the Dutchman little reminders that he remains a member of the Pawtucket Red Sox family: yearbooks and media guides and Christmas cards. And every now and then, Mondor will receive an update from the Netherlands. How a pitcher who once threw fastballs into the nine-ties sits in a wheelchair, in a nursing home, in a country whose national pastime is not baseball, and says to no one in particular: *I pitched in front of millions.*

In 2008, Bruce Hurst will visit Remmerswaal at his nursing home in The Hague, where the wall behind his hospital bed is adorned with Win Remmerswaal baseball cards and a Pawtucket Red Sox team photograph. Hurst, one of the straightest, most earnest men ever to play baseball, strong and strapping in white shorts and a red-and-blue polo shirt, will sit beside Remmerswaal, one of the oddest, most col-orful men ever to play baseball, bent in his wheelchair, his tan-and-white polo shirt stained by a coffee spill. Although they will manage to communicate, haltingly, for a few minutes, Hurst will leave with the sad sense that his old teammate "had a thousand things he wanted to say."

Tonight, though, Remmerswaal feels invincible. He strikes out Logan on three pitches. He is living inning to inning, and here comes the 21st.

The existential questions that might arise from the twinning of a never-ending baseball game with the resurrection of the Lord are not posed. No one is asking, in the argot befitting the setting: What in the name of Christ are we doing here? Instead, those on the field, in the dugout, and scattered throughout the stands accept this night for what it is, and in small ways are taking care of one another. The public-address announcer has spread the word that hot chocolate and coffee are available for free at the only concession stand still open. The batboy, Billy Broadbent, has trotted out to the plate with three Snickers bars for the umpires. The home plate umpire bequeaths his candy bar to his first-base colleague, whose hands are frozen because 6 innings ago he bequeathed his gloves to his third-base colleague. In this way they complete a Tinker-to-Evers-to-Chance act of umpire charity.

Of course, not everyone embraces the wonder of the hour. Lee Graham, the sweet and easygoing center fielder for Pawtucket, runs up to Lou Schwechheimer and demands, through trembling lips, that he end this thing. Schwechheimer smiles at the very idea that he, a twenty-three-year-old kid from the front office, could halt a Triple-A baseball game. But Graham, a child of Florida now chilled to his essence by the outfield wind blowing through him, is not joking. With eyes locked on Schwechheimer, Graham says it again, almost as a threat: End this thing!

There is also the eternally dyspeptic Angelo Cataldi, the *Providence Journal* sportswriter who would prefer to undergo anesthesia-free root canal than to be here at McCoy. The night, the game—the whole place!—is absurd. Whenever he goes to the men's room to relieve himself, for example, what does he see but that stupid mural of a bunch of McCoy inhabitants staring at him—including Angelo Cataldi! "I could literally take a leak while looking at myself," Cataldi will say years later. "There was something really off-putting about relieving yourself while looking into your own eyes."

But these acts of hope and kindness and frustration, these thoroughly human moments so touching and true to our condition, seem only to amuse the night. In a mischievous mood, the night decides to have some fun, and begins to play with McCoy the way a black cat might with a white ball of yarn.

Win Remmerswaal, so loose-limbed and free, begins the 21st inning by striking out the first Rochester batter. The second batter, Mike Hart, whose five-game major-league career has already ended at one major-league hit, singles now to left field. Then Bobby Bonner, the shortstop, hits a grounder to third; he is thrown out at first, but Hart advances to second. With two out, Rochester's catcher, Dave Huppert, stands at the plate, ready, nervous, fresh to the Triple-A, and eager to get his first hit in this young season.

Huppert, twenty-four and built for endurance, is more skilled behind the plate than at it. He already senses that he is being "groomed for an emergency," as he will later say, in case the starting Baltimore catcher, Rick Dempsey, gets injured. He has dedicated himself since high school in Southern California to a singular pursuit: squatting down and catching a ball and standing up and throwing a ball and squatting and standing, squatting, standing, all so that one day he can squat and stand for a major-league baseball team. This is what he has done for six hours straight tonight, two ball games plus, squatting, catching, standing, throwing, squatting, catching, standing, throwing, trudging to the dugout and back onto the field in clattering catcher's equipment, the shin guards, the chest protector, the mask, all of which have to come off whenever he has to bat—eight times already tonight, with four strikeouts—and then be put back on so that he can squat, catch, stand, and throw.

Huppert's manager, Doc Edwards, has not forgotten that the kid has already caught 20 innings. Edwards was a catcher himself, remember, so he knows how taxing even a 9-inning game can be. He also must have noticed that his managerial counterpart, Joe Morgan, took out his starting catcher, Rich Gedman, hours ago; Roger LaFrancois has been catching for Pawtucket for more than 10 innings now. So Edwards keeps asking Huppert whether he's tired and in need of a break. But will the exhausted and hungry Huppert ever acknowledge to his manager that yeah, he's kind of beat, and wouldn't mind coming out of the game?

Never.

Because who knows? At some point this season, or next, one last spot may need to be filled on the major-league team's roster. Or maybe, God forbid, Rick Dempsey gets injured, and the choice for a replacement comes down to Huppert and some other minor leaguer. Let's say they're both catchers, with good hands and weak bats. It's a toss-up, the powers that be are looking for reasons to pick one over the other, and someone says, Remember when Huppert asked out of a game that time? No need for anyone to say quitter, or loser. The silence would say it for them, as the powers that be move on to the next order of business, like the mill owners of old, without giving another thought to this Huppert. To which Dave Huppert says, in his own silence, never. He has inhaled the infield dust from Buena Park, California, to Bluefield, West Virginia, and he plans on a long major-league baseball career. Ten years would be a good length of time, he figures, although he will ultimately have to settle for far less: a total of seventeen games with the Baltimore Orioles, and just one hit. But Huppert will be so proud of that one hit—a single off future Hall of Fame pitcher Phil Niekro in Yankee Stadium—that, decades later, he will refer to it in his official biography, as the manager of the Lehigh Valley IronPigs of the International League. But to get there, to Baltimore and Yankee Stadium and Helena, Montana, and Stockton, California, and Birmingham, Alabama, and every other way station leading up to the Lehigh Valley of Pennsylvania, he must first succeed here and now, early on Easter Sunday in Pawtucket, Rhode Island. Momentarily freed of his confining armor, Huppert waits.

With two outs and two strikes, he lofts a fairly routine fly ball to right center field. Now the night steps in to have its fun, intercepting the ball in its windy grasp. The more that the center fielder, Graham, runs for the ball, the more the wind blows the ball away from him. It's as though man and ball are magnetic opposites. By the time the night blithely releases the ball, Huppert is standing on second base, the proud owner of a wind-tossed double that has driven in the go-ahead run, a run that looms like five runs at this late hour. After a groundout by Eaton, Huppert hustles back to the dugout to don his armor one more time, already imagining the happy embrace of grateful teammates in three short outs.

And the night chuckles.

Steve Luebber, the Rochester pitcher, is also anticipating the slaps on his back and the win on his record. He gets Russ Laribee to fly out to right. Now Dave Koza: a lot of power, a bit of a free swinger, not too difficult to fool. But somewhere in the stands, where maybe fifty people now sit, a young blond woman roots against Luebber, thinking, *Come on, Dave.*

Koza tries to muscle one out. Instead, he launches a short, sky-scraping pop fly out toward right field, for what Luebber is already calculating as an easy out. The second baseman, Tom Eaton, trots toward the outfield and calls "You've got it" to the right fielder, Mike Hart, who replaced Drungo Hazewood days ago, it seems. But Hart calls back, "No, it's yours!"

No, it's the night's. For the night has again cupped this ball, once destined for right field, and is wind-carrying it back toward the infield, creating the illusion of a midair turnaround. Tony Maners, the first-base umpire, will later remember seeing the ball "hit pretty well toward right field," only then to notice poor Tommy Eaton, who had just run toward the outfield, running flat-out in the opposite direction. Eaton is proud of his defensive skills, and he knows this one is on him, no matter that the night has set him up as its plaything. Running, running toward the pitcher's mound, he lunges, but the ball kicks off the heel of his glove, and the only words that he can think of, and he is not a profane man, but the only words that come to his mind are two: "Oh" and "fuck."

A pop fly lands somewhere behind the pitcher's mound—a few dozen feet from the plate—and Dave Koza is standing on second base with a double. Luebber and the rest of the Rochester Red Wings agree: Oh fuck.

Now Wade Boggs is doing that thing he does in the dirt before stepping into the batter's box, that Hebrew sign for life, or luck, or whatever it is that helps him to focus, along with imagining that his batting helmet is his "thinking cap." No one cares tonight about the many strange rituals of a slow minor-league third baseman who does not hit for power, but that will change. Years from now, the entire country will come to know him as perhaps the purest hitter of his generation. He will collect more than 3,000 hits, silence doubters of his fielding ability, and appear in two World Series. His loyal wife, Debbie, sitting and suffering now in the McCoy stands, will sit and suffer again, during an acutely embarrassing television interview with Barbara Walters in which her husband will discuss a years-long extramarital affair. He will diagnose himself as a sex addict after watching a Geraldo Rivera talk show episode on sex addiction. He will become a client and pitchman for a hair-restoration company, have cameo television appearances on both *Cheers* and *The Simpsons*, and be worshipped by a generation of college students more impressed by one unverifiable statistic—that he would drink sixty to seventy cans of Miller Lite on cross-country flights—than by any statistic related to his hitting. He will be admired and reviled, and he will never let the Red Sox front office forget how they underestimated him when he played in Pawtucket. He will often refer to himself in the third person, but to many he will simply be: Boggsy.

Boggsy works the count to 2 and 1, then hits a classic, classic Boggs double, opposite field, to left. Koza rounds third base and easily scores, tying the game, 2–2, in the bottom of the 21st inning, sometime after two o'clock in the morning.

Standing on second base, a triumphant Boggs looks into his team's dugout along the third-base side, where cold, huddled men stomp their cleats on the concrete floor to regain feeling in their toes, and a fire emanates from an oil drum, and he sees—well, he's not quite sure what he sees. Do his teammates want to hug him for tying up the game? Or do they want to slug him for tying up the game—maybe pummel him with those bad-habit-infected bats of theirs? Is this typical Boggs, coming through in the clutch with another clean hit to left? Or is this typical Boggs, putting self before team—in this case, putting self before the team's collective need for sleep?

Sweet Billy Broadbent, the batboy, wants to yell for joy, but one quick look around the home dugout tells him to keep his happiness to himself. Many of these ballplayers just want to go home, and the last thing they need is some sixteen-year-old kid yapping about how great this is. Billy also knows that the sudden change of fortune in this protracted ball game means trouble for him at home. He knows that a half mile away—down Division Street, past the factories and freight trailers, across the railroad tracks, and up a street called Greeley—his worried mother has already stepped out of their bungalow and looked to her right, to make sure that the stadium glow still emanates from beyond the low-slung industrial horizon; that her two sons, the bat-boys, Billy and Kevin, are safe. But she cannot be happy. She'll be call-ing any minute now, if she hasn't already.

Sam Bowen grounds out to shortstop, which keeps Boggs in check at second base, and the catcher, Roger LaFrancois, is intentionally walked. Two out now, with tired men on first and second and in both dugouts. Julio Valdez, Pawtucket's popular, flexible-as-Gumby shortstop, comes to the plate. He was called up to Boston briefly last year (he's one of the chosen five who are depicted hitchhiking on Interstate 95 in the official program), and he will be called up again later this year. He will stay with Boston as a utility infielder for all of 1982, and then, in 1983, he will be arrested by the Boston police—in the dugout—on a charge of statutory rape involving a fourteen-year-old runaway. The charge will be quickly dropped for lack of evidence, but he and his .120 batting average will be sent back to the minors, never to play another game in the major leagues.

All up to Valdez now, as spindly thin as the bat he's choking. A left-handed batter, he stands in wait for Luebber's pitch, the stadium light winking off his blue helmet.

Three pitches.

Three strikes.

Third out.

The end of the 21st inning and the start of the 22nd.

The telephone in the front office rings. General Manager Mike Tamburro answers. The caller asks: They can't still be playing, can they?

And Tamburro tells the worried mother of the batboys:

Yes, Mrs. Broadbent. Yes, they can.

Pawtucket manager Joe Morgan,
asserting once again that the umpire is
incorrect.

On the other side, past the rolls of tarp and the chain-link fencing, past the billboards for tuxedo rentals and oil changes, beyond where the stadium's vaporous glow presses against the infinite dark, Pawtucket sleeps. Its people sleep, too, though they never tire of defending their city's hardscrabble honor, and all but dare you to disparage a place that only they have license to call the Bucket—which they rarely do. They know: the lost textile industry, the quiet downtown, the triple-decker claustrophobia that pervades certain tree-poor streets. Still. Just try to find a parking space when St. Raphael Academy and Tolman High School renew their football rivalry every Thanksgiving. Just try to refuse the prime rib special down at the Checker Club, or to resist that first bite of a Sunday doughnut from Korb's Bakery. And if you don't understand their deep, almost tribal allegiance to this flawed place, read the cheeky editorial in yesterday's Pawtucket *Evening Times*:

> Do you know how you can always tell an outsider to this city? Sure you do: the way he pronounces its name.
>
> Don't listen to his claim that he's familiar with the area or has heard of the community's concerns. When that guy says PAW-tucket, watch out. . . .
>
> You don't live in PAW-tucket. You live in P'-TUCK-it. (If you say it right, it sounds like you're spitting.) And anyone who says it differently, grammarian or Washington, D.C., bureaucrat, just doesn't have our best interests at heart.

So here it is, P'-TUCK-it, at rest.

Main Street, nearly as still in the day as it is now at night, has recently been converted into a pedestrian mall as part of yet another "revitalization" effort, with canopies of clear plastic installed to shield pedestrians from the elements. These hideous, translucent coverings will only bake the sidewalks come summer—but they're worth a try. Nearby looms the grand Leroy Theater, once home to the largest Wurlitzer organ in New England; closed and quiet for a couple of years now, it is beginning its fitful surrender to making way for a Walgreens—but people are vowing to restore the place. True, the Ten Mile River is so polluted that residents along its shores can barely abide the stench—but there is talk of remediation. True, the population has dropped by more than 10 percent since 1950, to about seventy-one thousand people—but the city has felt overcrowded anyway.

True, the tireless entrepreneur believed to own more property than any other city taxpayer is a mob associate named Albo Vitali. He owns a trailer park near Narragansett Park where Dave Koza and other Pawtucket players have lived over the years, and he is vowing at the moment to restore the beloved Leroy. He has also been identified by the state police as an accomplished bookmaker, gifted mover of stolen goods, and convicted felon. So close is he to Raymond L. S. Patriarca, New England's steel-eyed, liver-lipped crime boss, that he once posted Patriarca's considerable bail. A couple of years ago, this prominent Pawtucket landowner and businessman pleaded guilty to selling quarter-shaped counterfeit coins that might, say, trick a vending machine into coughing up some candy Chuckles. True, true; all true. But don't you admire the hope in Vitali's felonious alchemy? The hope of transforming slugs into money?

Hope, after all, is the motto of Rhode Island. Hope has a seat on the public buses, those thirty-five-foot green whales, their insides musty with urine at certain hours of the day, sighing through their blowholes as they stop and start past machine shops and old mills. One of the drivers, Scott Molloy, who will soon embark upon a long career in academia, is occasionally assigned the Pawtucket route. And for all the urban despair he sees, especially late at night, when that despair as-

sumes the drape of gloom, he is struck by a small group of ragtag Pawtucket regulars, a couple of white guys, a black guy, and a woman, who
routinely make the transfer to the dog track in Lincoln. Broken people,
really, but made whole somehow by one another, and by the shared
hope of a winning day at the track—of returning home on a RIPTA
bus with a hundred-dollar score on a two-dollar bet. Never happens.
Maybe tomorrow.

At this hour, these small-time bettors must be asleep, dreaming
of greyhounds. At this hour, in the declining Slater Park Zoo, poor
Fanny the Elephant, chained for the last two decades to concrete covered in hay, enjoys brief, somnolent respite from her captors; someday
she will be rescued and taken to a Texas ranch to live among other
pachyderms, but for now, whatever visions of liberation Fanny might
harbor go undisturbed. At this hour, the socializing in social clubs has
ceased: in the Lily, beside McCoy Stadium, for instance, where a door-
banging raid by the cops will someday curtail its central business of
bookmaking; in the Dante Alighieri, on Hurley Avenue, where Albo
Vitali dreams of turning lead into silver; in the Irish, on Pawtucket
Avenue, where white-haired Pat McCabe, the County Armagh sprite
of a barman, truly understands the propriety of the last call, it's time,
it's time.

It's nearly Easter dawn, he might say. Sleep, why don't you?

Most of Pawtucket heeds this sensible advice, including some of
the few still remaining at McCoy. In the Rochester clubhouse, a couple
of ballplayers, long since removed from the game, have given in to the
tranquilizing effects of many cans of beer. In the parking lot, Kenny
Laflamme is in deep slumber in his stepfather's Ford Pinto, unaware
that he has accidentally activated the car's headlights, which are slowly
draining the battery. And in the owner's office, under a secondhand
desk, a child sleeps: a brown-haired girl of two, a spray of freckles upon
her cheeks, worn out from drawing in her coloring book and nestled
in a bed of blankets and coats. Her name is Meagann Boggs. Dad is at
work, playing third base for the Pawtucket team, and Mom is close by,
sitting with Ben Mondor in the modest partition so grandly called the
owner's box.

So a child sleeps, and intoxicated ballplayers sleep, and the book-makers and proprietors and residents of Pawtucket sleep, and a shack-led elephant sleeps, and, four hundred miles away, the New York city of Rochester sleeps, though some are half dozing to the Rochester-Pawtucket lullaby flowing through their radios from the creaky press box of McCoy. Two Red Wings employees, Bob Drew and Pete Torrez, each of them out of place in his own way, broadcast the game as if of-fering a late-night glass of warm milk.

"We're going into inning number twenty-two right now," says Drew, his voice as soothing as a bedtime storyteller's. "Williams steps in there, still looking for his first hit of the night, or the day, or whatever you call it. There's an attempted bunt, foul at the plate. . . ."

Wait!

What's that sound? That song! A lilting, Irish-tenor song of ire, echoing now through the radios of Rochester! It is Joe Morgan, the man-ager of the Pawtucket Red Sox, screaming at the home plate umpire. And because the stadium is nearly deserted, his angry ditty rises up from home plate to the press box, where it is being captured clearly by two small microphones, transmitted through the black-box mixer attached to a phone jack, and sent by phone line back to a small radio station in Rochester, where the only on-duty employee, a man named Howie, ensures its broadcast to the city of the Kodak Tower and the George Eastman House, to the many neighborhoods and suburbs, the Nineteenth Ward and Irondequoit, Upper Monroe and Penfield. It is a place where baseball matters: where the home team, formerly known as the Bronchos and Hustlers, among other names, and now called the Red Wings, has mattered since the nineteenth century. People in Roch-ester care about their Red Wings, and to those faithful still listening in, Joe Morgan sings an Easter Sunday hymn for which the refrain appears to be:

"I don't give a shit!"

Here is what has brought Morgan to the point of speaking in tongues. Rochester's speedy leadoff hitter, Dallas Williams, the twenty-three-year-old center fielder, is having a miserable night at the plate. He is 0 for 8 so far, and he has tried to drag-bunt his way onto first base and out of the hitless ignominy that awaits him. But the batted ball appears to have jumped up and hit him in fair territory as he ran from the batter's box. The umpire, Denny Cregg, has called it a foul ball, but Morgan is colorfully asserting that the umpire is incorrect. Williams, he is shouting, should be out.

Through the oval opening of his hooded sweatshirt a few feet from the commotion, ten-year-old David Cregg sees his uncle walking away, trying to avoid confrontation with the animated, persistent Morgan. In the off-season, Denny Cregg, thirty-two, works construction, roofing, anything that will sustain him until baseball season, when his compensation is $1,000 a month, plus expenses and the priceless feeling he gets by stepping onto a baseball field—"It's like a drug," he will say, decades later. His hope is that someday a roving supervisor named Barney Deary, Major League Baseball's one-man Umpire Development Program, will see him in action and say: Next year, you're calling balls and strikes in the big leagues. It will never happen. Cregg will give up his dream five years from now. But he will remain in baseball as a supervisor for the Professional Baseball Umpire Corporation, evaluating other aspiring umpires on how they handle myriad situations, such as this one, in which an argumentative manager refuses to leave the field.

"Okay, Joe Morgan has just been thrown out of the ball game," Drew tells his listeners, chuckling. "And I think it's because he said, 'I don't give a darn,' or something like that. Yeah—that Joe Morgan has been tossed here in the twenty-second inning."

That Joe Morgan. He's not going anywhere. Not yet.

Nearly thirty years later, on another inclement spring day in New England, Joe Morgan will nestle into a comfortable chair in his living room in Walpole, Massachusetts, his hometown. His feet will be shod in blue slippers, each one crowned with a red capital B—for Boston Red Sox. His wife, Dottie, will busy herself in the kitchen. On a wall there will hang a sign that reads: "A baseball fan lives here . . . with the woman he never struck out with." It will be a nice scene, a tranquil scene, until Morgan recalls that distant play.

"He ran toward first and the ball jumped up and hit him in the foot!" the white-haired man, nearly eighty, will say. And the 22nd inning of this long-ago ball game in Pawtucket will unfold again in his living room.

"He's out!"

Joe Morgan's baseball passion never cools. The son of immigrants from County Clare, he starred in baseball and hockey at Boston College, where he learned how to apply a Jesuitical rigor to the rules and nuances of the game, and continued his studies during summers by playing for the Hopedale mill town team in the Blackstone Valley League for $30 a week. He'd spend the day working—in a mill one year, at an inn two other years—then play baseball at night against mill workers, college students, and crusty baseball professionals, including a few former major-league pitchers who knew how to snap off a 12-to-6 curve ("I found out how good I wasn't in a hurry," he will say). Once he earned his bachelor's degree in American history and government, he set it aside to embark upon a long career as an itinerant baseball man, his every port of call remaining so vivid in his mind that he will summon them in a laconic Yankee recitation, like a salty Robert Frost asked once again to deliver "The Road Not Taken."

"Well, the first team I played for was the Hartford Chiefs in the Eastern League. Next year I was at Evansville, Indiana, in the Three-I League. Following two years I was in the U.S. Army as a ground pounder."

Ground pounder?

"A guy that's in the army is a ground pounder just by walking around."

Where was he? Oh, yes. The Hartford Chiefs, in 1952. The Evansville Braves. Then down to the Jacksonville Braves in the Sally League. The Atlanta Crackers in the Southern League. The Wichita Braves in the American Association. The Louisville Colonels. The Charleston Marlins. Back to the Atlanta Crackers, now in the International League, for a couple of years. Then back to Jacksonville, but this time for a team called the Suns. Then, at the age of thirty-five, down to the Raleigh Pirates, in the Carolina League, in 1966. Sprinkled among those thirteen years in the baseball wilderness were bits of four seasons in the major leagues, with the Milwaukee Braves, the Kansas City Athletics, the Philadelphia Phillies, the Cleveland Indians, and the St. Louis Cardinals. He was more than a cup-of-coffee guy, but not much more: two cups and maybe a doughnut, to go with a .193 batting average and an ever-expanding repository of baseball knowledge and lore.

He will describe the heat-baked infield at the ballpark in Keokuk, Iowa, as the worst he ever played on; explain why Jimmie Foxx was the best all-around ballplayer in history; remember the name of a long-forgotten minor-league pitcher, Al Meau, who hit a ball through a tire hung in right field in Bluefield, West Virginia, winning enough money to pay his rent for the 1947 season; vividly describe a strange dinner that he and Dot shared with Ted Williams and his girlfriend; and discuss, with professorial authority, the many ballpark stunts he witnessed over the years, including this:

Joe Engel, the gimmick-loving owner of the Chattanooga Lookouts and acknowledged "Barnum of Baseball," would cover the infield with hundreds of dollar bills, along with a fin and a sawbuck here and there. The players from both teams would be positioned along the first- and third-base lines, while a lucky fan standing at home plate would be told that he had thirty seconds to pocket as much of the money as he could, after which the players would dive in. But it would never get to thirty seconds. Shortly into the countdown, one of the ballplayers would feign a move, tricking other ballplayers into crossing the line, and a monetary free-for-all would ensue.

"I found out the best way to do it was to run out there and fall on the ground, and cover as many as you could, reach around the side, scoop up and then get 'em underneath you," Morgan will recall. "I think I got seventeen bucks one time."

After his playing career ended, Morgan continued his baseball peregrinations as a manager: Raleigh, North Carolina; York, Pennsylvania; Columbus, Ohio; Charleston, West Virginia; a year as a coach with the Pittsburgh Pirates; and then back to Charleston. Meanwhile, he and Dottie were raising a family and paying a mortgage in their native Walpole, so he took any job he could find in the off-season—so many, in fact, that he once compiled a list of them and filed it in a small wooden box, along with other idiosyncratic information: every horse to win at least fifty races; the countries that produced the most baseball players, besides the United States and Canada ("Ireland had a shitload of them in the early going"); prominent players who played just one year with the Boston Red Sox (Jack Chesbro, Juan Marichal, Orlando Cepeda, Tom Seaver . . .).

"I was a substitute schoolteacher. I was a bill collector. I took the census in this town. I was an oil man. A coal man. Construction worker. I worked for Polaroid. Raytheon. American Girl Shoe. I worked for Uncle Sam for two years in the U.S. Army; can't forget that. I went to winter ball, four years. I coached the Boston neighborhood hockey team. Oh, yeah, I worked for the post office for a couple of years."

In early 1974, the team in Pawtucket, just twenty-five miles south of Walpole, had an opening for a manager. Sensing another faint chance to manage in the major leagues someday, Morgan expressed his interest to the midlevel executives in the Boston organization. When nothing came of his inquiries, he boldly called Dick O'Connell, the Red Sox general manager, at home.

O'Connell's initial response: How the fuck did you get my telephone number?

Morgan's initial thought, rendered in Morgan-speak: Holy Christ, that's negatory.

But Morgan plowed on, saying he was the man for the job in Pawtucket. O'Connell floored him by responding: There's a ton of people who want this job, but nobody's asked me about it, and I'm the boss around here. You got the job!

So began New England's gradual embrace of its prodigal son, a baseball savant whose managerial decisions were rooted not in statistical analysis but in what he had learned from the Jesuits and those Blackstone Valley veterans, and from all that time spent in places large and small, in Milwaukee and Keokuk, playing beside the great and the forgotten, for teams called the Cardinals and the Crackers. He won over most of his players with his paternal bluntness and his ability to say I've been there; I've been cut, demoted, uncertain of my future; I've been in your cleats. He charmed fans with his on-field histrionics and odd linguistic style, a kind of Walpole meets Canterbury, in which his nonsensical catchall phrase, "Six, two and even," seemed to add up somehow. And he earned the respect of umpires for his deep knowledge of the rules of baseball, although they found his goading, exhibitionistic manner less than endearing. After being ejected one time in Columbus, Morgan did not leave until a sheriff arrived to escort him from the field, after which the unamused sheriff declined his invitation to share a clubhouse beer.

For all his antics, Morgan possessed the maturity that comes from hard-earned perspective. He understood the essential truth of baseball: that to be paid to throw and bat a ball around is a blessing. Real work came after the last game of the season, when he returned to the ranks of the stiffs, doing whatever he could to provide for his family. Soon after landing the manager's job at the Pawtucket Red Sox, he began working the off-season with the Massachusetts Turnpike Authority, mowing the last of the grass, picking up garbage, plowing snow. He'd clean up around the toll plazas, and when he found an errant coin, he'd pocket it.

Joe Morgan and Pawtucket, then, were a perfect fit: modest, time-tested, underestimated. He and the owner, Ben Mondor, understood and respected each other. After every road trip, for example, Morgan would return to McCoy to find a fifth of Chivas waiting for him, courtesy of Mondor—except for the time the team lost nine of ten on the road. Left on his desk was a miniature bottle of scotch: an airplane nip. He laughed his ass off.

One night, Ben and Madeleine Mondor treated Joe and Dottie Morgan to dinner at the Lafayette House, an upscale colonial remnant on Route 1 in Foxboro, not far from Walpole. After a couple of drinks, Mondor got down to business, saying to Morgan: If you promise to be my manager for the rest of your baseball career, your family will never have to worry about another dime again. College. Money. You won't have to worry.

After a pause, Morgan gently gave his answer: I can't, Ben.

Why not?

Indeed: why not? After thirty years of wandering the country in pursuit of a game, Morgan was being offered a dream of an opportunity by a multimillionaire friend whose word was gold. Stop your traveling. Stay in minor-league baseball. Commit to Pawtucket. All will be well. It sounded so inviting. Why not?

Because Morgan, not yet fifty, was still, at his core, a professional baseball player, and professional baseball players are conditioned to take one step, one base, and then the next base, and the next, and not stop until they have made it home. And home means only one thing.

I can't, Ben.

Why not?

Because someday I want to manage in the big leagues.

Deep in his comfortable chair, his box of lists by his side, Morgan will smile at the memory of his long career as the manager of the Pawtucket Red Sox: nine years, from 1974 to 1982. The good teams. The lousy teams. The bottles of Chivas. The characters. Win Remmerswaal, for example, that crazy Dutchman, imploring Morgan not to put him into a game until the 8th or 9th inning because he was still adjusting to the time zone. For a moment the man in Red Sox slippers will disappear into that distant place, where his office was a glorified closet, and the clubhouse showers scalded his skin, and the stadium was so empty and cold some nights that it felt like a morgue—and he will want to go back.

"Those were good times," he will say.

"I don't give a shit!"

So shouts Morgan, among other expressions of his disbelief. "How the hell can you say he was in the batter's bawx?" He yells at the home plate umpire, turns his profane attention to the third-base umpire, then back again to the home plate umpire, rousing from fitful slumber the forty or so fans still in the cavernous ballpark, as well as who knows how many radio listeners back in Rochester. One of the umpires threatens to call the cops if he doesn't leave the field, to which Morgan shoots back: Where the hell are you gonna get a cop at this hour?

"We're in the twenty-second inning here at Pawtucket and Joe has to take a shower," Drew, the Rochester broadcaster, says. "At least he's going to be in where he's warm, anyway—I wonder if we can get tossed out."

Morgan finally, reluctantly, leaves, serenaded as he goes by the affirming cheers of the lonesome McCoy congregation. Some of those tethered to this game—like the broadcasters—wonder whether the crafty veteran has orchestrated his ouster to find shelter from the cold. In truth, Morgan sneaks off to a favored hiding spot behind the backstop and under section 9, a corner of the McCoy underbelly where wood is stacked and rubble thrown and equipment stored. He knows that back here, if you pull a little on the forest green plywood fastened by wire to the chain-link fence, you can create a secret portal to the grass-and-clay spectacle of a baseball game, the unnatural light streaming into the dusky shadows. You are close to the action, yet unseen by all. But you can be heard. In the past, Morgan's mutterings of "Horseshit!" have betrayed his secret hiding place, prompting umpires to tell him to get the hell out of there. "Horseshit" might also reflect his opinion of the Boston Red Sox front office. A few years ago, he applied for the manager's job in Boston and was all but ignored. And just this past off-season, after the firing of manager Don Zimmer, he applied again, going up to Fenway and meeting with Haywood Sullivan, the organization's general manager.

Sullivan: Are you here for the same reason you were last time, Joe?

Morgan: Yes, I am.

Sullivan: Well, the answer is still the same.

For tonight, for now, Joe Morgan keeps his counsel. Here he stays, in the cold that comes from being shunned, surrounded by maintenance equipment in storage, one foot resting on a pile of wooden pallets, hands shoved into the pockets of his navy blue warm-up jacket, eyes trained on the game that gives him purpose.

From above, Drew and his sidekick, Pete Torrez, have been broadcasting for six hours now, with most of the burden carried by Drew, the play-by-play man. He has announced every pitch and catch with the faintest note of urgency, as if to suggest that despite its relentless routine, all of this matters. Just a few moments ago, he told Howie back in the studio to start recording the game, not knowing—how could he?—that at least one listener back in Rochester is doing that very thing. Now his every utterance is recorded for posterity, including an ever-so-faint belch.

"Excuse me," he says. "And here's the oh-one pitch to Williams."

Believe it or not, general managers do not normally go on the road with their teams, let alone broadcast them. But Drew is on the outs with his bosses. Within days he will be fired.

"Low for a ball, evens the count at one and one to Dallas Williams."

Drew, fifty-one, is a veteran minor-league executive who became Rochester's general manager two years ago, in the midst of a difficult time for the Red Wings franchise; among other problems, its home field, Silver Stadium, needs millions of dollars in repairs. Attendance and profits have risen under Drew's tenure, but so have tensions, as he and Bill Farrell, the president of the team's board of directors, have clashed over who, exactly, is in charge. After being pressured by Farrell to force the resignation of Pete Brown, a beloved veteran radio broadcaster who had recently undergone bypass surgery, Drew submitted his resignation, citing "personal reasons" (a polite way of saying that he cannot stand Farrell), but he has agreed to stay on until season's end— and is now performing the duties of the man he was forced to fire. At the moment, though, Drew is planning one last power play: to withdraw his resignation as long as he doesn't have to deal with Farrell—a lame gambit that will only expedite his departure.

Tonight, at least, Bob Drew is the reassuring voice of the Red Wings, describing the pirouettes of shortstop Bobby Bonner, the assuredness of third baseman Cal Ripken Jr., and other matters of more import to the fan than the front-office bloodletting going on behind the scenes. He wonders in vain whether anyone back in Rochester is listening, aside from Linda, his girlfriend and future wife, and so he imagines that he is talking directly to her, pitching baseball woo:

"There's the pitch. Ground ball on the right side. Koza's got it, flips to Remmerswaal covering, for out number one."

Before the game, Drew went into the Rochester clubhouse in search of someone to help him fill the air, and found Torrez, twenty-six, a tall, thin relief pitcher who is on the disabled list and near the end of his playing days. Although his halting performance in the booth tonight might argue against a next career in broadcasting, Torrez has gamely kept up with Drew through the long night, and occasionally has provided the insider's insight one desires from a color man. For example, he did not hesitate to say Morgan might have been right in arguing the call that led to his ejection: "I tell you, Bob, Joe is really mad. And I think he has reason."

"I tell you, Bob"—a verbal tic of Torrez's that accumulates over the hours.

And just as the puckish wind is vexing the players on the field, so too is it flummoxing the two men describing the game. After Ripken pops out to third baseman Wade Boggs, who has to run to the first-base line to track down the ball, pinch hitter Floyd Rayford walks. Then Dan Logan makes contact. "Looping fly ball into left field," Drew says, his flat tone suggesting that nothing unusual is occurring, but then turning panicked, as though his words cannot keep up with the action. "Chasing it, can't get it, as Walker—there's the throw into third base. And over to third base is Floyd Rayford!"

"And, Bob, that was a routine fly ball," Torrez says. "Chico just misjudged that ball because the wind's blowing so hard. . . ."

"So it's going to be a base hit for Dan Logan," Drew says. "And that's why I didn't get too excited about it. It looked like a routine fly ball. But then I look out there and Walker's having trouble with it, as the wind is blowing back in. And it drops in there."

The crazy wind seems to be affecting behavior throughout the press box, injecting a certain loopiness into the broadcast. "Here's the pitch," Drew says at one point. "High, ball one, and we've got a nice fresh hot cup of coffee. Mmmm, that tastes good." But every so often, Drew pulls back, as if startled by what he is about to say: "So Barrett steps in, his *tenth* time at the plate tonight. Some of these things sound a little ridiculous, don't they? *The tenth time at the plate?* One out away, in the *bottom of the twenty-second*?"

Remember that nice postgame dinner of chicken and pasta that Hood, the clubhouse manager, lovingly made for the Rochester team? It has long since turned to macaroni mush. A dispirited Hood has laid out the meal for anyone who wants it. But to the famished and frozen Red Wings hustling in and out, his culinary effort ranks with anything they'd find among the fine Italian restaurants on Federal Hill in Providence. This is not quite the tip-inducing feast that Hood had in mind, but still: Bon appétit.

Remember Harold Cooper, the missing-in-action president of the International League, the only one with power to stop this craziness? Mike Tamburro has called Cooper's home again after another frustrating go-around with the umpires, who are refusing to postpone the game. This time, Cooper's wife, Eloise, has answered the telephone to say that her husband is not in.

This is what Tamburro thinks: Not in? At—what the hell time is it—at two o'clock on Easter Sunday morning?

This is what Tamburro says: Well, would you please tell Harold to call Pawtucket as soon as he gets in? We're still playing baseball here! And we have to figure out how to stop this game!

Remember Danny Card, the boy who struck a deal with his father to stay until the end of the game? Well, Danny is reconsidering. His father seems fine, joking with other stragglers on the first-base side about when the number of innings will surpass the temperature, which hovers now just above 40 degrees. But Danny, a self-described McCoy rat, a beggar of balls, a kid who, in a couple of years, will write a paper for Miss Rini's class at Nathanael Greene Middle School on Pawtucket's backup catcher, Roger LaFrancois, has had enough of the night's cruel bluster and athletic drudgery. Hard to believe, but Danny Card has had enough of baseball. His thin body is cold and his heavy-lidded eyes have taken in all 22 innings. He tells his father that he wants to go home.

One day, Danny will become skilled enough at baseball to play catcher, just like LaFrancois, for Rhode Island College. Then he will wait tables at a Federal Hill restaurant. (It is owned by a very nice man who, years earlier and unbeknownst to Danny, joined one of the restaurant's regular patrons—another very nice man, by the way—in murdering a handsome local hood who was called Onions because he supposedly made all the girls cry. They buried Onions in a secret hiding place that would not be revealed for thirty years, and only after the last of the killers, in the final stage of a terminal illness, decided to give it up, which was very nice of him.)

Danny will spend twelve years in the navy, become a contractor for the Department of Defense, and pass on his abiding passion for the game to his own son. And whenever he remembers the Easter of 1981, he will think of his late father, Ron, who struggled with his weight, who tried but could never quit smoking those cigarettes, who died too young, at fifty-eight, of cancer and other complications—and who, on this night, said:

No. We're staying.

Danny Card will come to understand that his father's insistence has less to do with a love for baseball than with the sanctity of their pact to stick out the game no matter what. "I learned what a promise meant," he will say.

The sandy-haired boy settles back into his seat, beside his father.

Not far from where Danny Card desires to leave, the batboy, Billy Broadbent, desires nothing more than to stay. His mother has driven to McCoy Stadium from their two-bedroom cottage on Greeley Street, intent on collecting Billy and his younger brother, Kevin, the visiting team's batboy. She is now in Mondor's box at the lip of the field, asking—demanding, actually—for custody of her two sons. But Mike Tamburro is gently stalling her, explaining that the batboys play a vital role in the game. Billy is avoiding her gaze and pretending that he cannot hear her, even though every spoken word now seems to resound through the stadium's emptiness. He does not want to go home. He cannot go home. His team needs him.

Just think. A year ago, he showed up at McCoy's doorstep, a baseball-

besotted boy with no father at home, freshly cut from the Tolman High
School baseball team, dreaming of the outfield. He asked for a job in
the stadium's concessions and wound up becoming a batboy. How anxious was Billy that first year? He was so awestruck by the athletes pad-
ding about the clubhouse that, as one player later put it, "He would step
in front of a car if you told him to," and so nervous, or so enthusiastic,
that he got tagged with the clubhouse nickname of "Panic." He fretted
over everything, from the proper arrangement of bats in the dugout
to the supply of towels available to players coming in off the field. He
even developed anxiety over the infield practice balls. After warm-ups
before the start of every inning, first baseman Dave Koza would lob the
infield practice ball toward the dugout, making sure that it bounced, as
though presenting itself obediently to Billy, who would be waiting with
open glove. But Billy would attach outsize importance to the ball, approaching it as though it were live and in play (*"Ground ball, hit sharply
to Broadbent . . ."*). As this inconsequential ball bounced toward him,
he would work up the fear that he might make an error in front of the
thousands of fans taking absolutely no notice of him. And whenever
he did muff the ball, someone in the dugout would say, "E10." Error—
batboy.

But nothing caused him as much heartache last year as the time
he got ejected from a ball game. That's right: Wide-eyed, anxious, and
painfully earnest Billy Broadbent, all of fifteen, got tossed from a ball
game in an episode that made the news.

Batboy Ejected.

Oh, Billy.

It was the second game of a doubleheader against the Charleston
Charlies, and things were testy. Joe Morgan had already been thrown
out for arguing balls and strikes with the home plate umpire, Zach Rebackoff, who was also known as "the Flying Birdman" for his elaborate
delivery of certain calls. "It was an out call that I made," Rebackoff will
say years later. "I'd be in a crouch position and all of a sudden I would
jump high, forward, and land. The whole bit. The fans liked it."

One of the duties of a batboy, meanwhile, is to provide the home
plate umpire with a continuing supply of fresh baseballs. But among

Billy's various apprehensions was the fear of getting hit by a pitcher's warm-up throw. So he would wait at the on-deck circle like a scared puppy until the pitcher had thrown his last warm-up, just before the start of another half inning, then trot out to home plate with a handful of balls. Billy's habit of waiting, though, began to annoy Rebackoff, who suspected it was one of the sophomoric ways that the Pawtucket bench was getting back at him for having just ejected Morgan. "They were a pain in the ass, by the way," Rebackoff will recall. "The truth of the matter is that the team takes on the personality of the manager. With the manager being such a fucking nuthead, those guys picked it up like it's allowed."

As Billy will remember it, Rebackoff kept yelling at him to get over here—now!—with more baseballs, in barking snatches of words that got nastier with each passing inning. Finally, the men in the Pawtucket dugout noticed how upset Billy had become; the boy had no poker face. *Hey, Panic, what's blue saying to you?* When Billy explained that the umpire was riding him for not supplying the game balls fast enough, the pitcher Bob Ojeda, the trainer Dale Robertson, and a few others saw opportunity. They could teach a boy how to be a man *and* set fire to a dull June day at the ballpark. They told Billy that the next time he runs out to home plate, he must tell Rebackoff to go fuck himself.

Words like these did not skip freely over Billy's tongue. But here he was, stinging from his clubhouse nickname and eager to prove that he belonged—that he was part of the team. He looked up to these men in the dugout. He worshipped them. He was fifteen.

This is how Billy will forever remember the moment. In the brief period between the pitcher's last warm-up throw and the commencement of another half inning, a shy batboy hustled up to a flamboyant home plate umpire, handed him some fresh baseballs, and softly said:

Go fuck yourself.

The umpire may not have trusted what he had just heard. If he understood the lowly batboy correctly, this would be the baseball equivalent to Oliver Twist defying the beadle Bumble. *What did you say to me?*

The boy's body trembled like a grass blade as he whispered in reply: *Go fuck yourself.*

In Billy's memory, the umpire did not contort into one of his elaborate play-calling gestures, with face flush and finger pointing to an imaginary shower stall somewhere beyond the diamond; there was no variation of the Flying Birdman. Rebackoff just said—politely, when you think about it—he just said: *You're not working anymore tonight.*

When Billy returned to the dugout, ashen and confused, the ballplayers pestered him until he finally admitted that, like Morgan, he had been ejected from the game. Now here was a story for the ages, a story to break up the monotony of long bus rides and endless practice drills—a story of distinction and pride. Ojeda, one of the batboy's profane muses, may have felt guilt, or he may have simply wanted to prolong the absurd, diverting moment. Whatever his motivation, he began screaming and tossing baseballs onto the field until he, too, was ejected.

Reporters in the press box took note of Ojeda's ejection, of course, since he wasn't even in the game. Their postgame questions led to other questions, which led to a reference in the Pawtucket *Evening Times* to the ejection of "one of Pawtucket's peerless batboys, for conduct unbecoming," which led to an account of the incident in the *Sporting News*, the baseball bible with a national circulation.

Rebackoff, though, will have a somewhat different recollection. He will say that Billy defiantly dropped the baseballs in front of him, and refused to pick them up. He will say that he was being shown up by a fifteen-year-old kid who didn't seem that bright, and that he had no choice but to throw the boy out of the game. And he will say that the notorious episode would become one of the reasons why the Flying Birdman never became a major-league umpire.

Thirty years after this otherwise uneventful minor-league doubleheader, Billy Broadbent will shake his head no as he eats dinner in a Fort Myers restaurant, following another day of working at spring training camp for the Boston Red Sox. He will have become the indispensable video coordinator for the Red Sox, the man who helps the team find advantage in the slightest on-field moment. Remember when the pinch runner Dave Roberts stole second base off the New York Yankees pitcher Mariano Rivera in the bottom of the 9th inning of the fourth game of the 2004 American League Championship Series? A steal that led to a victory that changed the course of the series and propelled the Boston Red Sox to their first World Series championship since 1918? Billy Broadbent helped Roberts to prepare for that moment with videotaped breakdowns of Rivera. Billy Broadbent has a piece of that World Series.

So, no. The umpire is wrong. Shy Billy Broadbent was, and is, very, very bright.

But Broadbent will not smile when he remembers his only ejection from a baseball game, even if Ben Mondor and Mike Tamburro and Lou Schwechheimer and Bob Ojeda and so many others continue to tell the story with humor and affection. He will never take pride in his role, nor forget how livid his mother was upon hearing of his brief insolence. In fact, for years after, while working as a clubhouse manager in Pawtucket, he will share a sanitized version of his story with many of the wide-eyed teenagers working their first baseball jobs at McCoy.

Its lesson: Be careful with your trust.

Tonight, as he avoids his mother, Billy knows that his manufactured ejection last year at least had the intended effect of making him more mature. And it is true; he is much more assured this year. He is sixteen now. He weighs 115 pounds, up 15 pounds from last year, thanks to some off-season weightlifting. And when Dave Koza throws the practice ball toward the dugout before the start of every inning, Billy catches it with confidence.

Broadbent rifles a throw to first—in time!

"I hope you're still with us," the broadcaster Bob Drew says to the night, a note of desperation in his voice. "And if you are still with us, drop a postcard or letter to the Rochester Red Wings, Post Office Box—no post office box—the Rochester Red Wings, 500 Norton Street, Rochester, New York 14621.

"Tell us that you were listening on this historic night, as the Red Wings and the Pawtucket Red Sox break a record for the longest game ever played in the International League. As happened here last night into this morning, on this Easter morning, as we are going into the bottom of the twenty-fourth inning. You let us know that you stayed with us all the way through by sending us a postcard or a letter and we'll send you two tickets to a future Red Wing game. Just for sticking with us."

Who, exactly, is sticking with them? Who, exactly, cares that this game is now the longest in International League history, surpassing some Rochester–Jersey City contest back in 1950?

Here is another question: Is this even a baseball game anymore? Maybe it has morphed into some kind of extravagant form of performance art, in which the failure to reach climax is the point; in which the repetition of scoreless innings signals the meaninglessness of existence. Then again, maybe the performance is intended to convey the opposite message: That this is all a celebration of mystery, a divine reminder that the human condition is too complex and unpredictable, so enjoy this party while you can. Shake off the chill by dancing to "The Candy Man" and "Thank God I'm a Country Boy," two of the songs looping over and over on the stadium's sound system. Take a sip of the champagne that one of the fans has smuggled back into the stadium, along with a few chocolate Easter eggs. Treat yourself to whatever you want from the only concession stand still open, courtesy of the house.

The game's halo glow is now attracting the strays of the night, from an insomniac walking his dog to a couple of cops tired of patrolling Pawtucket in its slumber. Somewhere in the stadium's bowels, a man suddenly appears beside Joe Morgan, the ejected but ever-present Pawtucket manager, who is peering through that private window of his behind the backstop. Drawn like a moth to the ballpark's brightness, the stranger has entered through the unguarded doors of the stadium with an ease that would impress none of the neighborhood kids, who routinely break into McCoy to collect the old baseballs on the roof. He has walked through a second set of unlocked doors and down a narrow hall, past rakes and bags of lime, to identify himself to Morgan as a doctor at Memorial Hospital, fresh from having delivered a baby, and he has a question: What's going on here?

Morgan explains that a baseball game is being played—a game now in the twenty-something inning. The doctor does not believe him. So Morgan steps aside and invites the man to see for himself.

Yep. A baseball game.

The two men take turns sharing the view through Morgan's magical portal.

Pitching for Pawtucket now is Joel Finch, a tall right-hander who is blessed in the knowledge that once this season ends, barring some extraordinary development, he will return to his home state of Indiana to create a life disconnected from professional baseball, the pursuit that has dominated most of his years. He is twenty-four, and his head is spinning.

Just two years ago, during a road trip to Toledo, Joe Morgan called Finch to his hotel room and said the words every minor-league ballplayer yearns to hear: You're going up. Suddenly, Finch was staying in the best hotels in cities across the country, having his bag carried, being given the VIP treatment wherever he went—so much so that he began to feel guilty. With memories of Pawtucket, and less modest Bristol, and Elmira, oh, Elmira, fresh in his mind, he found all this luxury to be unfair. It was reward enough just to be in the major leagues!

Before Finch could catch his breath, he was being summoned from the bullpen—immediately after the warm-up catcher had candidly and unhelpfully told him, "You've got nothing"—to pitch in front of twenty-six thousand people on a June night in Kansas City. He pitched 5 innings, gave up no runs and just two hits, and struck out two—including the great George Brett, caught looking.

If only some of his other games had gone as well. That loss against Tommy John in Yankee Stadium, when he surrendered a home run to Reggie Jackson. That second game of a doubleheader in Cleveland, when he allowed eight hits before being pulled in the 4th inning. And that game against the Toronto Blue Jays in Fenway Park, at the very end of the 1979 season. He was winning the game, 3–1, going into the 8th inning, but gave up a triple to the leadoff batter, Alfredo Griffin, the American League co–rookie of the year.

And Joel Finch, just plain rookie, was yanked, forever, from major-league baseball.

That was almost nineteen months ago. Since then, Finch could tell that he had lost both some speed off his fastball and the support of his employer. An injury or two hadn't helped. This spring, he had barely made the Pawtucket team, and he knew that his only hope was to dazzle and be traded, neither of which seems likely. Just two years ago, he would run out to the mound, convinced, absolutely convinced, that he was about to win another ball game. Now, inconsistency has replaced that confidence. He's throwing harder to make up for his lost velocity, a counterproductive mind-set. He's married. And he is thinking, more and more, about Indiana.

His life seems as complicated as the first inning he pitches tonight, the top of the 23rd. Bobby Bonner singles off his first pitch. Dave Huppert lays down a sacrifice bunt, sending Bonner to second base. Eaton rockets a ground ball to third base, but Boggs makes a nice stop to hold Bonner at second and throw Eaton out at first. And poor Dallas Williams grounds out to second; he is 0 for 10.

Meanwhile, now pitching for Rochester, the gangly left-hander Jim Umbarger, who some 10 innings earlier was being razzed by his punch-drunk teammates for wearing a warm but silly outfit that made him look like a lanky Dr. Seuss character. That silliness is shed the moment he is summoned into the game; this is his life, his future. An introspective man, he thinks that every step in his professional life, every success and every failure, every injury and every front-office encounter, pleasant or otherwise, has led to this very moment on this mound, a mound so chewed up after 22 innings that he has decided to pitch from the stretch. In other words, no windup. Just stand there and throw. Fastball, curveball, slider. Throw.

Umbarger grew up in Southern California. His father was an aerospace engineer, his mother a homemaker who struggled with her health. After starring as a pitcher for Arizona State University, he signed with the Texas Rangers in 1974 for $15,000 in cash and a $7,500 sweetener, and embarked upon a life of baseball. He pitched one year in the minor leagues, in Pittsfield, Massachusetts, where the setting sun at the ancient, wooden Wahconah Park shone into the eyes of batters and where the players' showers had six inches of standing water. The next year he made the leap to the majors, playing for the Texas Rangers and its genius madman of a manager, Billy Martin. He pitched in relief on Opening Day, and induced the first batter he faced—Rod Carew, the hitting virtuoso and future member of the Hall of Fame—to ground out.

Umbarger played for four years in the major leagues, pitching for Texas and the Oakland A's and then Texas again. But he had trouble with his arm and trouble with some of his superiors, including one who supposedly bet that Umbarger would *not* make the 1978 Rangers (a bet the man lost). Other health problems followed, including a bout with a debilitating viral illness, and soon Umbarger was paying the minor-league dues he bypassed at the beginning of his career, in Tucson, and Tulsa, and Charleston, and, now, Rochester. His struggle to return to the major leagues has been defined by close calls and near call-ups—a good stint in Tulsa missed by the scouts, word trickling down that Baltimore manager Earl Weaver really likes him, but . . .

Discouragement is taking hold. He is, after all, twenty-eight years old.

Just the other day, Umbarger had a very private conversation about his future. He asked the Lord to please send some indication of what He wanted him to do with his life. *Do you want me to keep trying to make it in baseball, Lord? Then please, Lord, send a sign.*

Now here he is, on this cleat-ravaged mound, seeing nothing but the brown target of a catcher's mitt, open, waiting, beckoning. Put it right here.

In the bottom of the 23rd inning, Umbarger strikes out Laribee, swinging; strikes out Koza, swinging; and gets the hitting machine, Boggs, to ground out to second. He feels pretty good. Great, in fact.

It's Easter Sunday. Is this the sign, Lord? To keep playing?

Is anyone out there?

Is anyone out there? Is anyone listening, as radio announcer Bob Drew describes one of the strangest games in professional baseball history, pitch by pitch, against a background of the press box telephone ringing with questions (*What the hell's going on?*), and the press box men laughing in delivering the only answer (*Baseball infinity*)? As he wishes his listeners a happy Easter, followed by, "There's a pitch, outside, ball two." As he says again that this game is "all tied at two," followed by, "You're probably getting very tired of hearing us say that." As he continues to share statistics and observations never before uttered in a baseball broadcast:

"And behind the plate, Dave Huppert, who's caught twent-e-e-e— he's going into his twenty-fifth inning behind the plate. That's a long night. . . .

"Chico Walker steps in, and I've lost count. That's about his twelfth trip to the plate. In order to find out, I have to go to three score sheets. . . .

"For the Wings in the twenty-sixth, nothing doing. So, at the end of twenty-five and a half, this game is still tied at two."

Again, Drew seeks a sign. "If you're listening out there, we'd like to know how many people we still have with us. So why don't you give Howie a call at WPXN, 325–5300. Or is that 5500?"

"Fifty-five-hundred," his booth partner, Pete Torrez, answers, mistaken.

"325–5500," Drew says, repeating the mistake. "Give Howie a call down there and we'll count you when you call in. See how many people we have still with us on this Easter Sunday morning, listening to Rochester Red Wing baseball here on WPXN."

In other words: Is anyone out there?

Yes.

Back in Rochester, hundreds are listening: the tired but riveted, the sleepless, the faithful. In a house on the road called Flower City Park, a man is intently listening, no matter that in a few short hours he has to help his eleven-year-old son deliver the Sunday newspapers. On Westchester Avenue, a couple is entertaining friends, former Rochesterians who are home for the holiday weekend, and they are all listening. On Edgemere Drive, a man in his mid-fifties who has been up and down all night, and who will die in little more than a year, is listening, and having one of his last great times.

In a colonial home on Sydenham Road in Irondequoit, Norma McNair, twenty-seven, is lying on the floral-pattern couch in the living room, where a portrait of the Holy Family hangs above the fireplace, and she is listening through the earphone of her transistor radio. A clerk in the order department at the R. T. French mustard company, she adores the Red Wings and has been a season ticket holder for seven years now, always sitting in the second row on the first-base side of Silver Stadium, where she has begun to take many, many photographs of her favorite player, Cal Ripken Jr.—enough to one day fill two leather-bound albums. He and the impossibly tall first baseman, Dan Logan, are always the last ones out of the clubhouse after a game, which means she has to wait that much longer for autographs. But Cal is great; always seems to have time to say hello, pose for a photograph, sign his name. Did you know that Norma and Cal share the same birthday?

Norma loves baseball because each game presents a new narrative with no scheduled ending, and because each game reminds her of her father and namesake, Norman, dead five years now. Back when he was working as a factory shipping clerk, he'd occasionally come home with free tickets to a Red Wings game, courtesy of some trucking company, and he would take his Norma on a spontaneous date to the ballpark. In the hours to come, Norma and her mother, who has long since gone to bed, will be attending the eleven o'clock Easter Mass at St. Ambrose Church. And in the years to come, her mother will pass away, the French mustard company will move away, and her beloved Cal will belong to the entire nation. But she will continue to live in this house, her childhood home, on Sydenham Road, and she will continue to root for her Red Wings, her boys, just as she is doing now, alone, on a couch in the living room, where a photograph of her father sits on the mantel.

Two miles away, in a split-level home on Parkview Drive in Penfield, John Ambrosi is lying on a bed, entranced by words and sounds traveling four hundred miles across the northeast terrain and directly into this darkened upstairs room. The hour is very, very late, or very, very early, but this young man believes that if he turns the radio off now, he will be muting history in the making. He is twenty-one, a student at the University of Rochester, home for spring break, and he is mesmerized. *This is history.*

Earlier tonight, John went out for a couple of beers with his younger brother Marc and a friend from high school. When the three returned to the Ambrosi house, John did what is customary for so many Rochesterians during the baseball season: He turned on a radio to see how their Wings had done. *Guys*, he announced. *The Wings are still playing!* After listening for a while, John's friend and brother gave up; the first went home, the second went to bed. John, though, unplugged the radio from its kitchen socket and carried it upstairs to the small back bedroom reserved tonight for the home-again college boy. He set the volume low, so as not to disturb the sleep of his parents and younger siblings, and laid himself down on the narrow bed. He is five feet six or so, and muscular, thanks to hours spent lifting weights in the family's basement. His brown hair is close-shaved on the sides, a look that, in this time of fashionably long hair, sets him apart. He is a member of the Naval Reserve Officers Training Corps, and is planning to join the navy, or maybe the marines. Yes, it will be the marines. A decade from now, he will fight in the first Gulf War, joining the invasion of Kuwait as an artilleryman with the First Marine Division. He will eventually leave the military with the rank of captain, return to Rochester, earn a graduate degree, marry, and pass on to a son his love for baseball— a love that deepens tonight, as the distant murmurs of strangers, the echoing claps of connecting bats, and the mere words of a broadcaster conspire to cast the stadium lights of Pawtucket upon a small dark bedroom in upstate New York. *History.*

Finally, maybe four miles away, there listens the very person to whom Bob Drew directs his play-by-play patter: his future wife, Linda DuVal. Her first husband died four years ago, nine months after the youngest of their four children was born. Now she works long hours as the owner of a trophy shop, filling orders for bowling trophies and Little League trophies and high school sports trophies. Given that athletics often figure in her business, it was only natural that at some point she would meet the general manager of the Rochester Red Wings, Bob

Drew. And only natural, then, that after they became a couple, she would tape-record the radio broadcasts of the voice of the Red Wings, its general manager in exile, her boyfriend, in case he wants to hear how he sounded on the air.

Tonight, in the raised-ranch house that Linda bought after her husband died, chosen because it was across the street from her best friend for life, Carole Blauvelt, the four children are asleep and the small cassette recorder hums. The game has gone on for so long that Linda has replaced the tape several times and run out of new ones, reluctantly recording over some 1950s rock-and-roll music, even going so far as to use the tape of Elvis Presley that her cousin recorded for her as a birthday present. The melting serenades of the King (*Take my hand, take my whole life too, for I can't help falling in love with you*) erased forever, replaced with the soporific crooning of Bob Drew and Pete Torrez:

The count remains two and two. . . .

I tell you, Bob . . .

Easter Sunday morning will be hectic. Linda's kids all expect Easter baskets, and she and Carole usually stage an egg hunt in the backyard. But this baseball game refuses to end. She's been around long enough to know about the standard practice of a curfew. Shouldn't someone have called the game by now, on account of basic common sense? She knows that Carole Across the Street is usually awake at this hour, fixing something to eat for her husband, a truck driver who often doesn't finish his run until early morning, and so she reaches for the phone:

Carole, the Red Wings are still on—

Soon the two women, who have been friends since forever, are drinking coffee. They are listening to the radio, to Linda's Bob. And they are trying to visualize this strange place called Pawtucket that has men in its thrall, and will not let go.

You know, of course, that this traffic jam will clear. You know that the brake lights ahead will eventually stop their angry red stare, the stutter and halt will ease. You know that this airplane, idle on the tarmac, will eventually launch into the sky; that this subway train, stalled between

stations, will soon shudder into movement; that this sermon will con-
clude and life will reanimate. It must. Still, Rochester's center fielder,
Dallas Williams, feels so trapped by the night—a night in which he has
yet to get a hit—that he's beginning to fear this is it. This is the end of
the world and this is where he will die, in a never-ending game from
which he cannot escape. And the only way that he can release his frustrations and worries is the liberal use of one particular epithet:

Fuck this, fuck the cold, what the fuck are we doing out here, fuck,
fuck, fuck.

Williams speaks for many. Until now, in the bottom of the 26th inning,
the ball-playing inmates of the McCoy Correctional Institution have
believed that liberation would eventually come, most likely in the
form of a home run. Sooner or later—later, it now seems, rather than
sooner—the perfectly timed swing of a hard-ash bat would make a fair
ball disappear, and that will be that. But even without so dramatic an
ending, some combination—walk-steal-double, or error-single-walk-
walk, or double-steal-sacrifice—will surely score a run, pop the lock,
set us free. Every ballplayer here knows this, as well as they know that
dawn follows night. Baseball games do not continue ad infinitum.
Right?

Dave Koza lines out to right field.

Wade Boggs strikes out swinging.

Sam Bowen, right fielder, approaches the plate.

A baby-faced country boy from the coastal marshes of south
Georgia, he is an unassuming presence: neither tall, at five feet nine,
nor imposing, at 170 pounds. And when he takes his place in the batter's box as a right-handed hitter, he doesn't wave his bat with an air of
controlled aggression, because he believes that less movement means
less a chance of doing something wrong. With body nearly still and
feet planted a good foot off the plate, he looks as though he could
be waiting for a bus whose arrival time is of no concern to him. But
everyone in the International League knows that you underestimate
Sammy Bowen's power at your peril. Yes, everyone knows Sam Bowen,
or thinks they do.

For all his outward calm, Bowen wants to catch that bus and get the hell out of here. Don't get him wrong. He loves the Pawtucket Red Sox, and Mondor, and Tamburro, and all the others. He loves living in neighboring Central Falls, where he knows that if you give the local kids a scuffed baseball or broken bat, nobody messes with your truck, and where his friends always have his back, from Pat the barber to Al down at the fruit market, who stocks Dr. Pepper just for him. But this is Bowen's fifth year in Pawtucket, and he might be overstaying his welcome. Just the other night, he hit his seventieth home run as a Pawtucket player—an achievement that is both a team record and an indication that he has been around too long. "I used to look up the ladder at the Triple-A guys . . . and I thought, 'Why don't those old guys get out of the way?'" he will say. "They were twenty-five, twenty-six, twenty-seven, twenty-eight years old. Then all of a sudden you blink, and you're there. And you're twenty-five, twenty-six, twenty-seven, twenty-eight, twenty-nine, thirty, and then you say, 'But I'm only this far away. All I'm needing is a break.'"

Bowen is twenty-eight. And, lately, he feels misunderstood.

Some might say that Sam Bowen has already lived the dreams, and nightmares, of others. His parents, both alcoholics, split up when he was young. When he was sixteen, his mother shot herself to death in the restroom of a bar. A couple of years later, his father, an itinerant construction worker who'd give you the shirt off his back, along with a drink, died of a brain tumor. Bowen's young friends claimed to be jealous; no parents meant no curfew. But he was miserable, angry, immature, and able to experience joy and affection only on the baseball field. Baseball was his ticket out, he will later say. "I wanted something better than what I had seen."

After finding that baseball affirmation at Brunswick Community College, in North Carolina, and then at Valdosta State College, in Georgia, Bowen was drafted by the Boston Red Sox in 1974, and quickly worked his way up to become a Pawtucket star and Boston prospect. His first major-league at bat came on a late August Sunday in 1977, before thirty thousand fans in Fenway Park and against the Texas Rangers relief pitcher Paul Lindblad, who, at thirty-six, seemed ancient to Bowen. The old man caught him looking, a called strike three. In the clubhouse afterward, Boston's superstar catcher, Carlton Fisk, handed Bowen a beer and said: Ain't no place to go but up.

He found himself back with Boston in the summer of 1978, when the Red Sox were in first place, the hated New York Yankees were in third, and the possibility—the probability—of an American League pennant electrified New England. Imagine being Sam Bowen as he raced around the bases in Texas after hitting a home run—his first major-league hit!—for the first-place Boston Red Sox, with his famous new teammates waiting to clap him on the back, the season aligning in their favor, and Bowen, just twenty-five, a part of it all. Although the Red Sox lost the game, he will never forget how Fisk, Pudge himself, handed him another clubhouse beer and, this time, said: Way to go, big guy.

No time to savor the moment. The very next day, a Boston regular came off the disabled list, sending Sam Bowen back to Pawtucket.

Just two summers have passed, but that giddy night might as well belong to another century, so effective are the coping mechanisms of grief. The Red Sox dithered and the Yankees caught fire. Then came the drop-dead playoff game in October, when New York's slap-hitting shortstop, forever known northeast of Middletown, Connecticut, as Bucky Fucking Dent, somehow hit a three-run home run to help the Yankees win the game, the pennant, and, eventually, the 1978 World Series. As for Sam Bowen, he had been called back up from Pawtucket, and so watched Dent's home run from the dugout shadows. With Rice, Lynn, Evans, and Yaz taking turns in the outfield, there seemed to be no place for a Triple-A-plus ballplayer who was extremely good, but not good enough.

In 1979, Bowen led the International League with 28 home runs and 75 runs batted in. Although he batted only .235 and struck out, on average, about every fourth at bat, his power impressed the Detroit Tigers enough to set a deal in motion. Last May, the Tigers and the Red Sox announced a trade: Sam Bowen for veteran pitcher Jack Billingham. Suddenly, here was Jim Campbell, Detroit's general manager, on the telephone in Ben Mondor's office, asking to speak to his new acquisition. What an opportunity! Finally, Sam Bowen could escape from Boston's deep dugout shadows and redefine himself as a full-time major-league ballplayer! Dave Koza and Wade Boggs could only dream of such fortune. Bowen reached for the telephone receiver.

But something happened during that long-distance conversation, something that would change Bowen's life by keeping him where he was. The moment he hung up the telephone, the Bowen-for-Billingham trade was in jeopardy. Within hours, it was dead. Sam Bowen never went to Detroit.

As he placed the receiver to his ear and heard Detroit's general manager say the words you live to hear—Welcome aboard, we just traded for you and we want you to start for us tomorrow night—Bowen considered not mentioning the hamstring pull in his right leg, an injury that had kept him on the sidelines for the entire spring. He had recently run a few sprints and taken some fielding practice, and Boston officials had determined that he was ready to play, but Bowen had his doubts; he thought that he was at least a few days away from game-ready form. Deciding that he did not want to begin his career with Detroit on a false note, Bowen told Campbell of his injury, explained that he wasn't healthy enough to play in Pawtucket, much less Detroit, but assured the general manager that he would be ready to play soon.

"He went berserk," Bowen will recall.

After the stunned Campbell told him to "sit tight" until he called back, Bowen assumed that the deal would go ahead as planned. He said his good-byes in the clubhouse, packed his belongings, returned the furniture he had borrowed, arranged to have the power in his apartment shut off—and waited for a callback from Detroit that never came. Then, the next night, the two teams issued a joint statement that said the trade had been "restructured," although the way it was reported in the *Boston Globe* was, effectively:

Bowen Refuses to Go.

At first, Bowen's efforts to correct this interpretation seemed to lack emphasis. He sounded more wistful than excited at the prospect of moving to Detroit. "I've bounced around quite a bit, and I really liked it here," he told the *Providence Journal*, a few days after the trade was killed. "I felt I had a home here. I realized I'd have to say good-bye to all my friends, not to mention the guys on the club." He went on to say that after overcoming the initial shock, he began to feel "pretty good" about the trade, and realized that a promotion to the major leagues, whether in Boston or Toronto or Detroit, was "what it's all about." But his words came too late, both for the trade and for his reputation.

Bowen's teammates, along with Red Sox executives in Boston and Pawtucket, gleaned two possible reasons for his deal-breaking candor with the Detroit Tigers. One: That with the major-league ballplayers considering a strike, Sam Bowen feared losing a steady paycheck, and would rather make modest money in the minor leagues than no money at all. Or two: That Sam Bowen was afraid of failing. For years now, since childhood, the likes of Dave Koza and Wade Boggs and Danny Parks and Marty Barrett have dedicated themselves to reaching the major leagues. The idea that someone would jeopardize a rare opportunity by sharing too much information just didn't make sense. Unless, that is, Bowen actually preferred the easier, less pressurized setting of Pawtucket, a theory that gained traction after reporters got their hands on a heartfelt letter he had once sent to Ben Mondor. If he was destined to play his entire career in the minor leagues, Bowen had written, there was no place he would rather be than here, in McCoy Stadium, in Pawtucket, among friends.

Bowen felt betrayed by the dissemination of the letter, as well as by what he thought was the willful misinterpretation of its context. His honesty about his injury and about his affection for Pawtucket had been purposely distorted, he thought, to make him look weak. He became angry.

"I was honest with Detroit," he told Steven Krasner of the *Providence Journal*, his every word weighted with frustration. "I was hurt. And I was willing to take the consequences. I'm in the minors. I'm not content being in the minors, but I'm here.

"Listen, they can take away my money, they can take away my uniform," he said. "But I'll be damned if people are going to take away the concept of what kind of person I am."

Now, coming off a lackluster season in 1980, Bowen knows the end is near. His performance on the field and on the telephone clearly did not impress the parent club, and no other major-league team is expressing interest in him. Some might say that he is exactly where he wants to be: Pawtucket.

And this is where Bowen is now, standing in the batter's box in Pawtucket, waiting for that bus. Ball one. Ball two.

The rest of this year will peter out, and he will not be called up again to Boston. Come spring training in Winter Haven next year, he will find validation, if not a major-league job, from the great Ted Williams, who will tell him: Sammy, I've seen you play, and you can play this fucking game. The oracular words will all but carry him up to New England, where he will learn that, despite manager Joe Morgan's vow to play the best nine, Sam Bowen was no longer a starting outfielder for the Pawtucket Red Sox. He will become so enraged during a confrontation with Morgan that he will knock everything on the manager's desk onto the floor.

Done.

Thirty years later, Sam Bowen will have a wife and three kids, and a job as the director of marketing and advertising for the Sport Seasons athletic footwear stores in Tennessee. He will reminisce about having those clubhouse beers with Pudge Fisk; recall, with evident pain, the details and the aftermath of that phone call with the Detroit Tigers general manager; profess his enduring affection for Rhode Island; and describe himself as another Crash Davis, home-run heartbreak of the minor leagues. But he will also be candid about his brief major-league career. Three for twenty-two, with one home run, one run batted in, and a batting average of .136. "When I got my chance, I just didn't do well enough," he will say, leaving it to others to question why that chance was so brief.

Ball three.

But then the Rochester pitcher, Umbarger, makes a mistake in his next pitch to the man who almost played for the Detroit Tigers. A ball right down the middle, and you just don't do that with Sam Bowen at the plate. He gets all of it, the sound of bat meeting ball cracking over the radio like a thunderclap.

"Uh-oh," says Bob Drew.

The ball rockets out of the infield, bound for some distant place well beyond the left-field wall: Division Street, maybe, or the junior high school parking lot, or the Massachusetts town of Attleboro.

"One of the hardest balls ever hit off me," Umbarger will say. "Going straight to left field, and it's out of the ballpark."

"Over the light tower," Wade Boggs will say.

"When he hit it, everyone was, like, al-l-l-l right," Pawtucket's clubhouse joker, Mike Ongarato, will say.

"A lot of the players on the field put their heads down," Rochester's catcher, Dave Huppert, will say. "They really thought it was over. A lot of them probably wished it was."

Rochester's left fielder, John Hale, who had replaced Chris Bourjos a dozen innings ago, races to the wall as if prepared to escape this ball game by making a run for it; as if he might burst past the billboard come-on for the Fournier dealership on Newport Avenue, where you can buy an odd-looking car called the Pacer. Suddenly, at the warning track, Hale turns back toward the infield and waits to receive his gift from the mischievous wind, which is once again toying with the desires of men to get this over with and just go home. The hardest-hit ball of the night, one that seemed destined for a different zip code, halts in mid-journey—"like it hit a wall," according to Rochester's shortstop, Bobby Bonner. The ball plummets to earth, spent, and comes to rest in the leather bed of John Hale's glove. *Fop.*

"He makes the catch for out number three." Drew sighs. "Wow. That was close." Sitting a few feet away in the press box, Mike Scandura jots three words in red ink into his scorebook: "To Warning Track."

Bowen cannot believe that the ball did not carry over the wall. Instead of being embraced by relieved teammates gathered at home plate, he takes the solitary trot to the Pawtucket dugout, telling players from both teams as he passes by: If that thing's not going out, boys, we're in for a long night.

Save for the pitcher, Umbarger, who feels as though he has just been given new life—*Thank you, Lord*—players on both teams now sense the encroaching fear of eternal stasis. In the Pawtucket dugout, Wade Boggs lies down on the bench, exhausted, in disbelief. We are not going to score, we are not going to score, he keeps saying. This will go on forever.

At the dawn of the 27th inning, the night gives a sleepy nod to posterity.

"Howie's gotten twenty-five calls back there at the studio, and four lines have lit up, and that's pretty good, considering I gave you the wrong phone number," Bob Drew confesses. "It's 325-five-*three*-hundred. . . . Give Howie a call and tell him you're listening, 'cause the Red Wings and the Pawtucket Red Sox just set an all-time baseball record for the longest game ever played in both the minor leagues and in the major leagues. This game is now entering its twenty-seventh inning, making it the longest baseball game ever.

"How about that!"

How about that. On the annual celebration of Christ's resurrection, in the drive-by New England city where Samuel Slater encouraged the industrial revolution, at a tired ballpark that Mayor Thomas McCoy all but willed to float on water, baseball history is quietly realized. Without fanfare. Without cameras. With two journalists as witnesses, one cranky, one content, and neither able to report the event for their newspaper employers, so late is it, and so early. History.

The fires in the fifty-five-gallon drums continue to burn on the fuel of broken bats, with ballplayers warming their hands or heating their bat handles to make the pine tar stickier to the touch. In the Pawtucket clubhouse, the men hustle in and out, looking for coffee, warmth, and maybe some common sense, though they will not find their teammate, Luis Aponte. By now everyone on the team has heard how Aponte's wife was so upset by his late return and his lame excuse—*We're still playing!*—that she sent him back to McCoy. But a little while ago, after having pitched the best he will ever pitch, he quietly left the stadium, walked down Columbus Avenue, and knocked once more. This time, Xiomara Aponte opened the door, stepped aside, and, as he will later sweetly recall, "let me sleep beside her."

Meanwhile, in the Rochester clubhouse, Larry Jones, who pitched the first 8-and-some innings of the game, is telling everyone that it's been a couple of days now, and he's rested and ready to return. Amid some empty beer cans, a couple of players are passed out, sprawled across a table, tucked up near a wall heater. Hustling into the clubhouse to thaw out between innings, Umbarger will soon encounter Jeff Schneider, the Rochester pitcher who left the game back in the 15th inning. "Jeez, you guys still playing?" Schneider will say. "We have already showered, dressed, had a few beers, gone to sleep and gotten back up and have hangovers already!"

Some time back, the public-address announcer, Bob Guthrie, broadcast the license-plate number of a black Pinto—"RC 977"—with its lights on in the parking lot. Imagine the press-box hilarity when everyone realized that the car was owned by Dick Courtens, the scoreboard operator, sitting just a few feet from Guthrie. Courtens eventually puts two and two together: His teenage stepson, shy Kenny Laflamme, who eons ago went out to the car to sleep, must have tripped the lights while trying to get cozy. The duty-bound Courtens, though, cannot leave his post. With every zero he posts on the scoreboard, his car lights grow dimmer and dimmer.

But the lights in the kitchens of certain houses, here and there, in northern Rhode Island and southeastern Massachusetts, continue to burn holes into the blanketing darkness, as family members fear the worst. Their loved ones left for a stupid baseball game half a day ago and have yet to return. McCoy is receiving so many worried telephone calls that Mike Tamburro has developed a rehearsed speech: "No, everything is okay. But they're still playing ball out there. That's why he's late. The score is tied. . . ."

Up in the Massachusetts town of Dudley, Francis Cregg, father of a boy named David and brother of an umpire named Denny, both missing, calls his brother's new house in Webster, just across the French River, and wakes up his pregnant sister-in-law, Kathy. They have the kind of conversation you dread, something like: Denny and David aren't home yet, oh my God, something's wrong. Francis promises Kathy to find out what that something is. He calls the local police to check for any late-night reports of an accident or, God forbid, foul play, involving a boy and a man. Nah. Then he calls the Massachusetts state police and poses the same frantic question. Nah. Then he calls the Rhode Island state police.

Why do you ask?

Because my son and my brother went to the PawSox game last night, my brother was umpiring, and they haven't come home.

Extra, extra innings, a Rhode Island state police officer explains, as though reciting the rote answer to a routine question. Go back to bed.

At the same time, in a first-floor apartment on Providence's East Side, Joelle Card is making her own worried telephone rounds in search of her husband and son, while her five-year-old daughter sleeps in another room. First she calls Miriam Hospital, just down the street, then Rhode Island Hospital, on the other side of the city, and then Memorial Hospital, in Pawtucket, a few hundred yards from McCoy. Three times, then, she braces to hear affirmative answers to the anxious question she asks: Have you had any accidents involving a man and a boy named Card? Ronald and Daniel Card?

Three times the answer is no, thankfully, though the central question—Where are they?—remains unsettled. This wife, this mother, has no choice but to sit in the living room, with the television on. Waiting.

A hack's poem to the 27th inning:

Top.
Strikeout, swinging. Single to right.
Grounder, out. Walk, intentional.
Strikeout, swinging.
Bottom.
Grounder, out. Grounder, out.
Strikeout, swinging.
Scandura of the Times *takes note:*
Fiftieth strikeout of the game.
Twenty-eighth inning.
Top.

*   *   *

"And believe me, folks, it is real cold here in Pawtucket," Bob Drew tells Rochester. "Pete and I have been standing up since about, I'd say, around the fifteenth inning, just trying to keep warm. . . . One, two, three, four, five, six, seven, eight, nine, ten, eleven, twelve, thirteen, fourteen, fifteen, sixteen, seventeen, eighteen, nineteen, twenty, twenty-one, twenty-two, twenty-three, twenty-four, twenty-five, twenty-six, twenty-seven—there are twenty-eight fans left in McCoy Stadium, Pete."

"Twenty-eight loyal fans, Bob," Torrez says in agreement.

"We started out with seventeen hundred; we're down to twenty-eight," Drew says, before issuing a mock request of fans in Pawtucket, who cannot hear him. "Would you people down there give us a—let us know when you're leaving so we can keep track."

Pawtucket Red Sox officials have tried to shepherd the remaining stragglers into one section, thinking that this might create some collective body warmth. But Gary Levin, who left his family's Seder last night to see this ball game, is too busy at the moment, wandering the empty stands, searching for discarded tickets. With a nineteen-year-old's missionary zeal, he has been digging through garbage cans, hunting under seats, asking the girlfriends and wives of ballplayers for their tickets. His own date, Lisa, got a ride home several hours ago. She will eventually marry someone else and move to the Midwest. Gary, who will remain single, will at least have these fourteen ticket stubs to remember the night. He will donate five stubs to be auctioned off for the Jimmy Fund charity, and store the nine other stubs in a vault at his father's jewelry-plating business on Mineral Spring Avenue. Over the years he will give most, but not all, of the stubs away, one by one, to people who would understand the worth of the relic.

Another fan, Bob Brex, has respectfully waved off the invitations to sit with the others, though not because he is trying to be aloof, or antisocial. He simply prefers to experience the ball game in meditative solitude, sitting in his lonely wooden perch in the lower grandstand along right field—though when the wind stiffens, and his warm-up jacket fails to live up to its name, he takes shelter at the entrance between the grandstand and the box seats, beside the stadium's ancient concrete.

Brex is twenty-nine, a state government employee, unattached, overweight but shedding some of it, and expected at his grandmother's house in a few hours to help pound those veal cutlets for the family's Easter dinner. If there is church in his life, it is here, and now. He considers himself a longtime congregant of McCoy Stadium. He remembers the early days, the days under Joe Buzas and Phil Anez, when silly gimmicks overshadowed the game in the same way that a theatrical organist can detract from a Sunday service. Now, under Ben Mondor, the ballpark experience centers on the game and on community, however you define it.

At one point, Brex retrieves a foul ball that clatters in the gape of empty seats several rows behind him, the first he has ever snagged at a baseball game: a trophy. But racing over from the third-base side comes a boy, maybe ten years old and a few seconds late in the pursuit of the same foul ball. He looks at Brex with an expression that blends sleep deprivation with a baseball yearning, and what can the man do but surrender the ball to the boy. Then a young woman, either the girlfriend or wife of one of the Rochester players, notices Brex sitting alone, and walks over to hand him a cup of hot coffee. Two quiet, unifying gestures. Community.

A little while later, a Rochester player steps out of the Rochester dugout, sees that the woman is still here in the desolate stadium, and calls up to her: Are you crazy? And Brex wonders whether the question might as well be directed at him. Is he crazy for still being here? *Why* is he still here? Part of the answer reaches back to his childhood, when he and his father left a game at Fenway with Boston several runs behind, in what seemed certain to be a losing cause. But the Red Sox stormed back and won the game, after which Brex vowed to see future games to the end—not knowing, of course, that one day he would bear witness to a game without end. Mostly, though, he stays because he is mesmerized by the ball-and-strike rhythms, finding in its almost purposeful avoidance of conclusion an indefinable beauty. This singular feeling, of having entered into a soothing otherness, will stay with him forever, as he moves from Rhode Island to Connecticut, as he becomes the executive director of the Northeast Communities Against Substance Abuse, as his hairline recedes and his waistline shrinks, as his grandmother passes on. What he will also remember of this night is a quality not usually associated with a professional baseball game: the stillness.

Depending on how it is measured, the time is now either the top of the 28th inning or close to three in the morning. Bruce Hurst, a tall, well-built lefty, with dark eyebrows that emphasize the intensity in his eyes, enters the game as Pawtucket's seventh pitcher of the night. His teammates are probably chuckling that this is the latest Bruce has ever been up in his life. Hah-hah. Typical Mormon. Hah-hah.

One day, Bruce Hurst will rank among the toughest, most competitive pitchers ever to wear a Red Sox uniform. Fans will remember an almost unnerving game-day resolve, a locked-in steeliness that seemed all the more daunting because the rest of the time he came off as the affable Ward Cleaver of the clubhouse. Combining intelligence with great control and a mastery of several pitches, he often won games when his team most needed them. Revisit the statistics for the 1986 World Series, for instance, when the Red Sox came within one strike of winning their first championship since World War I, only to lose to the New York Mets. Before Mookie Wilson's elusive ground ball passed through the croquet-wicket legs of Boston first baseman Bill Buckner in the 10th inning of the sixth game, ensuring a doomed seventh, it was Bruce Hurst—not Roger Clemens, or Wade Boggs, or Dwight Evans, but Bruce Hurst—who was about to be named the most valuable player of the series. He won Game One, 1–0, giving up only four hits over 8 innings, then completed Game Five, to win 4–2. It was not until the 6th inning of Game Seven, after he had pitched 5 shutout innings, that Hurst proved to be mortal, giving up three runs in a Red Sox loss that brought winter early to New England. Still, if any Red Sox pride is to be found in the disastrous 1986 World Series, it is in the performance of Bruce Hurst. Tough; very, very tough. As the baddest of the Mets' bad boys, Darryl Strawberry, will put it: "Clemens is tough, but he's no Hurst."

All of this is five years in the future, and far, far from Pawtucket. That ground ball hit by Wilson; that error made by Buckner; that series-ending, knife-in-the-heart moment when Jesse Orosco launches his glove high into the New York night after striking out Marty Barrett. Marty is here now, harvesting and tossing away the infield pebbles that might lead to bad hops around second base. And Wade Boggs, who will weep in the Boston dugout after that World Series, is here, muttering curfew, curfew, isn't there any such thing as a curfew. And Rich Gedman, who will be unable to block an errant Bob Stanley pitch in the 10th inning of that fateful Game Six, allowing the Mets to tie the game, is in the bullpen, having left the game hours ago. And Bobby Ojeda, Hurst's brother in the slightly odd fraternity of left-handers, somehow convinced Joe Morgan to let him go home a few innings ago. Ojeda will also appear in the 1986 World Series, but for the New York Mets. In the moments leading up to the climactic seventh game of the World Series games, the two former teammates will spot each other, one in a Red Sox uniform, one in a Mets uniform, and their eyes will lock in wordless communication, conveying so much, including: Pawtucket.

Of all the Shea Stadium revelry that followed the last out of the World Series, Ojeda will remember one moment above the rest. He sees them now, two Red Sox players making their way through the champagne-soaked chaos of the Mets jubilant clubhouse, through a party at their expense. Boston's starting battery for Game Seven: Bruce Hurst and Rich Gedman, his Pawtucket brothers, coming to hug him and offer their heartfelt, heartbroken congratulations.

"I won't ever, ever forget it," Ojeda will say.

Tonight, though, the chance that Bruce Hurst might one day pitch in a World Series, much less dominate a World Series, seems as remote as Bruce Hurst one day walking on the fat moon above. It was only last year, while he was briefly up with Boston, that manager Don Zimmer dressed him down on the mound at Memorial Stadium in Baltimore for not being in the right place during a costly rundown. Zimmer yelled, Hurst said something juvenile in response, and Zimmer, a horse-betting, tobacco-chewing cuss who was not known for nurturing rookies, called for a relief pitcher—but not before screaming at Hurst to grow up or go home. This is fucking baseball.

Hurst, who had cried and nearly quit after Zimmer's humiliating reproach, understood the game. It was all the auxiliary stuff—the swearing in the locker room, the ribaldry on the bus—that sometimes disoriented him. He was raised by his Mormon mother in the small, lily-white Utah town of St. George. A goofy kid who threw a baseball well enough to be Boston's first-round draft pick in 1976, he was just a wholesome American boy, really, ready to play the wholesome national pastime. But when Hurst arrived for rookie-league ball in Elmira, wearing a suit and a tie with a pattern of tiny baseball pitchers, it was as though Andy Hardy had wandered into a production of *Hair*. He was taken aback by all the cursing and drinking and boasting of sexual conquests; taken aback, then, by aspects of professional baseball as elemental to the culture as pine tar and sunflower seeds. And in the clubhouse culture, if you let on that you are offended by something—if you let on that you even *care* about something—you set yourself up for endless abuse. Hurst let on.

Night after night, after every game, his chops-busting teammates— not above shoving porn or six-packs of beer into his locker—would go out to the bars to drink and carouse, and Hurst would go back to his room to telephone Utah. When Elmira won the league title, teammates showered him with champagne and beer, daring him to allow the liquor to pass his lips. Even in team victory, he was made to feel apart.

After Elmira came Winter Haven, then Bristol, then Pawtucket, where he quickly made an impression on Ben Mondor by becoming the first ballplayer ever to ask for two apartments: one for him and one for his girlfriend, for they were not yet married. Hurst often returns from road trips and talks to the worldly Mondor about the museums he visited while most of his teammates were sleeping off the previous night's antics. He has also endeared himself to Hood and Billy Broadbent, taking them out for hamburgers and ice cream, treating them with the affection and concern of an older brother. Here is a man who has the willpower not to succumb to the seductive clubhouse culture;

who sets himself apart by knowing what he does *not* want to do with his nights and his life.

But this isn't to say that Hurst necessarily knows what he *does* want in life; his consuming self-doubt is well known in the Red Sox organization. More than once, Mondor and Mike Tamburro have had to convince the left-hander to take a deep breath and stick it out, because he has the talent. And Lou Schwechheimer will never forget the sight of Bob Ojeda storming into Mondor's office, screaming that Hurstie, his good friend, rival, and fellow lefty, was quitting again, and someone has to stop him, because, goddamn, he can play.

Just three weeks ago, in fact, Hurst quit—again. After making it late into spring training with the Boston Red Sox, he was cut from the major-league roster and sent back to Triple-A. He returned to his apartment, wept, and decided to retire, even though he was only twenty-three. These were the "darkest days of my life," he would later say, days that he managed to work through by focusing on the long term, the still possible. He soon changed his mind and joined his Triple-A teammates, resolved to try—again.

This is not to say that Hurst's doubts have entirely lifted. Later this season he will quit once more, for three days, only to return after receiving a pep talk from a high-ranking elder in the Mormon Church. Though much has been made, and will continue to be made, of the cultural obstacles Hurst navigates as a devout Mormon—the "easy story," he will later say—most of his doubt is actually rooted in the universal questions now plaguing him.

"Am I chasing a pipe dream? Am I just a Triple-A player?"

But Pawtucket's beloved pitching coach, Mike Roarke, the pride of West Warwick, Rhode Island, will help to ease Hurst's worries. A longtime friend of Joe Morgan's—they were at Boston College together—Roarke played for four years as a catcher for the Detroit Tigers, then applied what he had learned behind the plate to become a revered pitching coach, known for his keen eye for mechanics and his dry, tension-puncturing humor. (In his 2006 induction speech at the Hall of Fame, former pitcher Bruce Sutter will single out Roarke for special praise and thanks.) Roarke will tell Hurst that the Triple-A is the "frustration league," where you can waste too much energy muttering to yourself, Why not me? Forget it, he tells Hurst. Put it out of your mind. Now listen: You need to keep your posture throughout your delivery. . . .

Tonight, Bruce Hurst is doing his best to suppress his many doubts, to hear from within the calming voice of Mike Roarke. The fatigue he has felt earlier in the night has given way to an adrenaline-pumping desire to win what he and his teammates now know is the longest game in baseball history. His 28th inning goes like this: out, walk, out, out, all on just eight pitches. His 29th is even better: walk, strikeout, strikeout, strikeout—looking.

The night wind is at his back. He is locked in.

But his Rochester opponent, Jim Umbarger, is benefiting from the same wind, and from the same sting felt in the chilled hands of batters anytime they make contact. He is also pumped up, perhaps too pumped up, gulping down vitamins and coffee between innings, soaking his hands in warm water, working his way through a tin of chewing tobacco. At one point Umbarger tells his third baseman, Cal Ripken, to watch for the bunt. Ripken, who does not take kindly to being told how to do his job by a pitcher, wearily replies that he's been watching for the bunt for 23 innings now.

You see, this is Umbarger's night, his chance; he feels it. What a turnaround from just the other day, when only the assurances of his fiancée and his agent—*People will be watching!*—kept him from calling it quits, after he didn't make the Baltimore team, and was then told he wouldn't even be a starter in Rochester. People will be watching. Someone will be watching. This Easter morning at McCoy, though, only two dozen people in the stands are watching, and not one is a scout bearing witness to perhaps the best performance of his career. No one will call Baltimore in the morning and say, Umbarger's ready to come back.

Jim Umbarger will not come back. He will play out his string in Rochester, never realizing his dream of joining the talent-packed Baltimore bullpen of Tippy Martinez and Sammy Stewart. In a couple of years, at thirty, he will retire after playing for teams from upstate New York to Hawaii, giving it his last best shot. Years from now, he will become a professional golf instructor, with a specialty in putting and a distinguishing back story that includes the four years he spent in the major leagues and the night he pitched in this long, long game, still unfolding.

His bottom of the 28th inning: groundout; strikeout, looking; strikeout, looking. Thank you, Lord.

In that ice chest of an owner's box along the third-base line, the open-air, cheap-wood domain of Ben Mondor, the remaining members of the PawSox family gather. Here are Ann Koza, Debbie Boggs, and one or two others, shivering in their theater chairs, watching a play without end. The toddler Meagann Boggs continues to sleep under Ben's used desk in the back, undisturbed by the constant jingling of the telephone. But the caller is never Harold Cooper, the president of the International League, who has yet to respond to Mike Tamburro's frantic message, left with Cooper's wife, that *We're STILL playing baseball here in Pawtucket!* Instead, time and time again, it is a worried someone looking for an absent someone yet to come home from your stupid minor-league ball game, and don't you know that it's after three on Easter Sunday morning? Still playing, Tamburro explains. Still playing.

At one point, the caller is Joe Morgan's wife, Dottie, who will not accept Tamburro's explanation that the game is still in progress, and who suspects that her husband and his baseball buddies have been raising their glasses to toast a win or drown a loss. So Tamburro summons Morgan from his peephole perch to convince his wife that, yes, we're still playing.

Mrs. Morgan: Oh yeah? Then how come you're answering the phone?

Mr. Morgan: Because I got kicked out in the 22nd inning, and— aw, forget it.

Mondor, ever the gracious host, offers his guests a beverage not available at the concession stands of McCoy: that fine blended Scotch called Chivas Regal. Take a swig, he urges. It'll keep you warm. So they pass the elegant bottle around, sharing glorious, chest-warming swallows, before someone with a sense of etiquette distributes a few plastic cups. These people are so tired that they cannot help but laugh, and so cold that they cannot stop from spilling the precious amber liquid in their trembling hands. Ann, who later jokes that she saw the Easter Bunny hopping through the outfield, keeps her cup under the blanket that cocoons her. It is the bottom of the 29th, her husband is leading off, and she prays again:

Come on, Dave. Get the hit. THE hit.

This is Koza's twelfth at bat of the night—three games' worth. He has a double and three singles so far, but he is not thinking about the uptick in his batting average right now. He is thinking about getting on base, starting something, getting the hell out of here. Unlike Boggs, Koza does not obsessively calculate his batting average, though Boggs might say that he wouldn't, either, if he put up numbers as low as Koza's (.239 in 1979, .235 in 1980). This is a touchy subject for Koza. Three years ago, at the beginning of the season in Pawtucket, he was sitting in front of his locker, lost in his depressing thoughts, trying to process the difficult news that he had been sent back down to Double-A in Bristol.

Just then, a voice spoke to him: Hey, kid, whattaya hitting?

The kid from Torrington, Wyoming, bound for Bristol, looked up and saw *the* Kid, Ted Williams, with that handsome box of a head, that once splintery body filled out with the weight of retirement, and those eyes, those piercing, 20/10 eyes. The greatest hitter who ever lived was working for the Red Sox organization as a hitting instructor, lecturing on the applied sciences to anyone worthy or talented enough, and now he was staring at Koza with those eyes that were said to see all. And the depressed kid from Torrington mumbled: What?

I said, whattaya hitting?

I don't even know.

Williams exploded. He screamed for maybe a minute, maybe an hour, who knows how long, because Koza can hear the man still, yelling that you should fucking know your fucking batting average at all fucking times. Then the god continued on through the clubhouse, having reduced this poor baseball mortal to tears. Yes, it was true: Ted Williams had made Dave Koza cry. But what do you do with this anecdote? Do you tell your children someday about the fleeting but intense emotional moment when one of the most famous Americans of the twentieth century made you weep? Do you learn from it? Do you vow from now on to know what your batting average is at all times, as well as you know your own date of birth?

No. Better to say: It is this at bat that counts. This moment, now.

Koza swings at Umbarger's first pitch and sends a ground ball skipping toward Rochester's shortstop, Bobby Bonner, arguably the best defensive player on the field, possessed of a baseball awareness you cannot teach. Occasionally someone on the bench will ask Rochester manager Doc Edwards why the hell Bonner's playing out of position, behind second base, or in shallow left center field? Doc will just say that Bonner must sense something the rest of us do not, something based on complex variables: the pitch about to be thrown, the stance of the batter, the shift in the wind. Don't worry about Bobby Bonner.

Bobby Bonner waits, his body crouched in what he describes to kids as his sitting-on-the-toilet position. But in keeping with the impish nature of this night, Dave Koza's ground ball takes a sneaky, screw-you hop, then rattles around Bonner's hands like a thing come to life.

"Bonner bobbles it, fires to first, in time," says the radio announcer, Bob Drew. "And Koza's out of there, six to three." Then Drew's radio-booth partner, Pete Torrez, adds: "Bob, that was a good play by Bobby that time."

A good play by Bobby that time. But everyone in Rochester knows about the other time, last year, in Toronto. For all his defensive prowess, it is a single ground ball that will forever elude him, and prove to be his undoing in baseball. But for that one ground ball, just one of many thousands that Robert Averill Bonner was born to catch, he would probably not be here in Pawtucket tonight, fussing with the disposable hand warmer in his back pocket and focusing on this early-morning absurdity. Instead, he would probably be asleep in a luxury hotel in Kansas City with the rest of the Baltimore Orioles, resting up for a Sunday game and another day as heir apparent to the team's brilliant but aging shortstop, Mark Belanger.

A single ground ball.

Bonner is only twenty-four, but he has already lived several lives. Growing up in Corpus Christi, Texas, all he wanted to do was play ball, ball, anything with a ball; ball was the first word he uttered. He developed his extraordinary hand-eye coordination by bouncing a golf ball off the walls of Richard King High School and imagining that each carom was a baseball in play. He would compete against himself, and not stop until a full 9 innings had been played. After starring in several sports at King, he focused on baseball at Texas A&M University, and did well enough to sign with the Baltimore Orioles, for $9,000, in 1978. He eased right in with the other baby birds, as they were called, playing hard, drinking hard, rarely passing up the chance to smoke a little dope on the side. He was a wild Texas mustang, and proud of it.

By the fall of 1978, though, Bonner seemed determined to compromise his talent and break up his young family. He was making more money in the oil fields than on the ball field, he was partying as much as ever, and the wife, the two little kids, the tiny apartment—it all seemed to conspire against him. He told his wife, Becky, that he wanted out of their marriage, but in the emotional tug-of-war that followed, she convinced him at least to join her for a service at the revival church she attended. And something happened. The fiery preacher invited to the altar those who were ready to accept Jesus as their personal savior, and Bobby Bonner went up, his athletic body convulsing with sobs, as he asked, again and again, forgive me. With his burdens lifted, he will later say, peace came.

Imagine what went through the minds of Dave Huppert, Brooks Carey, and all the other baby birds when Bonner, their good ol' drinking buddy from Texas, appeared at Biscayne College in Miami for spring training in 1979, baseball glove in one hand and a Bible in the other. Word got around in the Baltimore organization that something had happened to Bonner, something strange. All of a sudden he's talking about eternal salvation. What's more, he's not drinking!

Bonner wound up spending many nights alone. But his newfound religious devotion, now competing with baseball for his attention, did not seem to affect his game. As the starting shortstop for the Rochester Red Wings in 1980, he was voted the International League's rookie of the year, even though he hit only two home runs and batted just .241. He was simply that good in the field, so balletic that people said they'd pay to see Bonner take infield practice. His defensive ability sometimes took away the breath of Cal Ripken Jr., the up-and-coming kid at third. "One day I was playing in close at third when a high chopper bounced over my head," he later wrote. "When I looked back expecting to see the ball roll into short left field, there was Bobby, catching it while running full speed toward the line. Then he threw back across his body on a dead run to nail the fast runner at first. Amazing."

Executives in Baltimore's front office had all but chosen him as the shortstop of the future, with Ripken seen as the successor to the great Brooks Robinson at third. But Earl Weaver, the crabby, foulmouthed Orioles wizard, did not like being pressured into decisions. Not so goddamn fast, he was saying. *Not so goddamn fast!* This would explain the manner in which Weaver greeted Bonner when the rookie was called up to the major-league club in September 1980. Bonner will never forget the skipper's first words to him, although his Christian propriety will require that he sanitize the salutation in its retelling.

To wit: "Who the blankety-blank do you think you are?"

A few days later, on September 14, 1980, a ground ball changed everything.

Here are the once-vital, now-forgotten particulars: The second-place Orioles were hoping to gain ground on the division-leading Yankees with a win over the Blue Jays in Toronto's Exhibition Stadium, a challenging field of Astroturf more beloved by the scrap-scavenging seagulls of Lake Ontario than by those endeavoring to play baseball on it.

In the top of the ninth, Baltimore's first baseman, Eddie Murray, future Hall of Famer, hit his second solo home run of the game to tie the score at 2–2. Then, in the bottom of the inning, the rookie Bobby Bonner, sitting on the bench and minding his business, heard:

Bonnicker! Bonnicker!

Bonnicker? Or was that Boddicker?

It was Weaver, conflating Bonner's name with that of another rookie, the pitcher Mike Boddicker, but ordering this Bible-thumping, front-office favorite onto the field as a defensive replacement. Bonner hustled out to shortstop, where he normally felt at home, but at that moment did not. For one thing, he would always smooth the dirt in front of him—his left foot sweeping, then his right—partly to ward against bad bounces, but also to give the batter no sense of which way he was leaning in preparation for the next pitch. This was Astroturf, though; not much to smooth.

In the top of the 11th, Murray hit his third solo home run of the night to put Baltimore ahead, 3–2. All the Orioles had to do was get through the bottom of the inning, and Murray would own a night for the ages. But with one out, Toronto's Lloyd Moseby doubled to left field. Then Barry Bonnell, a decent right-handed hitter, planted himself in the batter's box, right foot first, then left, then a tap of the outside corner of the plate with his bat.

These next few moments never leave Bobby Bonner. Thirty years later, he will rise from his chair in the library of the Decatur Baptist Church in Decatur, Alabama, where he is working after decades of missionary work in Africa, and crouch like the shortstop he was, waiting for the pitch, his hands down, palms tilted slightly toward the imaginary plate, wracked knees bent as best as he can. At fifty-three, he will have been through two heart attacks, many bouts of malaria, and a spell of blackwater fever, all endured while building Christian schools and spreading the Good Word in various African outposts. And yet a wet night in Toronto will be with him wherever he goes. Here, in this church library, he is once again the shortstop for the Baltimore Orioles, an untested rookie, his body crouched in anticipation, his mind thinking one out and a runner on second.

The batter, Bonnell, was also a man of deep faith, a Mormon who, in Single-A ball in Greenwood, South Carolina, would tape a flashlight to the back of the school bus seat in front of him to read scripture on those long nighttime rides to somewhere. A few years ago, while he was playing for the Atlanta Braves, some young fans he knew from church in his hometown of Milford, Ohio, greeted him at Riverfront Stadium in Cincinnati with a banner that read, "Give 'em hell, Barry." He went over to the youths, told them that the sign's language was inappropriate, and strongly suggested they take it down, which they did. For this and other reasons, Bonnell's nickname is said to be "Preacher," although no one has ever called him that to his face.

Holding the bat upright and at the center of his chest, Barry Bonnell waited for Tim Stoddard, Baltimore's impossibly tall right-handed closer, to begin his motion. Then, as Stoddard started, he cocked his bat and bent his knees, just as Bonner opened his glove and leaned forward. Pitch, swing, connection. The baseball shot across the plastic field, just to Bonner's right. With the runner breaking for third, he was thinking, because he was always thinking: Catch and throw to third. This was his, all his.

But the line drive skipped on the wet Astroturf and zipped past Bonner, skidding into left center field to tie up the ball game and all but explode the white-haired head of Weaver in the dugout. The official scorer's debatable decision was E6, error on Bonner, and of course the Blue Jays went on to win the game in the 13th inning, 4–3.

After the game, Toronto's manager, an old shortstop named Bobby Mattick, expressed sympathy for Bonner, saying: "I'll tell you, that was a hard-hit ball. It skipped on him. It was a tough hit to come in cold and handle." And Cal Ripken Sr., a Baltimore coach, would tell his namesake that it was nearly an impossible play to make. But Weaver did not call the rookie over, put his arm around the young man's shoulder, and say, shake it off, we'll get 'em next time. No. That would not be Weaver. Instead, he bellowed profanely to the locker room, to the media, and to all of North America that this kid Bonner is a worthless front-office mistake, a so-called hot prospect at shortstop who can't even catch a fucking ground ball.

Even now, long after Baltimore players stopped referring to errors as "pulling a Bonner," this single ground ball, this single fucking ground ball, remains in play. If you talk to any of Bonner's contemporaries from the Baltimore organization, they will assert that the moment broke his confidence and wiped away his desire; whether they mean the actual error or the Weaverian fusillade of abuse that followed, it still comes down to this ground ball, which they vividly describe, whether they were in Toronto that day or not (a few will even insist that the ball went through Bonner's legs; it did not). Some argue that Weaver was cruel and out of line; others say that in his Darwinian style of managing, he was testing Bonner's ability to handle big-league pressure, and Bonner failed.

The ground ball has come to be seen as the bouncing embodiment of destiny, the catalyst for profound change—not just for Bonner, but for all of baseball. With that error, Bobby Bonner allows Earl Weaver to challenge the front office's contention that Bonner was the Orioles shortstop of the future. Then, in 1982, Weaver will make perhaps the most fateful decision of his storied career, moving Cal Ripken Jr. from third base to the open position at short, where Ripken will play without stop for what seems like a millennium, breaking Lou Gehrig's record for consecutive games and laying the statistical groundwork that will ensure his first-ballot induction into the Baseball Hall of Fame. All of which will add considerable value to the 1982 Topps baseball card No. 21, which features the photographs of three Baltimore Orioles "Future Stars": shortstop Bob Bonner on the left, pitcher Jeff Schneider on the right, and in the middle, third baseman Cal Ripken. ("I use that card sometimes when I preach, because there were three guys who were crucified: the one on the right, the one on the left, and the One in the middle," Bonner will later say. "The One in the middle is the One you need to look at.")

No right-thinking person can argue that Ripken would not be in the Hall of Fame if he had remained at third and Bonner had become the everyday shortstop. But a right-thinking person might say that Ripken's singular career at shortstop came about because of his exceptional talent, his indefatigable work ethic, his keen competitive streak, the foresight of Earl Weaver—and a certain ground ball hit in Toronto in September 1980, nearly a year before Ripken's first major-league game.

A single ground ball. Thirty years later, Barry Bonnell will have no recollection of even hitting it.

The ball well behind him now, Bobby Bonner will sit back down in the church library in Alabama to express satisfaction, not regret, over his life's journey since that defining evening in Toronto. He will not become the Orioles shortstop of the future, of course. He will hit .194 in 61 major-league games over four years, then retire in 1984 after a successful final season with Rochester. Of his old teammates, he will say, "I'd die for those guys." Of his first major-league manager, the irascible Mr. Weaver, he will say that the men met at an Orioles reunion a few years ago, and their teary conversation focused on forgiveness, and how some things happen for a reason.

Still, Bonner will sometimes question whether, in addition to that fateful error, his career was affected by his open commitment to live as a Christian. After all, his superiors often complained that his born-again ways were disrupting the clubhouse, and that he was violating baseball code by bringing his religion onto the secular field. Bonner will deny doing so, but at the same time he will not be shy about sharing his feelings.

"Jesus lives in my heart," Bonner will tell one manager. "He is with me wherever I go."

"Well," the manager will answer, "He ain't going to Baltimore."

Our baseball game continues its sleepwalk toward dawn. Like actors in an endless and mostly unwatched rehearsal, the ballplayers appear and disappear upon the stage of the dew-damp amphitheater, fulfilling the roles of futility assigned to them by some mad playwright.

Bonner grounds out to second. Huppert strikes out looking. Eaton strikes out.

Do it again.

Valdez grounds out to first. Graham grounds out to third. Barrett singles. Walker flies to right.

Again.

Williams grounds out to the pitcher. Ripken walks. Rayford strikes out looking. Logan grounds out to the pitcher.

Again.

Laribee grounds out to the pitcher. Koza grounds out to second. Boggs singles. Bowen pops out to short.

Again.

"Inning number thirty-two," says Bob Drew. "It's been tied since the twenty-first, for ten innings. My goodness. What a beautiful morning for baseball here in Pawtucket. We'll hear birds chirping anytime now."

A beautiful morning? Has Drew been mixing something in his coffee up there in the broadcast booth? The ballplayers on the field are hopping up and down to keep warm, while their frigid teammates in the dugout are wrapped like mummies, in towels and blankets, and just as still. Exhaustion and the elements are clearly conspiring with the two pitchers, the only ones enjoying themselves, to ensure that no one scores. Every now and then, Rochester's left fielder, John Hale, peeks out of the dugout and into the stands, as if to convince himself that there are people *still* watching this travesty. "You are truly troubled souls," he mutters. In the infield, the Rochester catcher Dave Huppert has been goading the home plate umpire to call sixteen straight balls and end this thing, while in distant center field, Rochester's Dallas Williams has continued his private chant of Fuck, fuck, fuck. Up in the press box, the *Providence Journal*'s Angelo Cataldi cannot believe his bad fortune. The last of his three deadlines has passed, and all he could file was a game-in-progress story, a story without a point. He will forever remember tonight as the single worst assignment in his long career. He buttons his coat and heads for the door, while somewhere below him, in the stadium's concrete bowels, Joe Morgan is getting angrier and angrier, seeing no evidence of common sense through that peephole of his, and damn if the wind-blown dirt whipping through the hole isn't stinging his eye.

Some beautiful morning.

Still. The peanuts-and-popcorn calls of wandering vendors and the conversational murmurs of the long-gone crowd have risen up to be swallowed and forgotten by the amnesiac night. The laughs, the coughs, the childlike bleats have evaporated, along with the repetitious music that tried so hard and for so long to muster cheers and foot stomps from a mostly empty stadium. Now the sounds are spare: the leather pops and wooden knocks, an umpire's grunt, a player's sigh.

Along the wind-whistling concourse, the three Pawtucket police officers working the McCoy detail find refuge in the concrete nooks and crannies. Among them is Bruce Germani, who is glad for the winter police coat he wears over his springtime navy blues, and whose childhood memories include seeing this stadium under construction. Strange how random moments of youth stay with you for the rest of your life. As a teenager, Germani played organized baseball at McCoy when the neglected field was a municipal embarrassment, a rock garden. He still sees this one ground ball coming toward him at short-stop. All he had to do was catch it and toss to second for a force-out. But the ball kicked off a large stone and that was that. Another ground ball, remembered forever.

Other Pawtucket officers are here as well, officers who have paused from their shifts in the dark town beyond. Tonight, a fight broke out on Woodbine Street. Two cars collided on Newport Avenue. Down at the Douglas Drug store, three men knocked down a woman after robbing her of $40. And over on East Street, someone stole five rabbits from a backyard cage—so happy Easter.

These lesser moments in our daily struggle will continue tomor-row, and the next day, and the next. For now, though, the police of-ficers, and the few remaining fans, and a baseball manager peering through a hole, bear witness to a radical break from the mundane. They see figures that seem charged by the stadium lights with a vital radiance, running in pursuit of something represented by a small white ball.

Cataldi, tired, annoyed, perpetually annoyed, pauses at the door. Sits back down. He cannot leave.

Somewhere in the top of the 32nd inning, somewhere close to four o'clock in the morning. One out. With runners on first and second, Rochester is threatening to score, with the count 1–1 against a pinch hitter, Ed Putman, who has briefly returned to the dugout, apparently to work out a kink. "I tell you, Bob, talk about somebody being stiff," Pete Torrez says. "Somebody sitting for thirty-two innings."

Time has lost its urgency. Waiting for Putman to return to the plate, Pawtucket's Wade Boggs lies down on the field with his head on the bag at third base. Then, in the middle of Putman's at bat, the third-base umpire, Jack Lietz, suddenly jogs off the field and disappears into the Pawtucket dugout.

"We don't know what the heck's going on," Drew says.

This is what's going on:

Harold Cooper, the president of the International League, in Grove City, Ohio, 735 miles away—whose name appears on each of the 150-odd balls used so far in this game—has finally returned that anxious phone call from Mike Tamburro. The same call in which Cooper's wife informed Tamburro that Harold was not home—at two o'clock on Easter Sunday morning—but that she would pass on the message: Pawtucket in crisis; cannot stop playing baseball.

Thirty years later, Harold Cooper, irascible, hilarious, revered Harold Cooper, so integral to professional baseball in central Ohio and beyond that a statue of him stands outside the new ballpark where the Columbus Clippers play, will pause from a bite of his Arby's sandwich to remember that telephone call. He will be eighty-six; his wife, Eloise, deceased; his health not great; his life a daily crapshoot. He is nowhere near as robust as his gleaming statue might suggest. But just about every week, Randy Mobley, a Cooper protégé and now the conscientious president of the International League, will stop at an Arby's before heading for Cooper's tidy, quiet town house. There, at the kitchen table, they will eat their lunch and talk the baseball of now and especially then, when Cooper was famous for getting what he wanted.

"I wasn't the nicest guy to work for," he will say, to which Mobley will respond, "Maybe some of them didn't like you, but they respected you."

Sometimes the two men will talk about the longest game, and how the strange disappearance of a single paragraph in the 1981 "International League Instructions for Umpires, Managers and Players"—the very paragraph that allows for a curfew after 12:50 in the morning—caused heartache and history in Pawtucket. Mobley will say that when he joined the league as an administrator in the fall of 1985, four years after the longest game, the process was the way it had always been: a secretary still adding revisions, typing out the document, making photocopies, and mailing out the manual to various parties. "Is it conceivable that it could have gotten dropped out?" Mobley will say. "It is conceivable."

Sitting at a kitchen table adorned with a floral display of opened fast-food wrappers, Cooper will remember the night. Back then, he was the acknowledged visionary and baseball know-it-all of Columbus—a burden as much as an honor. For example, a couple of guys on bar stools at midnight might begin arguing about, say, the number of home runs that Al Pilarcik hit for the Columbus Jets in 1956—Was it 18 or 19?—and decide that the only way to avert fisticuffs was to call Harold, at home. *Mr. Cooper? Sorry to disturb you, but me and my friend Eddie are down at Johnnie's Tavern, and we were just wondering* . . . After one too many of these friendly phone calls, Cooper instructed Eloise to pass on this standard message to late-night callers: Harold is not here.

But when Eloise explained the strange reason for tonight's late-night call, something about two teams *still* playing baseball in Pawtucket, Cooper decided to call back because this could not be the case. Eloise must have misunderstood. Taking his time, he finally reached Tamburro, whose panicked message—They won't stop the game!—has prompted Cooper to demand a word, immediately, with the head umpire, Lietz.

Jack Lietz is gone from the field for a minute, maybe two—only long enough to miss six pitches. Putman has struck out and the next batter, Tom Eaton, is in the middle of his at bat. As Lietz jogs back to his position behind third base, he gives his two colleagues a hand sign not found in any umpire's manual: a slicing gesture across the neck.

"Now the third-base ump, Jack Lietz, is back out on the field," Bob Drew announces. "I have no idea where he went. But I guess it doesn't matter at four o'clock in the morning."

Actually, it does matter. The exact words that Cooper used in his brief conversation with Lietz are lost to the night. The *New York Times* will later report that Cooper said, "If it's still tied at the end of the inning, suspend the game and get some sleep," while the account by the

Gannett News Service will suggest the conveyance of a more succinct message:

"Call the damn thing after this inning."

Two on, two out, and the count is now 2 and 2 against Eaton, Rochester's second baseman, who still believes that the wad of Red Man tucked in his right cheek gives him heft and power, and who sees, just beyond the pitcher, the possible key to the game's end: his teammate John Hale, whom he barely knows, a step off second base, waiting for what comes next.

Hale, twenty-seven, who joined Rochester a few weeks ago after a peripatetic career through the major and minor leagues, has gotten the hint. Just last night, he set his bags down in yet another Howard Johnson hotel room and told himself it was over. He grew up in the California farming town of Wasco, just north of Bakersfield, was drafted by the Dodgers before he turned eighteen, and played his first major-league game in the September heat of the 1974 pennant race. In the last two games of that season, he collected 4 hits in 4 at bats, including a double off the ferocious fastball pitcher J. R. Richard that nearly cleared the wall. After that, he will say, "It was all downhill."

Hale played for the Dodgers for parts of four seasons, then spent two years with the Seattle Mariners before being released in August 1979. His last appearance was as a 9th-inning replacement in left field, his career batting average, .201. He began the journeyman's wander through the minor leagues, where, he will later say, younger players "look at you with eyes that say, 'What are you doing here, old guy?'" By the time he landed in Rochester, less than a month ago, he more or less knew that he had joined the ranks of veteran ballplayers who bounce around, filling rosters, serving as seat warmers for prospects who have yet to reveal themselves. He knows what Baltimore's assessment of him is: This Guy Will Do for Now.

After tonight, Hale will continue to be a fill-in player with Rochester for a couple of months before being traded to the Denver Bears, in the American Association, where he will have a good enough season that his Pawtucket hotel epiphany will briefly lose its impact. He will think that, maybe, things might fall into place one last time; they will not. The 1981 season will be his last in professional baseball, and he will not fully appreciate the unforgiving separation—between those who play and those who played—until he finds himself chatting with a couple of old Indianapolis Indians teammates, now with the Cincinnati Reds, before a game in San Diego, soon after his forced retirement. He will be in civilian clothes, they will be in uniforms, and the chat at the railing will be pleasant. But with game time approaching, his former teammates will say good-bye, delivering the unspoken but clear message: Okay, it's time for us to go play baseball, and you're not coming with us.

The sweet ruthlessness of that moment will stay with Hale. Either you are part of the brotherhood or you are not. Soon enough, though, he will find perspective and move on, redefining himself as a husband, father, weekend sportscaster (very briefly), and successful commercial real estate salesman, not far from where he grew up. What's more, he will always be able to say that he hit a double off J. R. Richard, played beside some of the best baseball players of the 1970s—and once stood on second base in the 32nd inning of a twilight-zone baseball game in Pawtucket, Rhode Island.

Standing a step or two off second, Hale is hyperaware: of the slightest movement by the pitcher, Bruce Hurst; of the whereabouts of Marty Barrett (to his left, at second) and Julio Valdez (to his right, playing short); of the hand signals of Doc Edwards, his manager, coaching at third base; of the late hour, and the pervasive fatigue, and the slight chance he has to help win this game and prove to the decision makers of major-league baseball that John Hale, while an ancient twenty-seven, still has the speed of youth. Everyone knows exactly what will happen if the ball passes through the infield.

"You're listening to Rochester Red Wing baseball on WPXN in Rochester, New York, and this, the history-making ball game—the longest game ever played in organized baseball," says Bob Drew, his weariness evident in the repetition of his patter. "We're in the thirty-second inning, it's two balls, two strikes, to Tom Eaton, two outs, in the thirty-second inning, with two runners on base. Two, two, two, thirty-two."

"And, Bob, we've played exactly eight hours," says Pete Torrez.

"Eight hours of baseball here in Pawtucket, and McCoy Stadium," Drew answers. "The pitch . . ."

Eaton whacks a line drive into right field for a base hit, and Hale bolts for third, where Doc Edwards is swinging his arm like a windmill, signaling to keep going, keep going, as if there were ever any doubt. "How would you have liked to have gone back to face your teammates at four o'clock in the morning, and you held up at third base with the go-ahead run?" Hale will later say. "Everyone in the ballpark was saying, 'Please! Go!'"

Waiting at home plate is Roger LaFrancois, once the Red Sox organization's up-and-coming catcher, but now playing behind the younger, more powerful Rich Gedman, who is so gifted that in a few weeks he will be summoned to Boston, never to return. But Gedman left this game hours ago, back around the 10th inning, when sanity still prevailed. So it is Roger LaFrancois, now in his 22nd inning of the night, who waits, in shin guards and chest protector.

LaFrancois, twenty-four, grew up in Jewett City, Connecticut, about forty-five miles southwest of here. His French-Canadian father, a gifted ballplayer in his time, works the midnight shift at the Plastic Wire and Cable mill, a schedule that on some nights allows him to drive up to Pawtucket and play baseball again, vicariously, through his son. It is the mill that motivates Roger LaFrancois. A few years ago, when he was a talented but aimless athlete, just beginning to make some bad choices in his senior year in high school, his father dragged his ass down to the clanking, dirty, mind-numbing mill at three in the morning. "You had better get on track, son," his father had said. Message received.

Here, then, is Roger LaFrancois, six feet two, 215 pounds, and determined not to work in a mill, destined to make the major leagues next year, if only briefly, but long enough to collect 4 hits in 10 at bats for a career batting average of .400; his large mitt aches for the ball. Here, too, is John Hale, six feet two, 195 pounds, and almost ready for a new career, but not yet and certainly not at this moment, racing toward

LaFrancois, hell-bent on becoming the sliding exclamation point that ends this epic sentence of a ball game.

And here, in shallow right field, is Sam Bowen, Pawtucket's misunderstood outfielder, the one who has to keep denying that he torpedoed his own trade to Detroit last year, rushing toward a ball that nearly dies in the thick grass. At this late hour, who would blame him if he approached it too fast, or bobbled the ball just long enough? If he threw high? If he threw wide? Who, really, would blame him? Only everyone.

"Here comes the lead runner around to score!" Bob Drew shouts.

Sam Bowen's brief major-league career is behind him, and his reputation within the Boston Red Sox organization is irreparably damaged, and his professional baseball life will end next year, and this meaningless game is entering its ninth hour, and it is four o'clock in the freezing morning, but he *knows* he has a good arm, and no way will this runner score. In fact, he is thinking, No way will this runner even try. No way.

"I'll be damned if I look up, and he's rounding third," Bowen will later say.

With all that he can muster from his exhausted, 170-pound body, Sam Bowen heaves the baseball toward a spot at the distant center of the McCoy horseshoe, his fatigue working to reduce the chance that he might overthrow his target, home plate. The ball, the be-all and end-all, the white sun to this contained universe, arrives chest-high for the catcher-son of a mill worker. Perfect. Ball beats man to home by several feet. Roger LaFrancois, going up, tags out John Hale, going down.

"And they're going to get him."

"Ahhhhhh," exhales Pete Torrez, while all around him, the Rhode Island rooters in the press box whoo-hoo and clap in weary, joyous delirium.

The Pawtucket Red Sox go meekly in the bottom of the 32nd inning, three up, three out. It is 4:09 on Easter Sunday morning, and brightness limns the eastern horizon. Surrender.

As the public-address announcement is made that the game is suspended, the players and umpires trudge off the field, the only winners of this endeavor the cold and the wind and the dark. Along with the hundreds of people in far-off Rochester who are clicking off their radios, and the less than two dozen fans who are sleepwalking their way to the exits, they are just beginning to wonder what lessons the night has attempted to impart.

Here it is, eight hours after the first pitch, the score remains tied, 2–2, and in the judgment of baseball, nothing has changed and nothing will until the game resumes—who knows when. Then again, so much has happened during this protracted demonstration of endurance, commitment, and that great engine of human existence, ambition. With nothing and everything simultaneously unfolding, with eight hours becoming one hour and one hour becoming eight, the night seems to have said something about time itself: the deceptiveness of it; the dearness of it. Beseeched by the older ballplayers to slow the clock, and begged by the younger players to hasten it, the night chose instead to stop time; to place it under a stadium's laboratory lights and pin it to the Pawtucket clay. See? Between the past and the future there is the sacred now: the brush of shoulders between father and son; a wife's focused gaze upon a preoccupied husband; a boy's seamless fielding of a simple ground ball; a pitcher's effortless motion and a catcher's easy crouch. The spare moment of solitude granted to us between our many obligations; a moment in which we drop all defense and artifice and feel a smack from the wind that is like a doctor's slap to a newborn.

You are released now. Go.

A father and son return to their Providence apartment to ease the worry in the house. A solitary young man heads off to catch a few hours of sleep before joining his grandmother in her kitchen. Another young man leaves with pockets filled with discarded ticket stubs that he believes possess historic worth. An umpire collects his exhausted nephew and begins the long drive north to his pregnant wife and their new house. The scoreboard operator discovers that he needs to call a tow truck to jump-start his dead Ford Pinto, inside of which sleeps a stepson blissfully unaware of having activated the car's headlights hours ago. The official scorer, meanwhile, secures his precious score sheet— confirmation that this night did, indeed, happen—before taking the short drive to his home in Greenville, where his drowsy wife asks why he's up so early. He simply holds up the Dunkin' Donuts bag of Easter treats that she had asked him to buy for their two children, last night and so long ago.

Inside the stadium, a mother collects her batboy sons, while ballplayers and managers and front-office employees collect their things and their thoughts, which include the realization that in a few hours, Rochester and Pawtucket will set aside this unfinished game and start *another* game. The Pawtucket pitcher Keith MacWhorter, this afternoon's starting pitcher, will arrive in a little while to find a baseball in his locker. On it will be scrawled: "You're on your own."

They trudge from the stadium to be received by an awakening Pawtucket, where some hear birds singing good morning. Wade Boggs, dispensing with a shower, leaves at the same time as Cal Ripken, who jokes that this is the first time his postgame meal will be breakfast. Dave and Ann Koza make their way home to a tired triple-decker a few hundred yards down Pond Street, where a pimp named Wesley lives in one apartment, Mike and Jenny Smithson live in another, and the newlywed Kozas will fall asleep in a third, talking and laughing about their absurd night. And Joe Morgan, ejected from the game but never absent, climbs into his powder blue Mustang and begins his drive back to Dottie and home in Walpole, thinking of that Irish saying he has known all his life, something about how the sun dances for joy at Easter's dawn. Negatory.

At the Howard Johnson motor inn, Rochester's last pitcher, Jim Umbarger, orders a Ruthian breakfast: oatmeal with bananas, ham-and-cheese omelet, home fries, toast, three pancakes, sausage and eggs. He then attempts sleep in the room where his spent roommate, Bobby Bonner, is dead to the world, but sleep does not come—perhaps because of the twenty or so cups of coffee he consumed during the game. So Umbarger spends ninety minutes writing down his fast-coming thoughts in a spiral notebook, the thoughts of a man who has just done the very best that he can at his profession. He writes:

> Just this past Tuesday night, I was down, lonely and unhappy in Rochester, only because my desire to be in the big leagues again is so strong.

I had a chat with the Lord and asked Him to please show me if He still wanted me in baseball or to lead me wherever. Wow! Has He shown me.

Though Umbarger will never return to the major leagues, as he hopes and prays tonight, he will have this to keep: 10 innings of scoreless pitching, in professional baseball's longest game. Sleep, now, as the proprietor of the Irish social club might say. It's time.

Back at McCoy Stadium, the home team's owner, Ben Mondor, does not leave until he is satisfied that everything is under control; that the records of last night's game have been saved, and the plans for this afternoon's game are set. What a business this is, this *bazeball* business.

Mondor gets a lift from Mike Tamburro to his Dutch colonial home in Lincoln. He showers and shaves, and then he and his wife, Madeleine, attend the seven o'clock Easter Sunday Mass at St. Jude's Roman Catholic Church. Tamburro, fresh from Mass with his wife, Anna, at St. Maria Goretti in Pawtucket, returns to pick up Mondor. The two men come right back to McCoy, where the telephones are now jangling with calls from the disbelieving.

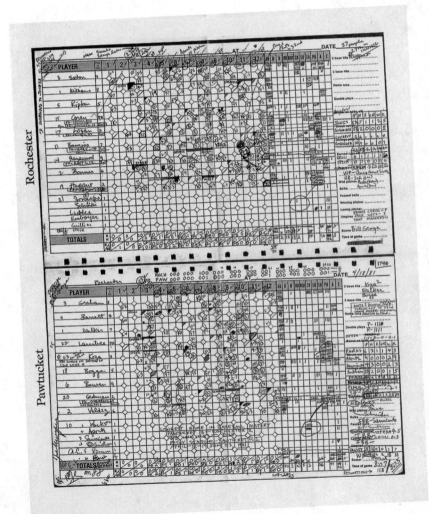

The rise of the Easter sun returned time to its natural rhythms. The hours once again lasted sixty minutes; the minutes, sixty seconds. The news of baseball's longest game, in Pawtucket, Rhode Island, made headlines around the country for a few days, then lost prominence as the relentless succession of other events, great and small, occupied the next two months. Police officers in Atlanta hunt for a suspect in a series of child murders. New Jersey senator Harrison Williams is convicted of corruption and sentenced to prison. The Federal Communications Commission makes a portion of the radio spectrum available for cellular telephones. A new musical, *Cats*, opens in London. Bob Marley dies, and a Turkish gunman seriously wounds Pope John Paul II in St. Peter's Square, and the Centers for Disease Control report an ominous strain of pneumonia surfacing among homosexual men in Los Angeles, and Major League Baseball goes on strike, and a prime suspect is arrested for all those children's deaths in Atlanta, and—

The hammering has stopped. Carpenters provided by the City of Pawtucket have built several rows of plywood tables behind home plate in section 7, creating a press gallery of World Series caliber for the 150 reporters and photographers about to descend upon McCoy Stadium. Yesterday, McCoy was just another decrepit Depression relic in another declining New England mill city. Today it is the hottest sports venue in the country, attracting several major-league television networks, a crew from *Good Morning America*, and reporters from *Time* magazine, the *New York Times*, *Rolling Stone*, the *Washington Star*, the *Philadelphia Inquirer*—even England and Japan—to a place that they will invariably pronounce as PAW-tuck-it, to the chagrin of its P-spitting natives. One after another, these big-league media players are passing the local landmarks—the historic Slater mill, the shady Lily Social Club—before making the turn at the Mei-King Chinese Restaurant, into an old ballpark on unsettled ground. Vital. Bustling. Significant. This is exactly what Mayor Thomas McCoy envisioned more than forty years ago, when he commanded workers to raise a stadium from the ooze of Hammond Pond. Dead these thirty-six years, His Honor wears an outfit appropriate for the occasion—light-weight tan suit, straw hat—and takes his seat in the section reserved for apparitions.

After decades of serving as a backup maintenance garage for the city, of seeing weeds in the infield and rot in the girders, of playing host to no teams and bad teams and teams that could only draw an audience with win-a-jalopy come-ons, McCoy is now blessed by a ser-endipitous twinning of events. First, the matter of the Major League Baseball strike. Eleven days ago, on June 12, the players announced a work stoppage over free-agent compensation. The owners are insisting that if a marquee player joins another team as a free agent, his former team should receive a player of equal worth. The players, though, see the demand as a threat to their hard-won right to test the market after they have fulfilled their contract. What the complicated issue means to the rest of the country is this: no poring over the box scores in the morning newspaper; no watching a baseball game on television after work; no drifting off to the nighttime lullaby of AM radio baseball, in which innings are counted like sheep and the broadcaster's canned baritone comes from someplace beyond the moon. The strike has the country out of sorts. The nation needs its baseball distraction.

As if divinely provided to fill the void, here it is: the continuation of the longest game in baseball history, which has lingered in between-inning limbo for two months—until now. Well before the major-league strike was declared, the Rochester Red Wings and the Pawtucket Red Sox agreed to pick up where they left off, in the top of the 33rd inning, when Rochester was next back in town. That would be today, Tuesday, June 23, 1981. The nation trains its fickle attention on Pawtucket.

The home team's owner, Ben Mondor, wandering about in his open-neck shirt and blue plaid pants, granting interview after interview, has spent $5,000 to have that makeshift press gallery built, and even more on the catered food he is providing his many out-of-town guests—cold cuts, potato salad, macaroni salad, pastries, soda, and beer. All worth it, though. The sellout crowd and the hundreds of telephone calls, seeking press credentials, asking for confirmation of the 6:00 p.m. start, have signaled to Mondor and his staff that today will be unprecedented. He could never have planned for the inability of two teams to score runs, for the mischievous wind to redirect balls in play, for that single paragraph concerning curfews to vanish from the umpires' manual—and now, for the game's resumption to take place during a Major League Baseball strike, an occurrence as rare as a Boston Red Sox championship. A gift ordained by Ruth, Cobb, Mack, and all the baseball saints in heaven! And Mondor plans to seize the opportunity to wipe clean McCoy's blemished past; to redefine the stadium as a pleasant, inexpensive place where you can see the future stars of the Boston Red Sox. Pure baseball. He's hoping for at least 5 innings, with the game ending on a bang-bang play that results in a Pawtucket win.

"I don't want to lose this sucker," he keeps saying.

Of the many Pawtucket Red Sox employees scurrying about to meet Mondor's edict that everything be perfect for this influx of suits and so-and-sos, none is more dedicated to the task than the excited young man working at the mimeograph machine in the front office, inhaling the fumes of the purple ink. This is Lou Schwechheimer, the team's one-man publicity department, who is busily printing and collating two hundred copies of the press packet—a kind of CliffsNotes, or Lou's Notes, to the Longest Game. If Bill White, the former All Star first baseman who is now broadcasting the New York Yankees games, wants to know how many plate appearances Dave Koza has so far, it's there (14); if Peter Gammons of the *Boston Globe* wants to know how many times Russ Laribee has struck out, it's there (7). Schwechheimer is twenty-three, yet every day he seems to bring to McCoy the enthusiasm of a nine-year-old boy attending his first baseball game. This is one of the reasons why, along with Mike Tamburro, he has been all but adopted by Mondor, who calls him by his given name, Ludwig, or by his nickname, Kraut.

Mondor, up from nothing, sees a version of his younger self in this earnest workhorse, beginning with the kid's modest New England circumstances. Schwechheimer grew up in a small housing project in Newburyport, a Massachusetts city on the banks of the Merrimack River. His father, a German immigrant, is a chief master sergeant in the Air Force Reserves and an expert carpenter; his mother, the daughter of New England clam diggers, works on the assembly line in an auto-parts plant. Hardworking, penny-saving, they will make sure that their four children graduate from college, including the oldest, their baseball-obsessed Ludwig, who long ago vowed that he would someday work for the Red Sox.

Two years ago, while still an undergraduate at the University of Massachusetts at Amherst, Schwechheimer got himself invited to the Red Sox front office at Fenway Park, where a top executive gave him a New England interpretation of Horace Greeley's famous counsel: Go to Pawtucket, young man. When the college student stammered that he didn't even know where Pawtucket was, the executive explained that a savvy businessman, Ben Mondor, and his assistant, Mike Tamburro, a UMass guy just like Schwechheimer, were trying to clean up a Triple-A franchise.

Go to Pawtucket.

Schwechheimer borrowed a tie from a college buddy and drove his used Volkswagen Beetle, with its rotten floorboard and broken heater, down to Pawtucket to be interviewed for an internship. Tamburro began the session by taking the applicant on a tour of McCoy, beneath its decaying canopy, past its mishmash of seats, some of them hand-me-downs from the old Narragansett Park racetrack. The tour was intended not to dissuade the young man but to inspire him, as Tamburro shared Mondor's determination to turn this rust bucket into a clean, inexpensive place where families could watch *bazeball* games. Struck by the simple, benevolent brilliance of the plan, Schwechheimer told Tamburro that he really, really wanted the internship.

Tamburro: Well, we've got dozens of candidates.

Schwechheimer: I will do whatever is necessary.

Tamburro: We can't aff—

Schwechheimer: I'll do it for free. This is where I want to be.

A few weeks later, Schwechheimer, all of twenty-one and with nothing to his name but a Volkswagen Bug with a dead engine, borrowed $500 and moved into a $25-a-month rooming house within walking distance of McCoy—where he was now, proudly, the Unpaid Intern for the Pawtucket Red Sox.

Schwechheimer stayed at the rooming house for several weeks, but moved out after a neighbor named Jimmy, whose chronic inebriation never impeded his polite inquiries into the fortunes of the PawSox, died in the communal shower, four doors down. With no money, the only place Schwechheimer could think to live was, of course, McCoy, where he slept for nearly a month on the trainer's table, in the clubhouse, even on Mondor's secondhand couch. He could hardly afford to feed himself, yet he never went hungry, thanks to the kindness of Mondor, Tamburro, and other McCoy colleagues: takeout from Mei-King, across the street; massive roast beef sandwiches from the House of Pizza, around the corner; late-night, early-morning breakfasts with Mondor at Sambo's, on Newport Avenue. Everything else in his life, apart from these meals and sleep, orbited minor-league baseball: compiling stats, running errands, stocking the souvenir stands, working the ticket office, hustling.

At the end of the 1979 season, the unpaid intern received a gift travel bag containing a Red Sox jacket, some golf shirts, a $500 check, and a note of thanks. Schwechheimer went back to college, but continued to pester Tamburro for work during school breaks and holidays. Then, after graduating with a communications degree in May 1980, he returned to McCoy to do it all over again, taking to heart Mondor's colorful words of advice: "Work your ass off, and we'll see."

Last August, toward the end of the season, the unpaid intern was summoned to the owner's office, where Mondor and Tamburro informed him that they were prepared to offer him a position with a starting salary of $4,800. It was only the organization's third full-time position, after theirs. Not a lot of money, they acknowledged, but if he accepted, who knows what this place, this franchise, could become. Lou Schwechheimer said yes—Yes!—before Mondor even finished presenting the offer. And he never left, rising to become senior vice president, general manager, and the integral third part to a McCoy trinity—Mondor, Tamburro, and Schwechheimer—that will last for more than three decades.

Right now, though, Lou Schwechheimer is in his very first year as a full-time employee of the Pawtucket Red Sox, wearing a short-sleeve shirt and a tie. Game days require ties. He can barely contain himself as he prints these press packets by the dozens—on a normal day he prints, maybe, six—and reads and reads again Mondor's understated welcoming address, and just inside the front cover:

> The Pawtucket Red Sox and the Rochester Red Wings would like to welcome one and all to the resumption of the longest game in baseball history. The game was originally played on April 18, lasting 8 hours and 7 minutes. Center fielder Dallas Williams will lead off for the Red Wings in the top of the 33rd inning.

Tickets, by the way, remain at the same customary price: $3 for a box seat, $2 for a seat in the grandstands. And an extra fifty cents off if you're a senior or a kid.

Standing room only. The PawSox have hired seventeen security guards from the Pinkerton Agency to help keep order, including a retired electrician named Walter Wassmer, who remembers working on the construction of McCoy Stadium back in 1938, when a five-ton truck disappeared into the swampy mire. Ted Dolan, a popular Pawtucket police officer who grew up across the street—and whose father was also among the legions of laborers who helped to build McCoy—is working crowd control, though now and then he adds to the crowd by waving in the occasional buddy without a ticket. One of these friends, a Massa-

chusetts state trooper, had called ahead to ask if he could bring his son
and a couple of his son's friends. Sure, sure, Dolan had said, anything
for a fellow guardian of the law. Only the trooper has shown up just
now with half his son's Little League team. Sweet Ted Dolan can only
shoo them in, joking all the while that his friend should have simply
invited the entire team.

When the umpires suspended this game at 4:09 on Easter Sunday
morning, two months ago, just nineteen fans were left, along with two
reporters. Time's passage has not improved Angelo Cataldi's sour opinion of McCoy Stadium, the Pawtucket Red Sox, and that godforsaken,
gonads-freezing longest night, only now he has found further reason to
hold the affair in contempt. From his press-box perch, he sees nearly
six thousand happy, well-rested people, all basking in the warmth of
a sunny early evening in late June—and all thinking they're now entitled to say that they, too, were at the longest game in baseball history.
Bullshit.

Even innocent Danny Card feels this way. Danny Card, the nine-
year-old boy who spent eight freezing hours watching that interminable game with his father, is now proud of his feat of faithful endurance.
Sitting in the same seat in which he watched the first 32 innings, yet
surrounded by hundreds of Johnny-come-latelies, Danny senses this
precious, personal thing of his slipping away. It's that feeling you get
when you try to explain a neat dream to someone else, but the dream's
enchantment melts away with every word you say.

The ache of possession shared by a boy, a sportswriter, and a band
of a happy few is understandable, yet unrealistic; this game no longer
belongs to them. Nor does it belong to Pawtucket, despite the national
attention the game is drawing to its striving existence. "Not since the
time they had to shoot the drunken camel at the city zoo has there
been this much excitement in Pawtucket," is how Bob Minzesheimer,
a reporter for the Rochester *Democrat and Chronicle*, began his setup
story today. This was true: A few years ago, at the fast-declining
Slater Park Zoo, the police shot and killed Kibubi the camel after it
trampled a friendly caretaker to death. Although the police suspected
that Kibubi was in the throes of a mating frenzy, Pawtucket's mayor,

Dennis Lynch, told Minzesheimer a more intoxicating version that involved the animal's supposed ingestion of a fermented apple. ("It was all over the networks," the mayor said of the incident. "I got letters from schoolchildren in Seattle saying what meanies we were to shoot the camel.")

There is no question that this baseball game grants to the city the rare publicity that is refreshingly unrelated to closed mills, a depleted downtown, or the execution of a zoo animal—or two. (Just two years ago, Frosty the polar bear died in a police SWAT team's barrage of bullets, after vandals set him loose to wander in a residential area.) Here is a television crew from London, the British flag affixed to the side of its camera, filming every stretch and toss by the players as they loosen up. Here are reporters from New York and Chicago and even Japan, hovering around the cage, watching Sam Bowen take batting practice. And a few days ago, producers from *Good Morning America* asked the two teams to provide one player each for a morning-after interview. Rochester's manager, Doc Edwards, immediately chose his third baseman, Cal Ripken Jr.: articulate, telegenic, on his way. But Pawtucket's manager, Joe Morgan, spent the night thinking about his choice before deciding on his first baseman, Dave Koza: steady, hardworking, uncertain. No matter which team wins, Ripken and Koza will be standing in front of a camera early tomorrow morning, telling the country about the biggest, longest game of their lives. That is, if the game is over by then.

The sun takes its time finding rest somewhere beyond the triple-deckers in the left-field distance, giving off enough warmth to allow the umpires to wear their light blue short-sleeve shirts. About the only element this cozy night seems to share with its cold Holy Saturday counterpart, in fact, is the leveling air of the absurd. In the dugout, a British reporter quiets the never-quiet Joe Morgan by asking the baseball lifer when he expects this "match" to end. In the press box, Bob Drew, who was fired as Rochester's general manager just days after broadcasting the game's first 32 innings, is preparing to call the 33rd inning for a Baltimore radio station, making him perhaps the first broadcaster in baseball history to start a game for one station and end it with another.

In the stands, the man in street clothes who casually sits down beside the sportswriter Peter Gammons turns out to be Win Remmerswaal, Pawtucket's enigmatic and, until this moment, AWOL pitcher, who was last seen a few days ago in Columbus, performing a late-night striptease in a bar, as if to live up to his nickname of "Last Call" Remmerswaal. And somewhere around here, maybe, just maybe, there lurks a prominent American novelist. A few weeks ago, a man telephoned McCoy Stadium to say that news of the longest game had inspired him to consider writing a play about it. He wanted to know how far Pawtucket is from Manhattan, and whether he could reserve a seat for this curious game's conclusion. The call could easily have been a prank or a misunderstanding. Just in case, a press pass has been set aside for a Philip Roth, never to be claimed.

All these reporters, scrambling to record the chorus of just-glad-to-be-here clichés. All these photographers, seeking that unguarded hint of ambition revealed in a Triple-A face. All these people in the stands, talking at once to create an ocean's hum that washes over the anxious players like an affirming wave. Elsewhere, Major League Baseball is on strike. But here, the cruel truth that professional baseball is an often ruthless business has been left outside the gate. What is unfolding at McCoy tonight is a purer interpretation of the game—baseball without sin—in which the story line includes the Pawtucket right fielder's throwing out a runner at home in the top of the 32nd inning, but not the freezing Rochester center fielder's mutterings to the cold, cold night, fuck, fuck, fuck. Up in Cooperstown, the Hall of Fame has already prepared an exhibit on this game, still in need of conclusion.

Taking in all the hoopla is a left-handed pitcher named Bob Ojeda, warming up now in Pawtucket's left-field bullpen. He's already acquainted with the major leagues, and he knows that he will return. The Red Sox front office has just informed him that he will soon be called up to Boston, no matter that his major-league debut last year was just short of forgettable. Still, he is grateful for the attention being paid now to beleaguered McCoy—grateful not for himself, but for his team-

mates, his brothers, many of whom will never know the rush of taking
your position on a major-league field, and sensing the respect, even the
adulation, of tens of thousands at once. He has experienced that high,
but what about the men he eats, sleeps, and travels with? Here are three
of them now, Boggs, Laribee, and Koza, heroic in their virgin white
uniforms of polyester, stretching their legs and swinging their weighted
bats along the left-field foul line, their shadows reaching far across the
outfield's olive grass. Boggs, left unprotected by the Boston organization over the winter, but attracting no interest from other major-league
teams. Laribee, a big deal in Double-A, but clearly out of sorts at this
level. And Koza, earnest, lionhearted Koza, with that big hole in his
swing; just can't seem to get his batting average up. Some of these guys,
you know—you just know—that they are not going to make it, Ojeda
thinks. But at least they will have this night.

Ojeda is twenty-three. Three years ago, he was the married father
of a six-month-old girl, working as a landscaper for his brother-in-law
in Visalia, the hub of central California's San Joaquin Valley, when the
Boston Red Sox offered him a shot. He signed for very little money
and a plane ticket to rookie league at the other end of the continent,
in Elmira, New York. He bought a suit, a pair of shoes, and a farewell
dinner for his parents. His father, who upholsters furniture, and his
mother, who works for the school system as an interpreter for Mexican
migrants, will always have a photograph of their smiling son, standing
at the doorway of a plane that will take him away.

What Ojeda knew of New York came from movies and television,
so he imagined Elmira to be a sophisticated suburb of Manhattan,
which it is not. Elmira is an old railroad and manufacturing city of
about thirty-five thousand people, some 235 miles to the northwest,
where a notorious Civil War prisoner-of-war camp was once located,
where Mark Twain once lived, and where Bob Ojeda experienced daily
discouragement. Owning no car and crammed into a shoebox apartment with his young family, Ojeda's enduring image of his time in
Elmira will be of pushing a wobbly cart filled with groceries down a
wet, busy road, while in the midst of compiling a record of six losses
and just one win.

But Ojeda had a determination about him that intrigued his superiors. He imagines that his evaluation back then read something like: "Sucks. But he's hungry. He's trying." He got himself invited to an off-season instructional league in Florida, where he became the willing student of Johnny Podres, a retired left-handed pitcher for the Brooklyn Dodgers who was known for his mental toughness. Podres taught Ojeda how to throw a changeup and how to give more snap to his curveball. The next year, in Single-A ball in Winter Haven, Ojeda was 15 and 7.

Last year, after pitching without distinction in seven games for Boston, where he half expected the security guards at Fenway to tackle him before he reached the mound, Ojeda was sent back to Pawtucket. When the season ended, he bought a weather-beaten Dodge van and drove the three thousand miles back to Visalia, where he promptly enrolled in a martial-arts class. If he had to drill a batter during a game, he wanted to be able to defend himself when that batter charged the mound.

Warming up on the sidelines now, his bushy brown hair billowing out from under his blue baseball cap, his mustache lending a touch of menace, Bob Ojeda has set aside his thoughts of gratitude for this special night. The longest game will be the career highlight for others, but not for him. He will pitch for the Boston Red Sox and then for the New York Mets; while with New York, he will beat Boston in a World Series game and share a championship at the expense of several of his teammates tonight. He will pitch for the Los Angeles Dodgers for two years. Then, in 1993, he will report to spring training in Florida for the Cleveland Indians, only to suffer a horrible head injury in a boating accident that will kill two of his new teammates. Four and a half months later, after scalp surgery and counseling and a mind-clearing trip to Sweden, he will return to the mound. His 2 innings in relief on that night will be remembered less for the home run that Cal Ripken Jr. hit off him than for the healing ovation he received from the Baltimore fans, and for the image of Bob Ojeda tugging on a baseball cap that covered the scars. After playing out the season with the Indians, Ojeda will pitch 3 poor innings for the New York Yankees in 1994, before accepting a major-league wink that it was time to retire.

Now, though, as Ojeda finishes his warm-ups, he summons the gritty resolve that will someday guide him through trauma and loss. He knows that a few hours ago, he cockily told Mondor not to worry: that the PawSox will win; that *he* will win. His thoughts turn to his Rochester opponents. Fuck these guys.

Time, again.

The same three umpires are back: Jack Lietz, Tony Maners, and, behind the plate, Denny Cregg. They shoo away the gaggle of photographers and camera operators curled around home plate, but not before posing for photographs with the Rochester manager, Doc Edwards, and Pawtucket's pitching coach, Mike Roarke, standing in place of the manager, Joe Morgan, who was thrown out back in the 22nd inning—sixty-five days ago—and is returning again to his secret vantage point, where he can watch the game from a peephole a few yards from home plate. It is the top of the 33rd inning, the score is tied, 2–2, and the country is listening and watching by radio and television broadcast, in Seattle, in St. Louis, in Chicago and Baltimore and Boston and New York. Pawtucket is everywhere.

Play ball.

The assembled ballplayers have waited for this rare moment—this exquisite chance to excel in the spotlight. "Being the hero of that game would be the ultimate," Wade Boggs said the other day. "You'd like to win the MVP, the batting title, things like that, but nothing compares to winning the longest game."

Angelo Cataldi agreed, writing: "Emerge as the hero in baseball's longest game, and everyone from Kennebunkport to Podunk is going to know your name and your story."

Right now, though, they are all nobodies, including Bob Ojeda, who stands on the McCoy mound, comfortable, at home. The Pizzeria Regina billboard over his left shoulder, the Miller High Life sign over his right: his wall art. The many fans: his guests. The Red Wings: fuck them. Easter's over. He waits impatiently for the lead-off hitter, Dallas Williams, to set himself at home plate. Williams is only twenty-three, but he feels the imminence of history's sneering judgment. He knows that the game's box score has shadowed him for weeks:

Dallas Williams: 0 for 12.

Flied to left in the 1st inning. Flied to right in the 4th. Grounded to short in the 6th. Laid down a sacrifice bunt in the 8th. Popped to third in the 11th. Flied to left in the 13th. Struck out in the 15th. Popped to third in the 17th. Lined to short in the 19th. Grounded to first in the 22nd. Grounded to second in the 23rd. Grounded to second in the 26th. Laid down a sacrifice bunt in the 28th. Grounded to the pitcher in the 31st.

Yes, he knows that the box score chronicles a game of singular futility by Williams, Dallas, center field. But here is another chance, probably his last, to get a hit and halt the repetition of failure reflected in the game's statistics. A left-handed hitter, he seeks the same comfort in the batter's box that Ojeda feels on the mound, setting his left foot at the back edge of the plate, then planting his right foot so that his feet and shoulders are square, natural. He prefers a lighter bat, a 31-ouncer, to help him be quick to the ball. He begins to spin that light bat now, finding in this athletic movement a winding up of focus. He does not believe in stillness. A few weeks ago, Earl Weaver, Baltimore's manager, told him that he needs to put up better numbers in Triple-A to justify a promotion to the major leagues. This game will not help that cause, but he has to put his previous 12 at bats, along with Weaver's words, out of his mind. Focus on this at bat.

Ojeda is fuck-you ready. It is left-hander against left-hander. He rears back, then snaps a hard curveball that paralyzes Williams as it pops across the plate for a called strike one. The game begins, again. The crowd calls out its approval in a collective "Yeahhhhhh."

His next pitch is a ball, his third a fastball that Williams can only hit foul to the left side. Then comes another nasty Ojeda epithet. Williams swings mightily, but a little late. The ball arcs into the air, toward left field.

The box score will never reflect that Dallas Williams grew up in the Gowanus Houses project in Brooklyn—a "red-brick mini-city" of five thousand

people, as the *New York Times* once called it; that he was one of ten children raised by a father who drove buses and a mother who sang gospel;
and that he almost chose singing hymns over playing baseball. The Williamses are a singing family, good enough to be known as the King Family
of the Gowanus Houses, and to have recorded an album some fifteen years
ago called *The Irresistible Gospel Chords*. Its cover features his mother and
his five older siblings, all smiles in their choir gowns of powder blue. Williams will hear them forever in his head:

> *Tell me, how did you feel when you*
> *Come out the wilderness, come out the wilderness*
> *Come out the wilderness, come out the wilderness*
> *Tell me how did you feel when you*
> *Come out the wilderness*
> *Leaning on the Lord . . .*

When he was old enough, Williams joined the group, eager to
entwine his voice with those of his mother and siblings. But he also
wanted to play sports, in emulation of his beloved older brother Mickey,
a school-yard star. Before long his two emerging talents, singing gospel
and playing baseball, were competing for his time, occasionally forcing
him to skip baseball practice at Abraham Lincoln High School to rehearse with his family. These interruptions, though, did little to hinder
his eye-opening skills as a hitter and a pitcher. In his senior year, he was
voted the best high school baseball player in New York City, and was
drafted in the first round by the Baltimore Orioles. So began twelve
years of wandering through the minor leagues; of stepping up to bat
more than five thousand times; of hitting a respectable .285; of constantly wondering why, why he was not getting much of a chance in the
major leagues. When his playing days end, he will have appeared in just
twenty big-league games, hitting 3 singles in 38 at bats for a lifetime
average of .079.

Williams will spend more time in the major leagues as a first-base
coach, first for the Colorado Rockies and then for the Boston Red Sox,
than as a player. But his career will remain mostly rooted in the minor

leagues, where he will coach in Hickory, North Carolina; Springfield, Missouri; Gary, Indiana; on and on. Still, as demanding and as frustrating as the game can be, he will find comfort in its essential silliness. Three of his nine siblings will succumb to the crack and heroin plague that will sweep through the Gowanus Houses and all of New York City in a few years, including Mickey, who will smile forever into the future from the cover of the family's gospel album. At times, Mickey's ballplaying younger brother will not be able to listen to that album without choking up. Thank God for the distraction, the game, the job of baseball.

The ball sails foul, and not that deep. The shortstop jogs over to track it down along the foul line. A lame pop fly to short. One out.

Williams trots back to the Rochester dugout, his legacy cemented. From now on, whenever the longest game is discussed, it will be customary to recall that Dallas Williams went 0 for 13. Reporters will joke that Williams had a bad month in one game. Players will assess their own poor performances with feigned humility before noting that at least they had a better game than Dallas Williams. His failure to get a hit will become an integral part of the game's lore, taking its place beside the refusal of Luis Aponte's wife to let him into their apartment, Sam Bowen's near home run, Russ Laribee's seven strikeouts, and Joe Morgan's ejection. The cold wind blew, broken bats burned, and Dallas Williams went 0 for 13.

But.

One down. "And here comes J.R.," a radio announcer from Baltimore says. "Cal Ripken Jr."

Ripken steps up to the plate, once again imagining himself whipping his barrel-heavy bat so fast it nearly bends. Every at bat matters; every at bat is with two outs, the bases loaded, in the bottom of the ninth of the seventh game of the World Series. Every at bat. He has been this way since he was a boy, wearing a baseball uniform as his everyday summer attire, emulating his father, committing himself to a life in which every at bat *is* life. It's just who he is.

What Ojeda is thinking, with all due respect, is fuck this guy. Ball one. A breaking pitch for ball two. Heater down the middle, strike one. Fuck this guy. Even after Ripken whips a single into left center field, Ojeda's interior reaction is who gives a shit? A single? Go fuck yourself. Who's up next? It's just who he is.

The batter is the catcher, Floyd Rayford, who entered the game back in the 18th inning as a pinch runner, which makes him a relative late-comer. He is twenty-three and goes by "Sugar Bear," a nickname that refers to his disarming, will-do-anything personality as much as to his roly-poly physique. Don't let the nickname fool you. Sugar Bear spent part of last year with the Orioles; he has already survived Earl Weaver in all his apoplectic glory. Bob Ojeda does not scare him.

Sugar Bear swings at a third strike for the 60th strikeout of the game.

Ojeda paces about the mound, wanting no interruption to his momentum, eager to face his next conquest, thinking: Whoever the fuck you are, just get in the box, make your out, and get out of the way. It's the pinch hitter John Valle, entering his tenth minor-league season at the age of twenty-six. By the time Ojeda graduated from high school, Valle had already played for the Clinton Pilots in Iowa, the Lakeland Tigers in Florida, the Montgomery Rebels in Alabama, and the Evansville Triplets in Indiana, all of which is to say that John Valle is not intimidated by the pitcher before him. His younger brother, Dave, will rise from the minors to play thirteen years as a major-league catcher, but John will never get there. After fouling off three consecutive pitches, he hits a harmless fly ball to left field, a footnote.

Three outs. Pawtucket roars. Ojeda jogs straight into the clubhouse, in search of a cup of tea to calm his nerves.

In the press box, Bill George can hardly contain himself, so proud is he to be *the* official scorer, the artist of the uncompleted score sheet— the Book of Pawtucket—that he carefully preserved for two months, and which is now a bit of an attraction for broadcasters, reporters, and baseball aficionados. Though he normally dresses casually for games, George is wearing a blazer and tie tonight; it seemed appropriate. He has decided to use green ink for the start of the 33rd inning.

Down in the home dugout, the batboy, Billy Broadbent, feels as though he is a part of a Yankees–Red Sox playoff game. He left his house especially early today, taking a shortcut up Greeley, across the railroad tracks, past the place that gives him a few bucks for recycled newspapers, past Palagi's Ice Cream warehouse, and across Pariseau Field—all to see how big a deal this day would be. The answer: Big; real big. When Koza tossed the warm-up ball to him before the top of the 33rd, it seemed as though six thousand people watched Billy Broadbent make the catch.

And in the third-base grandstand, Bob Brex, the state government employee who spent the longest night sitting by himself, in cold, mind-clearing seclusion, is now experiencing that night's opposite. For the last week, reporters from newspapers, television stations, and radio programs have been interviewing him about his recollections of being one of the hardy few to endure the first 32 innings. And just a few minutes ago, a producer from *NBC Nightly News* accessorized Brex's tan corduroy blazer with a remote microphone. The network apparently wants to share his reactions during the game's resumption—with the nation. Two months ago, he watched this game alone; now he will have virtual millions sitting beside him.

This faithful fan, the official scorer, the batboy, and thousands of others now watch as the Rochester pitcher strides toward the mound. A veteran of the major leagues, this pitcher, Steve Grilli, seems business-like calm as he takes his warm-ups. You wouldn't know to look at him, but not ten minutes ago, during the national anthem, he confided in a teammate that he hasn't felt stomach butterflies like this in a long, long time. He feels like an outsider—a rookie, really—because he did not suffer through the eight-hour cold two months ago, or see the wind stop Sam Bowen's sure home run, or share in any of the moments that have become part of the game's epic narrative. He is also taken aback by the outsized attention that this one game is receiving.

A child of Long Island, by way of Brooklyn, Grilli's decade of professional baseball includes two full seasons and parts of two others in the major leagues, working mostly as a fastball-slider setup man out of the bullpen for the Detroit Tigers. But he is thirty-two years old, he has spent the last two years mired in the minor leagues, and he strongly senses that professional baseball is trying to tell him something. The game tried first with polite silence in 1979, when he pitched well for the Syracuse Chiefs but was not included in the September call-ups by the Toronto Blue Jays—a team that, to Grilli, seemed inordinately obsessed with youth. By last month, though, the game could no longer keep silent, and was all but shouting at Grilli as the Chiefs released him during a road trip to Columbus.

Maybe Grilli should listen to the game. The road trips were getting harder, and he and his wife, Kathleen, have a two-year-old daughter, Stephanie, and a four-year-old son, Jason, who likes to play catch with his dad at their home in the Syracuse suburbs. Maybe the game was right; maybe it was time.

Then, a few days after Grilli's release, the game changed its mind. A Baltimore Orioles executive called him at home, around midnight, to offer him a job with the Rochester Red Wings, but said that the team needed an answer now, or else it would continue down its list of available pitchers and find someone else to fill the position. Although he was an experienced veteran, almost mentally prepared to start his life's next adventure, Grilli could not suppress the faint but so familiar sensation of the possible. Maybe something will happen. Maybe the breaks will fall his way. Maybe he can make it back to the big leagues.

If Grilli did not quite realize how old he seemed when he joined the Rochester team a couple of weeks ago, he got the message while making his introductory rounds in the clubhouse, and the young third baseman, Cal Ripken Jr., said he knew exactly who Steve Grilli was. He had seen Grilli pitch when Grilli was tearing up the Southern League for the Montgomery Rebels, and Ripken was with the Asheville Orioles—as its batboy. At this point, Grilli wishes the game would just make up its mind.

Pawtucket's leadoff hitter, the second baseman Marty Barrett, steps into the batter's box and raises his eyes to meet Grilli's downward glance, his uniform like a Rhode Island manifestation of Old Glory: blue helmet, white uniform, bright red number 4 on the back. Barrett plans to celebrate his twenty-third birthday today by doing something he rarely does, which is to swing at the first pitch. He expects a fastball. Grilli, who has faced the best hitters in baseball, winds up, throws—and releases a nervous pitch, one that catches Barrett unawares. He swivels to get out of the way, but the high-and-tight ball glances off his shoulder. In one seamless balletic move, Barrett drops his bat, breaks his fall with his outstretched hands, bounces up, and jogs off to accept the base he has just been awarded.

Pawtucket's acting manager, Mike Roarke, has said that if the PawSox win this game, he will accept all the praise, but if they lose, well, he was just following the orders of his friend and boss, Joe Morgan. Determined to advance Barrett to second base—where he can possibly score on a single—Roarke gives the signal for the hit-and-run, which means that Barrett will be running on the pitch to the batter, Chico Walker. Roarke figures that Grilli is a low-ball pitcher, Walker is a good low-ball hitter, and something good might happen. He figures right. Walker, crouched in concentration, his blue sliding glove dangling from his back pocket, grounds a 3-2 pitch past Grilli's outstretched glove and into center field, allowing Barrett to round second base and easily reach third base, no sliding necessary.

The murmurs and sporadic barks of the instantly invested crowd grow louder, as Pawtucket's designated hitter, big Russ Laribee, approaches the plate, carrying a heavy bat and the heavier burden of his statistics in this game. He has struck out seven times—so often that players on the Rochester bench have been arguing about what the baseball term is for such failure. Seven strikeouts! If three strikeouts is a hat trick, has Laribee completed a double hat trick plus one? Laribee feels the embarrassment of his multiple whiffs more than he lets on, and is eager, make that determined, to seize his moment of redemption. Attuned to the come-on cheers of six thousand, he plans to hit the ball high and far enough for a home run—or, at least, for a sacrifice fly. Barrett will score, and Laribee, big Russ Laribee, will be the game-winning hero.

This will not happen. The Rochester manager walks out to the mound to talk with his rattled pitcher, and their topic of discussion is so obvious that Laribee might as well participate in the conversation himself: intentional walk, a scheme to load the bases and create a force-out at home. And there is nothing that Laribee can do. An intentional walk is a formality in which the catcher stands to receive each pitch, purposely thrown far from the strike zone, and the batter is reduced to passive participant.

Ball one. Laribee aches to swing. Ball two. But he cannot. Ball three. Each pitch is beyond his bat's reach. Ball four.

The walk thwarts the plans of Russ Laribee, who, a few weeks from now, will quit the team. "I just wanted to redeem myself," he says after the game.

No outs and the bases are loaded, a baseball term that suggests imminent explosion. All this awaits the next batter, Dave Koza. Since the early-morning suspension of this game sixty-five days ago, Koza has known that when play resumed, he would be Pawtucket's fourth batter up. He has visualized this at bat on an endless loop in hotel rooms along the International League circuit and in his own bedroom just down the street from McCoy, his new wife snuggled by his side, the two of them talking so much about it that they finally agreed to stop talking about it altogether. He has dreamed of it, really, ever since his father strung up some chicken wire to transform a plot of Wyoming nothingness into a Little League ball field; dreamed of the pitch, his game-winning hit, and the world's joyous reaction. Now he carries the Louisville Slugger that the awed batboy placed in the bat-rack slot reserved for Koza, and he wears the blue helmet stained with the sweat of his teammate Mike Ongarato, a hat that lately seems to be granting him good luck at the plate. Moments ago, Ongarato urged him to wear this helmet once more, saying something that makes sense only in a baseball dugout: The helmet's got a lot of hits in it.

Across the field, Doc Edwards hitches his uniform belt and ambles out to remove the baseball from the grasp of a dejected Steve Grilli, who, in eleven quick pitches, has allowed all three batters he has faced to reach base. This will be Grilli's last season in professional baseball; he will not return to the major leagues—although twenty years from

now, his little son, Jason, always itching to play catch, will follow his
father onto the fields of the major leagues.

A new pitcher, a right-hander named Cliff Speck, approaches
from the visiting team's bullpen, a barren stretch beside a large roll of
green tarp, on the first-base side. Like Grilli, the six-foot-four Speck
only joined the Red Wings a few weeks ago, after his promotion from
Double-A, and so does not share the depth of emotional investment
that his teammates have in this game. Still, for all the disproportionate
hysteria surrounding what is really nothing more than another minor-
league game in Pawtucket, Rhode Island, he enjoys when everything is
on the line and up to him. Besides, he has no time to get nervous. It's
either do it or don't.

While Speck warms up, a thought occurs to Roarke, Pawtucket's
third-base coach and acting manager. He motions for Koza to meet
him halfway between third and home. With arms folded across his
chest, the veteran coach asks the young player: Have you ever laid
down a squeeze bunt? In other words, do you have the confidence and
bat skill to participate in one of baseball's most daring and difficult
plays by dropping a surprise bunt at the precise moment that Barrett
comes charging home from third? If you miss the ball, Barrett is a sure
out. If you pop the ball up, both you and Barrett are out. So, the question is, young man: Have you ever laid down a squeeze bunt?

The young man's stunned expression seems to suggest that one
of the two people in this conversation has suddenly gone mad. Never
mind, Roarke says. Go get 'em.

Koza steps into the batter's box to begin his brief maintenance routine of mind and space, smoothing out the dirt with his left cleat, working a chunk of Dubble Bubble chewing gum hard enough to tighten the
definition of his jaw. His chest pounds as his subconscious processes
all the hitting advice he has received over the years, from his father
on Torrington grass to Ted Williams in the Pawtucket clubhouse. Ted
Williams, who made him cry once. But Koza is clear-eyed now. Keep
the bat close to your body, he is thinking. Hold the handle light, on the
fingertips. Protect the plate, but don't get suckered. Drive the ball into
the outfield. Drive the ball.

Up in the stands, Bob Brex, wired with a microphone to the nation, fears a ground-out double play. He wishes for a sacrifice fly. He speaks for all of Pawtucket as he commands Koza from afar: Get it in the air! Get it in the air!

Before Koza even knows it, the count is 1 and 1.

"This is the most attention that the city of Pawtucket, Rhode Island, has had since a number of years back, when, believe it or not, the camel at the local zoo here got drunk," says Tom Marr, a radio announcer who normally handles Baltimore Orioles games. "That's true. It is true. And they got a lot of national attention because the camel trampled the watchman and had to be shot. Here's the next pitch. It's out of the strike zone, two-and-one count.

"Well, it happened. It actually happened. The camel went berserk, they had to shoot the camel, and animal lovers from all over the country sent nasty letters to the mayor of Pawtucket. Bases loaded.

"Here's the pitch to the next batter. It's fouled off again, two balls and two strikes the count."

With two strikes on him, Koza fouls off another pitch; in baseball parlance, he stays alive. Somewhere to his left, waiting to bat next, is Wade Boggs, so gifted a hitter that he will surely drive in the winning run if given the chance. And directly behind Koza, as always, is his wife, Ann, sitting in one of the choice seats reserved for the wives and girlfriends of the players. Every pitch seems to rob her of breath as she prays for Dave to hit a home run—a grand slam!—only to pull back, out of fear that she might be asking too much of God. A hit. That's all. A hit to win the game.

Speck is a statue, his very stillness a form of intimidation. He cradles the precious ball in his right hand, out of Koza's view, and peers from under the bill of his red Rochester cap in the direction of home plate. Koza steps out of the batter's box to compose himself. Two strikes. He engages again in an at bat's subtle formalities, equal parts courtesy, anxiety, and focus. He smooths the dirt. He takes a practice swing. He steps back in and taps his raised left cleat with the barrel of the bat held in his left hand. He taps the plate with the bat's nose at precisely the same time that he adjusts his blue helmet with his right hand. Finally, he points his bat at the pitcher in a manner that lacks any hint of threat; that says, almost politely, Ready when you are. Behind him, the crouching catcher, Floyd Rayford, waves his mitt down, down, down, reminding Speck to keep the ball low.

Koza catches sight of the ball just as it unscrews from Speck's grasp: a curve. A knee-buckler, spinning with the promise of evasion, heading directly for Koza. At this moment he is forced to confront his demon, the curveball, which, more than anything else, has kept him from playing in the major leagues. Undermining his years of hard work, making him look foolish, derailing his plans. He cannot escape it, the curve. Speck, meanwhile, bent at the waist and with his face recalibrating from the exertion, is happy with this low, away, and nearly unhittable pitch. He is thinking: "No way."

Koza's waist snaps, his upper body follows, his powerful arms extend. His bat of ash transforms into an extension of himself, all his hopes and fears carried in its barrel. He's chasing a pitch just as he has chased a major-league career, hoping to make contact with the elusive. He reaches out and, almost apologetically, connects. His discarded bat twirls to the ground, as time slows again in Pawtucket.

The softly hit ball flutters past the runner on third base, Marty Barrett, who stutters in place as he tries to discern its destination and meaning. It floats in a tease over the head of the helpless third baseman, Cal Ripken Jr., whose storied major-league career has yet to begin, and descends well in front of the defeated left fielder, Keith Smith, whose brief major-league career has already passed. Then, having served its purpose, the ball falls to deliver a good-night kiss to the grass.

Barrett scores, confirming the victory with a foot touch of home plate, his right hand raised to create what will become the game's iconic image. The Pawtucket Red Sox win, 3–2. After 33 innings, this game is blessedly, mercifully, over.

Only eighteen minutes were needed to finish what had taken eight hours and seven minutes to begin, an American opera whose cast included sons from the east and the west, the north and the far, far south; children of farmers and mill workers, bus drivers and truck drivers, firefighters and aerospace engineers, soldiers and toy-store owners and gospel singers, all trying to get someplace else.

Here comes a whooping Wade Boggs, clutching his unneeded bat, to slap Barrett's hand. Here comes Ojeda, now the winning pitcher of the longest game in baseball history, and Bowen, and Smithson, and Gedman, and Aponte, and Valdez, and the rest of the Pawtucket players, charging onto the field as if they have just won the major-league world championship, and not a midseason minor-league game of little consequence. Here comes Billy Broadbent, the batboy, to retrieve the bat for safekeeping, until it is forwarded to the Hall of Fame. And here, here is Dave Koza, who has leapt onto the first-base bag in triumph and is now jogging back to receive hugs and handshakes and helmet taps of affirmation. His giddy teammates, jumping up and down, create a cocoon around Koza as they all but carry him into the clubhouse, where a crush of reporters wait to chronicle his words and announce his heroics to a country deprived of its baseball. The conclusion elicits a prolonged exhalation from the ghosts and girders of McCoy Stadium, as the smoky voice of Peggy Lee teases from its loudspeakers:

Is that all there is? Is that all there is? If that's all there is, my friends, then let's keep dancing. Let's break out the booze and have a ball . . .

The official scorekeeper, Bill George, applies the final touches to his score sheet, a multicolored study of baseball codes that has taken more than two months to complete. He began recording this game in blue ink, then moved to red, then black. Now, in his ink of hopeful green, he meticulously prints the following at the bottom of his artwork, soon to be acquired by the Hall of Fame:

LONGEST GAME IN BASEBALL HISTORY

PAWTUCKET 3—ROCHESTER 2

33 INNINGS—8:25

MCCOY STADIUM—PAWTUCKET, R.I.

APRIL 18–19   JUNE 23, 1981

Who notices the others, the Rochester Red Wings, the bills of their scarlet caps pointed downward, following their long shadows toward the refuge of the dugout reserved for visitors? Their failure has rendered them all but invisible. A form of some redemption will soon come. Wise Doc Edwards will ease Steve Grilli's pain by sending him back out to the mound for tonight's second game, where he will pitch three nearly perfect innings in a Rochester win almost instantly forgotten. Years from now, as the father of a major-league pitcher, Jason Grilli, and as the approachable owner of a sports bar in Syracuse called the Change of Pace, Grilli will enjoy the distinction this loss grants him. Tonight, though, aching with the sense that he has miserably failed his new teammates, he exudes only maturity and class while answering question after question about how it feels to be the losing pitcher in baseball's longest game.

"This is more than a loss for Steve Grilli," he says. "I let the team down. I wasn't even here back in April when they struggled for the first thirty-two innings. I missed all that cold and all that wind. I come in and pitch one inning and lose it all for them."

His downcast teammate, Cliff Speck, who will briefly reach the major leagues five long years from now, is answering similar questions about history, and legacy, and how does it feel to give up the walk-off single that he still cannot believe Koza managed to golf for a hit.

"I guess I'll be like that fellow who gave up that homer to Bobby Thomson," he says, referring to the hit that won the National League pennant for the New York Giants in 1951. "What was his name?"

"Ralph Branca," someone answers, as if to confirm for the twenty-four-year-old how, in baseball, some moments do not fade.

A few paces from there, in the home team's clubhouse, a water pipe bursts to baptize some of the joyous Pawtucket players and to assert the old stadium's dominion, while Ben Mondor hugs anyone in a PawSox uniform, and Russ Laribee tells people how much he wishes he had gotten his chance, and Lou Schwechheimer helps to compile the eye-popping final statistics—219 at bats? 60 strikeouts?—and Joe Morgan keeps saying that the elevation of the hardworking Koza to hero is pure justice. "He's been here about as long as anyone," he says.

Ah, but for how long? Surely, Boston's front office will take notice that Dave Koza can hit in the clutch. And if there's no room on the Red Sox roster, every team in the country will know who Koza is by morning, when his name and photograph will adorn the nation's sports pages, and he and Cal Ripken Jr. will appear, live, on *Good Morning America*, his triumph shared between news of President Reagan's plan for the lagging economy and a review of *Cannonball Run*, a new movie starring Burt Reynolds, Farrah Fawcett, and Dom DeLuise. In a moment of pure, absurd Americana, Koza and Ripken will stand in McCoy's left field while the show's host, the urbane actor John Forsythe, who in his youth worked as a public-address announcer for the Brooklyn Dodgers, sits in a studio in New York City, directing his somewhat misinformed questions to a small television screen.

> FORSYTHE (*polished*): Now you, Dave, you tied the ball game, didn't you, in the 32nd inning. And then you won it last night. How'd you do that?
>
> KOZA (*nervous*): Well, we led off the inning. Marty Barrett led it off, he got hit by a pitch. Then Chico Walker came up—(*a pause to swallow*)—had a base hit up the middle. Doc Edwards, their manager, came out and decided to walk Russ Laribee. Well, there it was, bases loaded, no one out, and I'm up at the plate. I just—I just wouldn't want to be anywhere else right then.
>
> FORSYTHE (*joking*): You made sure you touched first base, though, didn't you?
>
> KOZA (*earnest*): Yes, I did. . . .
>
> FORSYTHE (*concluding*): Well, you've created history, fellas. It was a great ball game. And congratulations to you all, winners and losers.
>
> KOZA AND RIPKEN (*relieved*): Thank you.
>
> FORSYTHE (*moving on*): We'll find out how to take advantage of the hot weather to change your eating habits and get yourself in better shape. After this . . .

That will be tomorrow's glory. Tonight, the hero, still wearing his Pawtucket Red Sox uniform and cap, stands just outside the home team clubhouse, in front of a sign on the pale yellow wall that reads, NO ADMITTANCE, TEAM PERSONNEL AND CLUBHOUSE PASSES ONLY. He has blue eyes, shaggy brown-blond hair, and a full mustache that suggests he knows the wide-open spaces. Behind him stands a Pawtucket police officer, his distended belly testing the fabric of his light blue uniform shirt, his smiling face a beam of admiration and envy. And embracing the hero, his new wife, in crisp white shirt and dungarees, her blond hair lustrous and long down her back. He gently rocks her back and forth, as though preparing them both for their next springing step.

The ballplayer kisses his wife, and pulls her closer with a hand snug in a batting glove.

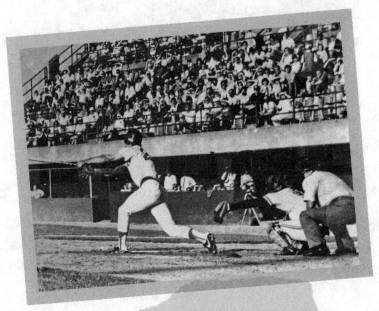

Koza connects.

Barrett scores.

Dave Koza at Ben Mondor's funeral,
October 2010.

Dave Koza stores his baseball memories in plastic bins that he tucks away in the spare bedroom of his small home in Pawtucket, less than three miles from McCoy Stadium. Pry open the lid to any one of these tubs and his boyish past is released: the intermingled hints of Skoal, Ben-Gay, and fresh-cut grass; the hand-clap echoes of hits, the swing-and-miss grunts, the last calls at My Brother's Pub. He keeps them all here, the bits and pieces of his baseball years, jumbled together, measured less by the passage of days than by the statistics of the seasons, the singular moments: 1976 (.281 batting average); 1979 (27 home runs); 1981 (the longest game).

In the thirty years since Koza ended a 33-inning baseball marathon with a soft, dreamy single over Cal Ripken's head, the story of this sporting event has proven susceptible to the truth-altering charms of myth and memory. There is no malicious intent in the retold tales, no evidence of self-promoting embellishment. But the improbable nature of that Holy Saturday night and Easter Sunday morning seems to have encouraged narrative embroidery, as though the participants and witnesses of baseball's longest game remain hypnotized by the flames dancing and writhing from the burning bats in the dugout barrels. Some will remember that a cold mist fell, that temperatures dropped below freezing, and that a car hit a transformer on a Paw-tucket street, knocking out power to the stadium lights right before the game's scheduled start; none of this is true. Some accounts will say that twenty-seven fans were present at the end of the 32nd inning;

Ben Mondor, the owner, swore by nineteen. Some will say that Harold Cooper, the president of the International League, did not pick up the telephone that night because he was at a wedding, or was driving home to Ohio from Indianapolis; Cooper said he was at home that night, asleep, when Pawtucket called with news of a runaway game. Some will insist that Luis Aponte, the pitcher whose unhappy wife turned him away at their apartment door, slept on the trainer's table; he insisted he returned home and slept cozily beside his wife. The Pawtucket pitcher Bruce Hurst, future major-league hero, genetically incapable of telling an untruth, often recalls how he struck out Ripken on a 3-2 curve at four o'clock in the morning. In his major-league career, Hurst struck out Ripken seven times in 45 at bats—but he did *not* strike Ripken out in the longest game. This is a reflection not on the decent, straight-up Bruce Hurst, but of the late-hour exhaustion that infused the night with certain enchantment.

Dave Koza often encounters these exaggerations. People will approach him at, say, Chelo's restaurant on Newport Avenue, or maybe at the Ground Round restaurant, next to where the old Howard Johnson motor inn used to be, and ask: Aren't you the guy who hit the home run to win the longest game? "No, no," he always answers, in a gee-whiz sort of way. "It was just a little base hit to left."

But these plastic bins of his, sitting in an extra room of his house, contain no embellishments or misunderstandings about the past. They hold only facts: baseball ephemera and personal scraps that, when assembled in rough chronology, tell part of the story of one man's heroic journey.

Plaques and photographs and Florida State League yearbooks. Some minor-league baseball cards. A couple of Association of Professional Ball Players of America identification cards. A photograph of Pawtucket first baseman Dave Koza standing beside Boston first baseman Carl Yastrzemski. A letter that Koza wrote to his parents in Wyoming, on Boston Red Sox Baseball Club stationery, back in 1979: *Baseball is still trying to treat me good. I've been hitting the ball better. 16 HRs, 45 RBIs out of about 45 hits! My average is .223. Darn that ave. anyway. . . .*

A copy of Koza's 1981 contract: *Club hereby employs Player to render, and Player agrees to render, skilled services as a professional baseball player for Club . . . For the performance of all of the skilled services as aforesaid by Player and for Player's promises herein contained, Club will pay Player, therefore, at the rate of $2,400 per month . . .*

Here are some videocassettes, labeled in pen along their black spines. One reads, "Dave Baseball"; another, "Dave—Ball—1981." A third reads, "*Star Trek* and *Good Morning America*," as if to confirm the oddity of that long-ago interview with John Forsythe, the two of them, Ripken and Koza, standing in McCoy's left field, talking by remote to an actor who once starred for Alfred Hitchcock:

"*Hello, fellas!*"

"*Hello.*"

"*'Lo.*"

Here is a yellowed letter from the United States Senate:

June 25, 1981

Dear Dave:

I might have known that it would take a Wyoming boy to end the longest game in the history of baseball. Congratulations!

. . . I hope things go well for you this season and throughout a long and distinguished career. If they would just settle this disheartening strike, maybe you could make your major-league debut yet this year.

> *Congratulations and best wishes,*
> *Malcolm Wallop*
> *United States Senator*

And here is a note that Ann Koza sent to his parents. She was always so diligent that way—the president, treasurer, and secretary of her own private Dave Koza Fan Club:

July 10, 1981

Hello Everybody!!! . . .
   Things are still coming in from that big game for Dave. He won a travel bag from the Gillette "This Week in Baseball" show. Fan mail is still coming by the heaps. He got a letter from his first-grade teacher in Florida. . . .
   Dave got another home run last night. Number 13. His average is now .280, give or take a point. Hopefully the strike will end and his chances of being sent up at the end of the season are looking mighty good. . . .

It never happened.

During the 1981 season, the Boston Red Sox summoned six players from Pawtucket. Dave Koza, the hero of the longest game in baseball history, was not among them. He finished the year with 18 home runs and a .268 batting average, learned that he would not be among the so-called September call-ups, again, and turned to Ann, again, to pose the question that she had no hope of answering: Why?

Then, as always, he filled the aching silence with an "Oh well," or a "Maybe it's not meant to be," and Ann just wanted to yell at him to say something, do something, let Boston know how you feel! "But I couldn't," she recalled, many years later, tears trickling down from her large eyes. "I didn't want to make him feel bad. And I would just feel—so bad."

Once more, they took that long 1,900-mile drive back to Wyoming, where some of the excitement and importance of the longest game got lost in transit between Pennsylvania and Colorado. People had heard about the game, of course, and were impressed by the letter Dave had received from a United States senator, but down at the Broncho Bar, a few still rudely asked why he hadn't made it yet—as though reaching the major leagues was merely a matter of promotion based on seniority. Cactus, his good buddy from Torrington, often changed the subject. Dave, meanwhile, returned to working construction, turned twenty-seven years old, got his head straight, and prepared for another spring by throwing a ball against the town gymnasium's concrete wall, *whop, whop, whop.*

For Koza, the 1982 season mirrored his 1981 season, save for the absence of any heroics worthy of national celebration. Of course, there was the time that Cactus and his wife surprised Dave by showing up at McCoy one night. Cactus arrived just as Dave was swinging a bat in the on-deck circle, and started calling out a nickname from the old days that only Dave would know.

"Hey, Hutch! Hutcher!"

The all-business mask dropped from Koza's face, the bat from his hands. He ran over and greeted his pal in the stands, who knew him when. "And then he hit a home run for us," Cactus later recalled.

They heard about this remarkable moment back in Torrington, but no one in Pawtucket, or Boston, particularly cared. Koza hit the same number of home runs (18), hit for nearly the same average (.259), and hit up against the same spirit-crushing disappointment. Ojeda, Hurst, and Gedman were up with Boston for good now, it seemed, and Wade Boggs had made the most of his long-awaited chance, hitting .349 to end any doubt that he belonged in the major leagues. Marty Barrett spent some time with the Boston Red Sox, as did Julio Valdez, and Roger LaFrancois—but not Koza. His exclusion from the list of September call-ups surprised several of his colleagues in Pawtucket, from the dugout to the front office. The Elkman, they agreed, at least had earned a sip of coffee.

By the end of 1982, with the Pawtucket Red Sox some 14 games out of first place, and winter approaching for the uninvited, Koza could no longer keep to himself a question that had nagged at him for the better part of six years. He had wearied of dreaming the same teasing dream, over and over, only to wake up to his Pawtucket reality. One evening in Syracuse, while shagging some fly balls during batting practice, Koza saw Joe Morgan standing alone, fungo bat in hand, and decided that now was as good a time as any to ask.

"What do you think, Joe?"

In many ways, these two men were east-west opposites. Morgan had that sideways Irish wit, and seemed to enjoy savoring the etymological

taste of every one of the many words to pour from his mouth; Koza
seemed to wait an extra beat before speaking a single earnest word.
Morgan externalized his anger; Koza kept his in, mostly. Morgan liked
to bet on horses; Koza liked to shoot elk. Still, they had spent much
of the last six years together, sharing in the daily dramas at McCoy,
traveling from Tidewater to Toledo and back again, staying in the same
damn hotels, eating at the same damn restaurants. They understood
each other.

Morgan, a dreamer himself, did not relish this part of his job.
You couldn't very well go around telling most of your minor-league
ballplayers that they'd never make the major leagues; if you did that,
you wouldn't be able to field a team. Still, Morgan never wanted to be
complicit in another man's delusions. He knew that baseball players
often need to hear someone else articulate the thoughts they harbor
but cannot bring themselves to say aloud. And if a young man, who in
baseball terms may not be so young anymore, asked Morgan straight
out—Hey, Joe, I won't hold nothing against you, but do you think I'll
ever play in the big leagues?—he felt morally required to provide either
encouragement or release. To say yes or no.

Now comes the Elkman, Dave Koza, seeking a way out of baseball limbo. Big, strong, mature. A calming influence in the dugout, and
someone who always had his teammates' backs. (Who can forget that
time a batter for the Toledo Mud Hens charged the mound, intent on
harming the Pawtucket pitcher Mike Smithson, and Koza came out
of nowhere and leveled the guy with a crushing tackle?) Good with
the glove. Strong arm. Lots of power. And no question: He had put up
some decent numbers over the years in Triple-A, the penultimate level
of baseball, an extraordinarily difficult game to play well.

But Dave Koza fell just short. He did not dominate. He lacked consistency. And Joe Morgan gently, firmly, told him so.

There it was. All those hot summers spent at that boys' baseball
camp in Oklahoma, raking the field, wearing itchy woolen uniforms;
all those dozens of games played in college and in the semiprofessional
summer leagues; all those hundreds of games with Elmira, Winter
Haven, Bristol, and, of course, Pawtucket. The endless fielding drills:

learning the proper footwork for covering first base; knowing where to stand as the cutoff man for a throw from the outfield; how to execute a 3-6-3 double play. The endless batting practice: Dave, you're dropping your shoulder; Dave, you've got your shoulder too high; Dave, hips ahead of hands. The many injuries, including the time he wore a batting glove for several days to control the swelling and hide the discoloration on a bruised hand he wanted to keep secret. All the little things, the little things. How about the time in Rochester, when he got hit in the head by a fastball that cracked his helmet and left him flat in the dirt, stunned, looking up and seeing the concerned faces of Sammy Bowen and Joe Morgan. The next night in Syracuse, in his first at bat: home run.

All of this, nearly two decades' worth, dedicated to one pursuit: to become a major-league baseball player—even if just for one at bat that might not last a minute.

His manager's words stayed with him on the trip back to Pawtucket, as he cleaned out his locker at season's end, and on the long ride with Ann, back to Wyoming for another winter. Whatever arguments he privately laid out before the Court of Baseball Fairness—Think of what I could learn just by being in a major-league clubhouse, talking baseball with major-league guys—were immediately shot down by the Morgan deposition, which might as well have been taken under oath. You lack consistency.

Dave Koza turned twenty-eight. Ann Koza became pregnant. And from a gymnasium in Torrington came the lonely echoes of a ball bouncing against the wall. *Whop. Whop. Whop.*

The Pawtucket Red Sox began the 1983 season with a new manager and a new first baseman. After nine years in Pawtucket, with nothing more to prove, Joe Morgan moved on to become a scout in the Boston Red Sox organization. Ben Mondor, the owner of the PawSox, who once offered Morgan the world if he promised to stay, understood: Joe wanted his shot, too. And after four years as the team's starting first baseman, Dave Koza was relegated to a secondary role as a late-inning defensive replacement, designated hitter, and bench warmer. The new manager who marginalized Koza had spent thirteen years in the minors, mostly as a first baseman, and had never played in the major leagues, while the player who replaced Koza at first was, like him, an inconsistent power hitter who would also never rise above Triple-A.

When the season finally ended, Koza had 14 home runs, 44 runs batted in, and a lingering case of the baseball player maybes. *Maybe I'm misreading the situation. Maybe another team will see what Boston clearly does not. Maybe the opinion of Joe Morgan, God love him, is not shared in Boston.* He called Boston and made an appointment with Ed Kenney, a Red Sox vice president who, for many years, had been the organization's director of player development. Soon Koza was taking the forty-five-mile drive to Fenway Park, a drive he had always imagined would be made under happier circumstances. His meeting with Kenney lasted ten minutes, if that. Their conversation was matter-of-fact, all business.

Koza: Mr. Kenney, I've come up here to find out where I stand.

Kenney: Well, Dave, you're a free agent now, and no other team has expressed any interest in you.

Koza: Does that mean that the Red Sox aren't interested in me, either?

Kenney: No, we're not.

Although the two men were sitting in an office in Boston, the moment drew Koza spiritually closer to all those brown-brick textile mills that defined his landscape in Pawtucket. A century and a half ago, an anonymous New England mill manager bluntly explained: When my machinery breaks down, I replace it; so too with my workers. And what was minor-league baseball, really, but pleasant millwork conducted outdoors? In exchange for setting aside your education and the development of marketable skills, you receive clubhouse pampering, fan adulation, and the faint chance of major-league ascension—but only as long as you stay healthy, put up numbers, and do not age. Ed Kenney had effectively informed Dave Koza, just short of twenty-nine years old, that he was a worn piece of machinery, no longer of use to the company. That most of us would love to play professional baseball—would gladly trade places with Dave Koza for the chance to hit even one home run before a cheering hometown crowd, in Pawtucket, or Bristol, or Elmira—only complicates the moment's essential cruelty.

The fired mill worker thanked the busy mill manager for his time, and returned to brown-brick Pawtucket. A few days later, his wife gave birth to their first child, Rebecca. His prolonged boyhood was over.

The Koza family headed west again, first to Tunkhannock, to see Ann's relatives, and then on to Torrington, where they moved in with Dave's parents for the winter. All they knew of their future was that it now included this precious baby girl. Dave, though, struggled with the uncertainty. He had always been a baseball player pursuing a big-league dream, and now, suddenly, he was not. Like so many professional athletes before him, his career had ended abruptly, against his will, and he could no longer count on a grassy buffer to separate him from the real world. His mother even gave him a lunch pail with a thermos, as if to say: It's time to go to work.

Ann Koza could not bear to see her husband suffer. She sent Dave's résumé to every major-league ball club, save for Boston, to alert them to the availability of Dave Koza, power-hitting first baseman, and the man who drove in the winning run in the longest game in baseball history. Several teams wrote back, saying that of course they knew who Dave Koza was, but, unfortunately, there were no suitable openings at this time. Without his knowledge, Ann also wrote a letter from the nonexistent Dave Koza Fan Club to the Boston Red Sox (going so far as to have a friend mail it from Rhode Island, so that the envelope would not have the telltale postage mark of Torrington, Wyoming). The letter all but begged Boston not to give up on Koza. No player gave more of himself.

The Dave Koza Fan Club did not receive a response. The regret, the pain—the grief, really, over the death of a career—began to strain the relationship between Dave and Ann. For so long she had lived and died with her husband's every at bat. Now she began to wonder whether Dave's failure to reach the major leagues was her fault. Maybe if they hadn't gotten married. Maybe if they hadn't started a family. . . .

After a vague offer for Dave to become a player-coach in the Dominican Republic fell through, the Kozas returned to Pawtucket to figure out what to do next. Dave understood that his primary role in life was to be a father—and Becky gave him such joy—but, as he will put it, he was still wearing his career around his neck, like a gold medallion that said, Look at me. He could still walk into any bar in Pawtucket, be recognized, and enjoy a drink or two on the house. But he soon wearied of being asked about how he had almost, almost made it to the big leagues; in effect, he was being celebrated for his failure. He stopped going to games at McCoy Stadium.

In 1984, a prominent local contractor, who had been a longtime booster of the PawSox, the kind of supporter who sponsored the annual Tenth Player Award, hired Koza as the manager and bartender of the Mill River Tavern, a restaurant in an old five-and-dime store in downtown Pawtucket that had been converted into a pleasant but unnervingly quiet warren of small shops. Koza had absolutely no experience in the food-service industry, but the job came with a salary and health benefits— plus tips. After more than a decade of worrying about curveballs and bat speed, he now focused on providing cups of soup and halves of sandwiches to the lunch crowd, then grappling with how to attract a dinner crowd to an emptied city core. He started taking a drink or two toward the end of his day to unwind and think.

You could say that Dave Koza had been drinking ever since he was a fifteen-year-old high school sophomore, and two older women—high school juniors—took him down to the canal, one of the preferred Torrington places for underage drinking, to sample some Boone's Farm apple wine. He did what most first-time drinkers do when this sickly sweet liquor passes their lips: He got dizzy drunk and puked. But a connection had been made. Here it was, courage in a bottle.

His career as a professional baseball player did not exactly discourage drinking. If anything, the postgame beer or two was part of the time-honored ritual. The clubbies stocked beer for the ballplayers the same way they stocked chewing tobacco and bubble gum. Then, after you left the clubhouse, you'd go down to My Brother's Pub to drink some more and relive the game just played, all the while commiserating over Boston's failure to appreciate what you had to offer. Christ, Morgan's fast to pull a pitcher in trouble. Jesus, did you see how far Sammy hit that ball tonight? Hell, we're all just insurance, in case Yaz pulls a hammy, or Eckersley goes on the DL.

Four for four? Let's drink.

Oh for four? Let's drink.

Koza always thought that he would never be as alcohol-dependent as his dad—a good, good guy, beloved by many, but it was no secret in small-town Torrington how, every once in a while, Dave would have to collect his dad down at the American Legion hall. But now, even with a child of his own, Koza felt handcuffed by the stuff that real life was throwing at him. In his misery, he felt entitled. After all, he was Pawtucket's own tragic hero, winner of the longest game in baseball history, and a guy who came within a bottle cap's width of making it to the major leagues.

Dave, that guy down the bar wants to buy you a drink. What'll it be?

In 1986, the year that several of his former teammates—Boggs and Barrett, Hurst and Gedman, and Ojeda—made it to the World Series, a new boss took over the restaurant and said he couldn't offer to pay Koza the same salary. While looking for employment, he never seriously considered uprooting the family and moving to Torrington. Beyond the lack of any jobs out there, he knew the arc that the collective conversation with his hometown would take.

Geez, you didn't make it.

Nope.

In 1987, Koza joined the Teamsters union and found a local job with the Yellow Freight System trucking company. He began working the dock at one of the company's terminals, driving a forklift, loading and unloading pallets of goods. Some of his new colleagues recognized him and began recalling this game-winning hit, or that game-saving catch, and wasn't he the guy who won the longest game in baseball history? Koza enjoyed the distinction that his baseball heroics had granted him, but he will later say that he was not particularly gracious to his colleagues. He still felt as though he rightfully belonged some-place else—holding a baseball glove in the clubhouse of the pennant-winning Boston Red Sox, for example, and not wearing work gloves on some loading dock. But on the loading dock he stayed, putting in his time; it was the only way to get promoted one day to driver.

And there was Koza, four years later, on the dock in the early spring of 1991, wearing work gloves and loading boxes onto a delivery truck bound for McCoy Stadium. And in those boxes were stacks and stacks of sixteen-ounce plastic cups, each one commemorating the tenth anniversary of the game that he had won.

McCoy Stadium

Home of Baseball's Longest Game

Pawtucket 3, Rochester 2

33 Innings, April 18–19, June 23, 1981

Koza got promoted to part-time driver just as his drinking intensified. He could guide a forty-five-foot truck through impossibly tight spaces, but he could not navigate everyday life without that liquid courage: vodka and beer, mostly. He and Ann were living with their young children—Becky, Samantha, and Christopher, whom everyone called Topher—in a large home on a double lot in Pawtucket, where Dave's alcoholism took up most of the space. He tried to control his drinking during the week by working the evening and overnight shifts, but he still seemed to measure every moment by the glass. The trip to Kmart, for example: a three-beer ride. Ann asked him to stop, then begged him to stop, but her pleas only made him more upset, which meant that he had all the more justification for a drink.

If you ask an old baseball player to name his worst year, he will often oblige with seasons that ultimately lowered his batting average, raised his earned run average, or fell far short of his usual capability; he might even cite an injury, or some crazy front-office decision, as the reason. But if you ask Dave Koza to name his worst year, it is 1994, a full eleven years after he stopped playing baseball.

In March of that year, when Koza's father came east to visit his son, daughter-in-law, and three grandchildren, he was proudly carrying a bronze coin inscribed with the words "To Thine Own Self Be True." It signified that Gene Koza, the gregarious alcoholic so often found at the American Legion, had achieved three months of sobriety by surrendering to the philosophy of Alcoholics Anonymous. One morning during his stay, Gene asked his son to find an A.A. meeting in the area, and Dave obliged, driving him to a church basement in Central Falls. As the father got out of the Ford pickup to make the noontime meeting, he asked his son to join him. Dave declined, in part because he had laced the coffee he was drinking with vodka. So he sat in his truck in the late winter cold, sipping his drink, and wanting, really wanting, to stop. But he could not.

Two months later, Gene Koza died of a heart attack in his bed in Torrington; he was sixty-nine. While home for the wake and funeral, Dave happened to open the top dresser drawer that nightly received his father's tossed fistful of loose change. He spotted the bronze A.A. coin, slipped it into his pocket, and kept drinking.

And three months after that, Ann told Dave that she had taken all that she could, and was leaving him. At first he thought she was testing him, the way a base runner might feign a steal to test a pitcher's pickoff move. But here he was, disbelieving and needing a drink, helping Ann load up a U-Haul truck and watching, with tears in his eyes, as she left him, taking their three children with her to her Pennsylvania home-town of Tunkhannock. He carried those wrenching images, of crying, uncomprehending children, back into his spacious, empty house, and closed the door. For the next several months, he drank, kept the shades lowered, drank, felt sorry for himself, drank, left for work, came home, and drank. Somewhere in this house, among his accumulation of baseball detritus, was that videotape of his triumphant *Good Morning America* appearance so long ago.

FORSYTHE: Dave, I understand your wife hung on until the bitter end.

KOZA: Yes, she did. I came out of the locker room the night we left off in the 32nd inning. I came outside. The sun started to come up, and I said, "You gotta be kidding me."

*   *   *

How short, now, the longest game seems. How ephemeral. On a night and early morning set aside for prayer, reflection, and everlasting joy, a baseball game insisted on the suspension of ordinary time. It gathered together a few dozen hopefuls in a poorly lit coliseum and refused them release for more than eight hours, providing them little comfort from the harsh elements beyond the heat generated by the burning of wood. It forced those watching the game to contemplate cosmic issues that transcend the successive crises of balls and strikes. The interdependence we all share. The inadequacy of statistics to measure one's worth. The existence of God. The dominion of nature over humankind, reflected by the howl of the night's wind, *whoooosh*, rising to muffle the profane howl of the Rochester center fielder.

Then, as if in jest, the game freed its captives to an Easter dawn's chorus of birds, only to summon them again, two months later, to complete the unfinished business of an unimportant ball game—a final point about the illusion of time. After 1 inning that lasted just eighteen minutes, the longest game released its participants for good, like a mother nudging her large brood into the world and wondering: What's to become of them?

What about the central player, McCoy Stadium itself, the weary concrete hulk that could never seem to shake the mucky cap-and-overall specters of its Depression-era birth? Today it is a renovated and remodeled pleasure of a minor-league ballpark, with ten thousand seats, an expanded concourse, a million-dollar JumboTron in center field—and, in the labyrinthine corridor beneath the stands, a shrine to that godsend for Pawtucket, the Longest Game. Among the holy relics on display is the home plate that received the touch of Marty Barrett's cleat as he jogged home, smiling with the knowledge that Dave Koza's soft line drive had found grass.

In 1977, the year that Ben Mondor assumed ownership of the Pawtucket Red Sox, the team had a paid attendance of a paltry 111,000, and the conditions at McCoy were so unappealing that the PawSox "couldn't draw maggots, let alone flies," as one sportswriter put it. Mondor, being Mondor, promptly framed the article. For the next thirty-three years, he, Mike Tamburro, and Lou Schwechheimer stayed together, executing their mission to provide working-class families with an affordable place to see the future stars of the Boston Red Sox. They saw the rewards of their labor in a rising popularity that consistently placed the PawSox among the top half dozen minor-league franchises in the country (in 2010, for example, the PawSox had a paid attendance of more than 600,000 for the seventh consecutive year). And Mondor, being Mondor, took pains every year to send a copy of that maggots-and-flies article to the offending author, as a polite but persistent way of saying screw you.

On a Sunday in early October 2010, Ben Mondor, eighty-five, died at his waterfront home in Warwick Neck, Rhode Island, his beloved wife, Madeleine, by his side. Several days earlier, in his bedroom on the second floor, he had gazed out the window at the gray-blue waters of Narragansett Bay, fully aware that he was terminally ill. After a few moments, he had shrugged his shoulders and said, with no regret: "I've had a good life."

The morning of his funeral Mass, a dozen uniformed police officers—several from Pawtucket, a few from a smattering of other departments—gathered outside the funeral home in Warwick, waiting to form an honor guard, while those closest to him said their last goodbyes. When it was time, Madeleine, along with Tamburro and Schwechheimer, emerged into the cool autumn morning, slightly ahead of the casket. One of the police officers, tears blurring his eyes, suddenly rushed over to hug Madeleine. This was Deputy Chief Michael Kinch of the Cumberland Police Department.

Hood.

After Hood composed himself, the officer leading the honor guard called out the commands of attention. Hood fell back into line and joined the other officers in saluting the casket of the man who had saved baseball for Pawtucket—a man who had been the private benefactor of so many people that McCoy's front office was still fielding stories of his generosity weeks after his death. Then Hood got into his black-and-white Ford Crown Victoria and joined the police escort that guided the funeral cortege the several miles to Providence, to the stone steps of the Cathedral of Saints Peter and Paul, where hundreds waited in the pews. Here was the governor of the state, Donald Carcieri; there, the former manager of the Pawtucket Red Sox, Joe Morgan. Here, Sam Bowen, and beside him, Dave Koza.

And what of the longest night's other elder statesmen? The two managers, who, through one degree of separation, linked the least known of the night's ballplayers to Hall of Fame teammates of theirs, Mickey Mantle and Whitey Ford, Hank Aaron and Warren Spahn? Rochester's Doc Edwards went on to manage the Cleveland Indians for a couple of years, and at the close of 2010 he was *still* in professional baseball, completing his fifty-third year in the game as the manager of the San Angelo Colts, in Texas's independent United League. As for Pawtucket's Joe Morgan, he was savoring his stature as Walpole Joe, New England icon, available for games of golf and the dispensing of baseball wisdom. After leveling with Dave Koza and leaving Pawtucket at the end of 1982, he became a Boston Red Sox scout and coach who seemed destined to retire without ever managing at the major-league level. Then, suddenly, in the middle of the 1988 season, he was reluctantly appointed the "interim" manager of the Red Sox by front-office suits who seemed impervious to the charms of his many minor-league anecdotes. Those suits never counted on what came to be known as "Morgan's Miracle." The Red Sox went on to win 19 of their next 20 games, catapulting a lackluster team to the front of the pack to win the American League East title. Soon, all of New England spoke in nonsensical Morgan-speak—"Six, two and even," and "See you in St. Paul"—and the Red Sox had no choice but to quickly name as its full-time manager a guy from Walpole who could tell you a thing or two about plowing snow on the turnpike, or how Win Remmerswaal—remember Win Remmerswaal?—would go AWOL for days at a time. Morgan's penchant for acting on hunches baffled and even irritated people at times, but he led the Red Sox to another American League East title, in 1990, before he was unceremoniously fired, in 1991. A few days later, a hundred people, along with the Walpole High School marching band, gathered on the front lawn of Joe Morgan's home, just to say thanks.

*   *   *

Finally, there are the others, scattered across the country, down to Latin America, and across to the Netherlands, many of them gone back to where they came from, many of them thankful for the salvation from obscurity that an endless night in Pawtucket has granted them. A poster commemorating the longest game hangs in South Bend, Indiana, in the home of Joel Finch, the former Pawtucket Red Sox pitcher, now a corporate account executive with a trucking company; in Tryon, Georgia, in the office of Dan Logan, the former Rochester Red Wings first baseman, now an insurance manager with the Georgia Farm Bureau; in Syracuse, New York, in Steve Grilli's Change of Pace. On the televisions at the Change of Pace and other bars, and on the televisions in their living rooms and recreation rooms and hotel rooms, they watched their fellow Longest Game alums move on to even greater glory, in the 1983 World Series, in the 1986 World Series, in various All Star games.

That skinny kid who played third base for Rochester that night? The one who banged his helmet to the ground after grounding out in the 6th inning? Cal Ripken Jr.? The bronze plaque from his induction into the Baseball Hall of Fame, in 2007, reads:

ARRIVED AT THE BALLPARK EVERY DAY WITH A BURNING DESIRE TO PERFORM AT HIS HIGHEST LEVEL. DEDICATION AND WORK ETHIC RESULTED IN A RECORD 2,632 CONSECUTIVE GAMES PLAYED FROM MAY 30, 1982 THROUGH SEPTEMBER 19, 1998, EARNING HIM THE TITLE OF BASEBALL'S "IRON MAN." IN 21 SEASONS, COLLECTED 3,184 HITS AND 431 HOME RUNS, AND WAS NAMED TO 19 CONSECUTIVE ALL-STAR TEAMS. WON ROOKIE OF THE YEAR HONORS, TWO MVPS, AND TWO GOLD GLOVE AWARDS. HIS ORIOLES WON THE 1983 WORLD SERIES AND HE HIT .336 LIFETIME IN 28 POSTSEASON GAMES.

And that ambitious bundle of superstition who played third base for Pawtucket that night? The one who used the third-base bag as a pillow in the late innings, while his little daughter slept under a desk in the owner's office? Wade Boggs? The plaque from his induction into the Baseball Hall of Fame, in 2005, reads:

A DISCIPLINED HITTER WHOSE COMMANDING KNOWLEDGE OF THE
STRIKE ZONE MADE HIM ONE OF BASEBALL'S TOUGHEST OUTS. ONLY
20TH CENTURY PLAYER WITH SEVEN STRAIGHT 200-HIT SEASONS.
REACHED BASE SAFELY IN 80 PERCENT OF GAMES PLAYED. BEGAN
CAREER WITH 10 CONSECUTIVE SEASONS HITTING ABOVE .300. A
FIVE-TIME BATTING CHAMPION WHO ALSO LED THE LEAGUE IN
ON-BASE PERCENTAGE AND INTENTIONAL WALKS SIX TIMES EACH.
A 12-TIME ALL-STAR, HIT .328 WITH 3,010 HITS AND 1,412 WALKS.
MEMBER OF THE 1996 WORLD SERIES CHAMPION YANKEES AND
WON TWO GOLD GLOVES. LEGENDARY FOR HIS SUPERSTITIONS.

Strange how life works out. A couple of years ago, Wade Boggs, of all people, wound up in Torrington, Wyoming, of all places, for a two-shot goose-hunt tournament that helps to promote economic development in Goshen County. And, of all people, one of his hosts in town was Paul Covello Jr., also known as Cactus. Boggs could not have been nicer to the people of Torrington and Goshen County. After going goose hunting down by the North Platte River, he attended the afternoon luncheon and the evening awards banquet, posed for photographs, autographed baseballs, and passed on some encouraging advice to a local ballplayer who was struggling a bit in the minor leagues. When young boys and girls approached him with their baseball caps on backward, Boggs would gently instruct them on the proper way to wear one; it's all about discipline. After the dinner, the gang headed through the snow drifts to Cactus's house for a cocktail hour that lasted until three in the morning. Over a few Miller Lites, Boggs and Cactus got to talking about their mutual acquaintance. Boggs said that Dave Koza just had the bad luck to be playing first base at a time when that position was clogged at the top with superstars—namely, Carl Yastrzemski and Tony Perez. He remembered how Dave caught everything and anything that he threw from third base, how Dave helped younger players in the clubhouse feel as though they belonged—how, when Dave drove in the winning run in the longest game, the batter on deck was yours truly, Wade Boggs.

Then the Hall of Famer asked: So, Cactus. You ever hear from Koza?

*　　　*　　　*

Dave Koza knows the many statistics of his career, but none better than this: He got sober on Monday, January 9, 1995.

On the Thursday before, he was whining and complaining about his life during a talk with his brother, Rick, out west, when Rick suddenly said: I think you've got a problem with booze. The words coming over the telephone nearly knocked Dave down. Though stunned, he was also relieved. If he wasn't fooling anyone with his impersonation of a sober person, he could finally be honest with himself. He reached for the Yellow Pages and looked up Alcoholics Anonymous.

That Friday, he attended an A.A. meeting in East Providence, half hoping to hear tips on how to drink responsibly.

That Saturday, he drank. He had always been a big weekend boozer and, well, it was Saturday.

That Sunday, he attended another A.A. meeting, this one at Jenks Junior High School, directly across Division Street from McCoy Stadium. There, at the meeting, a coffeemaker named Dave T. and a firefighter named Billy M. decided to take him under their wing. Billy's firehouse was a baseball toss away from the entrance to McCoy, and he had often seen Dave play. The two men told Dave not to drink, so he returned home and finished up what liquor he still had in the house.

And that Monday, the morning of January 9, the two men threw Dave in the back of Billy's twenty-year-old Oldsmobile and drove him to a meeting in the Salvation Army's Freedom Hall building on Pitman Street in Providence. He had his father's coin in his pocket. He hasn't had a drink since.

Koza traded the large house in Pawtucket for a small house in Pawtucket, and began focusing on doing his very best with every day, the way he once did with every at bat. As the days turned to weeks and then to years, the cheers he heard came not from thousands gathered at McCoy but from a few gathered in a church basement or some rented hall. They also came from Ann and the children, in long-distance conversations between Pawtucket and Tunkhannock, where she remarried, and then between Pawtucket and Las Vegas, where she relocated. When Dave reached his twelfth year of sobriety, Ann happened to be in Rhode

Island, and she decided to surprise him by showing up at the small celebration that would be part of his A.A. group's next meeting. She hid in a back room, and when the time came, she emerged with his twelfth anniversary cake, bringing him—and then her—to tears.

It was hard at first. For a while, Dave resented the fact that Ann had gotten remarried, but time and discussions with his A.A. support group have made him realize that Ann didn't leave him; rather, he—through his drinking—pushed her out of his life. Now Ann and Dave talk a few times a week. And when Dave comes to visit his kids, he often stays in a spare bedroom in Ann's house, where, tucked away somewhere, she has her own box of baseball memories, including a quilt that she and a few other PawSox wives started long ago to commemorate the longest game, but never finished. She can't get rid of the thing, she says, because that game, that time, remains a part of her. Who knows? Maybe some-day she'll finish the quilt.

If ten years after that game found Dave Koza working the load-ing docks and drinking heavily, twenty years after found him working on his seventh year of sobriety, making truck deliveries all over Rhode Island (including, on occasion, to McCoy Stadium, to drop off more of those souvenir cups)—and trying to be a good father to his three children. In August of that year, 2001, he drove from Pawtucket to Tunkhannock in his silver Taurus, and spent the Friday night with Ann and the family. Then, early the next morning, he and the three chil-dren—Becky, seventeen, Sami, thirteen, and Topher, twelve—drove the nearly three hours to Cooperstown. Sami was getting more and more serious about competing with the boys in baseball, and Topher, a Little League outfielder, had recently written a school paper about Jackie Robinson. But there was another reason for making the trip.

When they reached the Hall of Fame, they found an endless line snaking down Main Street. Koza noticed a members-only entrance to the side, and somehow summoned the nerve to approach the employee at the door and say that he thought he was kind of, sort of, in the Hall of Fame, but wasn't sure. I played in the longest game, he explained. I had the game-winning hit.

Within minutes he and his children were handed complimentary tickets and welcomed inside. And there, on the second floor of the Baseball Hall of Fame, this family from Rhode Island, by way of Pennsylvania and Wyoming, came upon a glass display dedicated to the Longest Game in Professional Baseball History. It included a scoreboard stretching for 33 innings; a photograph of several Pawtucket Red Sox players congratulating one another; the Louisville Slugger bat that was used to drive in the game-winning single; and a large portrait of the hero who swung it: Dave Koza, former ballplayer, truck driver, recovering alcoholic—dad.

Today, ten years after that family trip to Cooperstown, and thirty years after the longest game, Dave Koza no longer drives a truck for a living. Two decades of playing baseball, followed by two more decades of climbing in and out of his truck, loading and unloading, took their toll. After he required the replacement of one hip and both knees, his doctors told him the time had come to retire. He hits his A.A. meetings, attends several PawSox games a year, and gets out to Las Vegas as often as possible to see his three grown children and the couple of grandchildren who have come along.

But the man from Wyoming always comes home—to Pawtucket. Every once in a while, he agrees to speak at a gathering of baseball enthusiasts, answering their questions. What was it like to play for Joe Morgan? What was it like to play with Marty Barrett? Bruce Hurst? Rich Gedman? Wade Boggs? Then, of course, this question:

Why didn't you make it to the major leagues?

Not consistent enough, he will say.

And if you search Dave Koza's home for celebratory mementoes of his baseball past, you will not find much. In the bedroom, across from a display of the Serenity Prayer ("God, grant me the serenity to accept the things I cannot change . . ."), one of Norman Rockwell's baseball illustrations hangs on the wall. Near the bathroom, a framed copy of the Longest Game poster. And down in the basement, slightly askew, a small magnet bought in a Cooperstown souvenir shop.

"National Baseball Hall of Fame," it says. "DAVE."

The magnet is the smallest token of a trip that has come to stand out in the family narrative. The children will remember how their father drew Topher's attention to an exhibit about the African American baseball experience; how he pointed Sami to a display devoted to Dorothy Kamenshek and the other women who played in the All-American Girls Professional Baseball League; and how much he downplayed the Longest Game exhibit.

After lingering a long, long while in the corridors of a game's past, the Koza family left Cooperstown and began the journey back to Tunkhannock. Dave steered his sedan south onto Route 28 and then turned onto Interstate 88, hugging the Susquehanna River all the way. It was a pure August evening and baseball was breaking out all over. In New York, the first-place Yankees had just beaten the Anaheim Angels, thanks to an 8th-inning home run by Tino Martinez, while in Boston, the second-place Red Sox were planning to start their ageless knuckleball pitcher, Tim Wakefield, against the Texas Rangers. In Toronto, the gray-haired third baseman for the Baltimore Orioles was sitting out his team's loss to the Blue Jays; with two months to go before his retirement, though, no one would begrudge a day off to Cal Ripken Jr. In Chicago, the redheaded hitting coach for the weak Tampa Bay Devil Rays was also close to calling it quits; it seemed that what had made him Wade Boggs was not transferable.

And in a car moving west through the undulating hills of central New York, the talk was of baseball and nothing but baseball, until the children of Dave and Ann sleepily surrendered to the rhythms of the rutted road.

SOURCES, THANK-YOUS, AND CRACKER JACK

This is a book of informed imagination. It could not have been con-jured without the assistance of many people who generously shared their memories of a time, a place, and a game—from the two future members of the Baseball Hall of Fame to the clubhouse kid who made sure that McCoy Stadium was well stocked with Dubble Bubble and Skoal. I am grateful to all of them, but especially to Ann Life, who abided my disruptions with a rare generosity of spirit, and, of course, to Dave Koza. He allowed me to intrude upon his past and present not for his personal glory, but because he believed that the story of his life's journey might help someone else. He answered my many questions, en-dured my many visits, and never once engaged in self-aggrandizement. His humility humbles me. Thank you, all.

I lived in Pawtucket for four years, close enough to McCoy Stadium to hear the roars and sighs of the beckoning crowd. I played on a Sunday morning basketball team sponsored by the Weiner Genie Restaurant, found my day's fuel at the Modern Diner, and spent many evenings at the Irish Social Club. Pawtucket took me in, and I am forever grateful.

The idea for this book came to me while flipping again through *The Longest Game*, a charming children's picture book by Steven

Krasner, a former colleague of mine at the *Providence Journal*. That led me to call another former *Providence Journal* colleague, the gracious Paige Van Antwerp, who had gone on to work for a while for the Pawtucket Red Sox, and who put me in touch with Lou Schwechheimer, the vice president and general manager for the Pawtucket Red Sox. This book would not have been written without the ever-patient Mr. Schwechheimer. It bears repeating. This book would not have been written without the ever-patient Mr. Schwechheimer. With the blessing and encouragement of team owner Ben Mondor and team president Mike Tamburro, Mr. Schwechheimer tracked down former ballplayers, dug up old newspaper clippings and photographs, provided constant counsel, and brought to bear the formidable PawSox army, whose ranks include Becky Berta, Kevin Galligan, Bonnie Goff, Michael Gwynn, Mary Beth Kelly, Rick Medeiros, Eric Petterson, Augusto "Cookie" Rojas Jr., and Bill Wanless. I cannot possibly repay you all for your cheerful assistance. Thank you.

Dan Mason, the general manager for the Rochester Red Wings, double-checked obscure facts (Was the Rochester team once called the Bronchos or the Broncos?), and located a number of former Red Wings players. Randy Mobley, the president of the International League, provided access to historical records and arranged a memorable lunchtime visit with that singular baseball personality, Harold Cooper (who died in October 2010 at the age of eighty-six—less than a day after the passing of Ben Mondor). Gabriel Schechter, baseball savant, guided me through the game's dusty past, as did Freddy Berowski and Lenny DiFranza, of the National Baseball Hall of Fame, and the historian David W. Smith. Among those who tutored me in the history of Pawtucket and the Blackstone Valley were Chuck Arning, Albert Klyberg, Gary Kulik, William Jennings, Susan Millard, Scott Molloy, and the staffs at the Pawtucket Public Library, the Rhode Island Historical Society, and the Slater Mill Museum. In particular, I wish to thank Bob Drew, the former general manager and radio announcer for the Rochester Red Wings, whose broadcast of that game gives it breath, and Mike Scandura, the former Pawtucket *Evening Times* sportswriter, who patiently recited for me all 33 innings of balls and strikes, as rendered in his scorebook. Thank you.

I consulted many books during my research, among them *The Only Way I Know How*, by Cal Ripken Jr. and Mike Bryan, which remains one of the very best baseball memoirs, and the definitive *Ted Williams*, by Leigh Montville. Others include: *Boggs!*, by Wade Boggs; *The Pawtucket Red Sox*, by David Borges; *The History of Pawtucket, 1635–1986*, by Susan Marie Boucher; *Working Lives: An Oral History of Rhode Island Labor*, edited by Paul M. Buhle; *Shut Out: A Story of Race and Baseball in Boston*, by Howard Bryant; *The Red Sox Fan Handbook*, compiled by Leigh Grossman; *Pawtucket*, by Elizabeth J. Johnson, James L. Wheaton, and Susan L. Reed; *Silver Seasons: The Story of the Rochester Red Wings*, by Jim Mandelaro and Scott Pitoniak; *Trolley Wars: Streetcar Workers on the Line*, by Scott Molloy; *A Game of Inches: The Story Behind the Innovations That Shaped Baseball*, by Peter Morris; *A Common Man for the Common People: The Life of Thomas P. McCoy*, by Vernon C. Norton; *The International League*, by Bill O'Neal; *Diamonds in the Rough: Life in Baseball's Minor Leagues*, by Ken Rappoport; *Working in the Blackstone River Valley: Exploring the Heritage of Industrialization*, edited by Douglas M. Reynolds and Marjory Myers; *The Numbers Game: Baseball's Lifelong Fascination with Statistics*, by Alan Schwarz; and *As They See 'Em: A Fan's Travels in the Land of Umpires*, by Bruce Weber.

I also relied on various papers and monographs, including: *McCoy Stadium: Legacy or Folly*, by Chuck Arning and Kevin Klyberg; *Textile-Mill Labor in the Blackstone Valley: Work and Protest in the Nineteenth Century*, by Gary Kulik; *Pawtucket Village and the Strike of 1824: The Origins of Class Conflict in Rhode Island*, also by Mr. Kulik; *Triple A Baseball's Oldest Stadium Turns 60*, by Tom Mason; *The Longest Game in Baseball History*, an invaluable reference work by J. M. Murphy; *The Game That Wouldn't End*, by Scott Pitoniak, for the *Baseball Research Journal*; *Hardball Paternalism, Hardball Politics*, by Douglas M. Reynolds; *Samuel Slater: Father of American Manufactures*, by Paul E. Rivard; and *The Real McCoy in the Bloodless Revolution of 1935*, by Matthew J. Smith. In addition,

I came upon a valuable oral history provided by Jerry Sherlock, of Pawtucket, in 2007.

Several Web sites were indispensable, none more so than Baseball-Reference.com. Others that proved helpful were Baseball Almanac, the Baseball Biography Project (one of many contributions by the Society for American Baseball Research), Baseball Library, Ripken in the Minors, the Sons of Sam Horn, the Buffalo Head Society, and Oklahoma Sports Memories. There is also a striking Dutch documentary about Win Remmerswaal called *An Almost Perfect Game*.

Naturally, I read many stories from the archives of the *Providence Journal* and the Pawtucket *Evening Times*, with supplementation provided by the *Boston Globe*, the *New York Times*, the Rochester *Democrat and Chronicle*, the *Columbus Dispatch*, the *Torrington Telegram*, the *Baseball Digest*, and the *Sporting News*. Special note should also be paid to "Off the Field: Wade Boggs," by Monte Burke, Forbes.com, May 26, 2009; "Where've You Gone, Barry Bonnell?" by Spencer Fordin, MLB.com, January 24, 2003; "Pretty Fair for a Fowl Guy," by Peter Gammons, *Sports Illustrated*, April 14, 1986; "Sports News," by Michael Geffner, the Associated Press, June 30, 1984; "Baseball Town, Oklahoma: Glory Days," by Andrew Gilman, the *Daily Oklahoman*, July 1, 2001; "Dugout Fragrances and Sweet Memories," by Jerome Holtzman, the *Chicago Tribune*, July 1, 1986; "Longest Day a Nightmare No More 10 Years Later, 33-Inning Affair Recalled Fondly," by Matt Michael, the Syracuse *Post-Standard*, April 17, 1991; "The Long Haul," by Leigh Montville, *Sports Illustrated*, April 24, 2000; "Hurst Balances Life in Baseball with His Beliefs," by Bob Nightengale, the *Los Angeles Times*, March 17, 1991; "She's Been His Closest Fan for 30 Years," by Emily Nipps, the *St. Petersburg Times*, July 28, 2005; "Alone on the Hill: Bruce Hurst Might Not Fit In, but Padres Know He'll Pitch In," by Bill Plaschke, the *Los Angeles Times*, March 4, 1989; "Wade Boggs: 2005 Hall of Fame Inductee," by Dan Shaughnessy, the *Boston Globe*, July 31, 2005; "Return Is Victory for Ojeda," by Bud Shaw, the Cleveland *Plain Dealer*, August 8, 1993; "Long Memories from a Baseball Classic," by Dave Sheinen, the *Washington Post*, April 18, 2006; and "Where There's a Will, There's a way," by Leo Verheul, *Achilles*, April 2009.

This book greatly benefited from many kindnesses, large and small. I'd like to thank: Jack "Home Run" Baker; Richie Bancells; Dave Bloss; Billy Broadbent; Bryan Bullock; Rory Costello; Cactus Covello; Kevin Cullen; Julie Dalton; Scott Del Sole; Brendan Doherty; Ted Dolan; Jim Dorsey; Cate Doty; George Patrick Duffy; Peter Gammons; Bruce Germani; Tom Giordano; Jane Giovannucci, of the Pawtucket *Times*; Pat Heslin; Kathy Hill; Pete Khoury; Michael Kinch; Galway Kinnell; Sean Kirst; Topher Koza; Steve Krasner; Bill Malinowski; John Maroon; Mike McBurney; Bob Minzesheimer; Madeleine Mondor; Terry Moran; Mary Murphy; Bob Ojeda; Mike Pappas; Willie Rashbaum; Bill Reynolds; Joe Sexton; Dan Shaughnessy; Don Van Natta; Leo Verheul; Bob Weil; and Todd Willmarth. Special thanks to those who waded through early drafts and who buttressed my research and my spirits, including Dave Chmiel; Tom Heslin; John Hill; Len Levin; Colum McCann; and Rick Simpson.

I'd also like to thank my colleagues at the *New York Times* for their indulgence, including David Firestone, Rick Lyman, Rick Berke, Jill Abramson, and Bill Keller; my friends at HarperCollins, especially Kate Blum and Leah Wasielewski, for accepting the challenge to publicize a non-baseball baseball book; Barry Harbaugh, an extremely gifted editor with an unerring ear; and, of course, David Hirshey, who believed in this book from the beginning and whose enthusiasm never flagged. Gently coaxing and challenging, he made this book better.

As I round home, I'd like to thank, again, my agents, Todd Shuster and Lane Zachary, for their patience, guidance, and editorial gifts; my friend and colleague Michael McElroy, who checked and double-checked facts, read and reread copy, and was always at the ready; and the holy trinity of Pawtucket, Lou Schwechheimer, Mike Tamburro, and, of course, Ben Mondor. Ben's enthusiastic spirit—for "bazeball," for life—informs every word of this book. It was a privilege to have known him.

And now, as I make it home, there are the three who make it such: my daughters, Nora and Grace, and my wife, Mary Trinity, my first editor, my best friend, my love.

OFFICIAL BOX SCORE

ROCHESTER	ab	r	h	bi	PAWTUCKET	ab	r	h	bi
Eaton 2b	10	0	3	0	Graham cf	14	0	1	0
Williams cf	13	0	0	0	Barrett 2b	12	1	2	0
Ripken 3b	13	0	2	0	Walker lf	14	1	2	0
Corey dh	5	1	1	0	Laribee dh	11	0	0	1
Chism ph	1	0	0	0	Koza 1b	14	1	5	1
Rayford c	5	0	0	0	Boggs 3b	12	0	4	1
Logan 1b	12	0	4	0	Bowen rf	12	0	2	0
Valle 1b	1	0	0	0	Gedman c	3	0	1	0
Bourjos lf	4	0	2	1	Ongarato ph	1	0	0	0
Hale lf	7	0	1	0	LaFrancois c	8	0	2	0
Smith lf	0	0	0	0	Valdez ss	13	0	2	0
Hazewood rf	4	0	0	0					
Hart rf	6	1	1	0					
Bonner ss	12	0	3	0					
Huppert c	11	0	1	1					
Putnam ph	1	0	0	0					
Totals	**105**	**2**	**18**	**2**	**Totals**	**114**	**3**	**21**	**3**

No outs when winning run scored.
E – Eaton, Logan, Bonner, Valdez. DP – Rochester 4. Pawtucket 3. LOB – Rochester 30, Pawtucket 23. 2B – Koza 2, Walker, Boggs, Huppert. SB – Eaton. S – Williams 2, Logan, Hart, Huppert 2. SF – Laribee.

ROCHESTER	IP	H	R	ER	BB	SO
Jones	8⅔	7	1	1	2	5
Schneider	5⅓	2	0	0	0	8
Luebber	8	6	1	1	2	4
Umbarger	10	4	0	0	0	9
Grilli (L)	0	1	1	1	1	0
Speck	0	1	0	0	0	0

PAWTUCKET	IP	H	R	ER	BB	SO
Parks	6	3	1	1	4	3
Aponte	4	0	0	0	2	9
Sarmiento	4	3	0	0	2	3
Smithson	3⅔	2	0	0	3	5
Remmerswaal	4⅓	4	1	1	3	3
Finch	5	3	0	0	1	3
Hurst	5	2	0	0	3	7
Ojeda (W)	1	1	0	0	0	1

Parks pitched to 3 batters in the 7th; Grilli pitched to 3 batters in the 33rd; Speck pitched to 1 batter in the 33rd.
WP – Jones, Smithson, Hurst, HPB – by Schneider (Laribee), by Parks (Eaton), by Aponte (Bonner), by Grilli (Barrett).
T – 8:25. A – 1,740.

ABOUT THE AUTHOR

Dan Barry is a national columnist for the *New York Times*. He has twice been a finalist for the Pulitzer Prize and in 1994 was part of an investigative team for the *Providence Journal* that won the prize for a series on Rhode Island's justice system. He is the author of a memoir, *Pull Me Up,* and *City Lights,* a collection of his *New York Times* columns. He lives with his wife and two daughters in Maplewood, New Jersey.